ARMS, ARMIES
AND
FORTIFICATIONS
IN THE
HUNDRED YEARS WAR

ARMS, ARMIES
AND
FORTIFICATIONS
IN THE
HUNDRED YEARS WAR

Edited by
ANNE CURRY & MICHAEL HUGHES

THE BOYDELL PRESS

First published 1994
The Boydell Press, Woodbidge
Reprinted in paperback 1999

Transferred to digital printing

ISBN 978-0-85115-365-0 hardback
ISBN 978-0-85115-755-9 paperback

The Boydell Press is an imprint of Boydell & Brewer Ltd
PO Box 9, Woodbridge, Suffolk IP12 3DF, UK
and of Boydell & Brewer Inc.
668 Mt Hope Avenue, Rochester, NY 14620, USA
website: www.boydellandbrewer.com

A CiP catalogue record for this book is available
from the British Library

This publication is printed on acid-free paper

CONTENTS

CONTRIBUTORS

Matthew Bennett	Lecturer, Royal Military Academy Sandhurst
Andrew Ayton	Lecturer in History, University of Hull
Anne Curry	Senior Lecturer in History, University of Reading
Malcolm Vale	Fellow and University Lecturer, St John's College, Oxford
W.M. Ormrod	Lecturer in History, University of York
Michael Jones	Professor of Medieval French History, University of Nottingham
Michael Hughes	County Archaeologist, Hampshire County Council and Visiting Fellow, University of Southampton
John R. Kenyon	Librarian, National Museum of Wales
Robert D. Smith	Head of Conservation, Royal Armouries, HM Tower of London
Robert Hardy	Actor, and Trustee, Mary Rose Trust
Ian Friel	Keeper, Littlehampton Museum
Brian Kemp	Professor of Medieval History, University of Reading

PLATES

The plates appear between pages 110 and 111

English Armies in the Fourteenth Century

I   The battlefield of Crécy, looking south-eastwards from the observation tower thought to be on the site of the windmill from which Edward III viewed the field.

II   The battlefield of Crécy, looking north-eastwards from Edward's supposed viewing point towards the village of Wadicourt.

III   Bois de Crécy-Grange, near to which was placed the English baggage park behind the English lines.

IV   The battlefield of Poitiers.

English Armies in the Fifteenth Century

V   Sir John Cressy's retinue in the muster roll of 26 March, 1441 (PRO, E101/53/33).

The War in Aquitaine

VI   The castle of Beynac (Dordogne) on its promontory.

VII   The keep of the castle of Beynac (Dordogne).

VIII   The town defences of Libourne (Gironde).

War and Fourteenth-Century France

IX   The castle of Motcontour (Vienne), finally retaken by the French in 1372.

X   The port defences of La Rochelle, after 1372.

XI   The fortified church of Esnandes (Charente-Maritime).

XII   The town defences of Avignon, c.1355–70.

The Fourteenth-Century Franch Raids

XIII   Portsmouth: the seaward defences constructed in the sixteenth and seventeenth centuries.

XIV   Southampton: Back of the Walls excavations showing remains of late thirteenth-century dovecote and fourteenth-century half-round tower.

FIGURES

PREFACE

The Hundred Years War has long been a source of fascination for many, whether professional historian or lay enthusiast. In November 1991 an attempt was made to bring these two groups together by holding a weekend conference at Rewley House, Oxford University's Department of Continuing Education. The purpose of this event, as now of this book, was to bring to the attention of a wider audience recent developments in the academic study of the Hundred Years War. It also aimed at mixing historical and archaeological approaches, and at pursuing a wide range of topics in a lively yet informative way. Neither the conference nor the ensuing collection of essays can claim to be exhaustive either in content or coverage. Other themes could have been included, such as armour, and all themes which are treated could have been dealt with at greater length and in more detail. What we have tried to do is offer a taste of the research work now being carried out, with evaluation, wherever possible, of the source materials which have been used, and with full referencing so that leads may be followed up.

Some areas will be better known than others. Where topics have already received much historical and popular attention, the approach is revisionist. Matthew Bennett, for instance, in his opening paper on 'Battle tactics' tries to redeem the study of battles from what has tended to be anachronistic treatment, and to provide a more precise definition of what 'tactics' means. The warfare of this period was complex – the result not of accidental encounter and ad hoc response to crisis, but of deliberate and well thought-out forward planning and of impressive and amazingly bureaucratic organisation. Bennett shows how the English developed a plan of action and stuck to it, suggesting that 'personal experience and the passing on of information between contemporaries and even down the generations was crucial'. The bureaucracy generated by war is elucidated by three studies of English military organisation, all based upon what is, for all its gaps and losses, a very rich archive. An examination of the value and pitfalls of documentary sources is central to Andrew Ayton's study of the fourteenth-century army and Anne Curry's of the fifteenth. Both have been using computer assistance to deal with the vast quantities of administrative records, facilitating the elucidation of individual careers, such as Ayton's study of Sir Nicholas de Goushill, and Curry's of Sir John Cressy and his men-at-arms, as well as a more reliable calculation of army sizes and composition. Malcolm Vale adopts a regional approach, examining the war in Aquitaine, that part of France where English kings had ruled as dukes since the later twelfth century and where Anglo-French conflict long predated the Hundred Years War proper. Whilst much has been written on the role of Aquitaine in the origins of the war, less attention has been paid to the area during the war, perhaps because the 'exciting' battles all happened elsewhere. Vale tries to redress this by outlining the continuing military significance of the duchy, pointing out the potential for further study in the extensive central and local archives and the need for important sources to be calendared to make them more accessible. English royal archives feature prominently in Mark Ormrod's overview of the response in England to the Hundred Years War, providing an excellent guide in his notes to recent historical study. He shows too, through his graphs generated by his involvement in the recent European State Finance Database Project, how the computer can open new vistas onto the key issues of taxation and royal finance.

Michael Jones' paper on 'War and Fourteenth-Century France' provides a bridge between historical and archaeological approaches. Jones summarises recent French researches into the economic impact of war, looking particularly at the question of destruction and devastation, and showing how urban records can be used to reveal building activity and the purchase of defensive equipment. Documentary evidence is set against the findings of recent excavations at Southampton, Winchester and Portsmouth in Michael Hughes' study of the impact of the French raids on Hampshire and the Isle of Wight. Destruction can be detected as also the measures taken by the crown and the townspeople to improve defences. Such physical evidence also reveals much about contemporary attitudes to and perceptions of war. The question of coastal defences is explored in more detail by John Kenyon, again using the evidence of standing remains and focusing particularly on changes incumbent upon the increased use of artillery in the defence of castles and town walls. This study is complemented by Robert Smith's review of what is known (and unknown) about the artillery of the period of the Hundred Years War, lamenting the lack of work in this area but also pointing the way to future research. His consideration of the few surviving guns which can be reliably dated is paralleled by Robert Hardy's analysis of the *Mary Rose* bows, where modern technology has shed so much light on construction and fighting potential. Like Smith, he reminds us of the need for an inter-disciplinary approach, bringing together, in this case, study of the weapon and of the archer and of how both were deployed in the key actions of the war. Surviving remains are also drawn upon in Ian Friel's examination of ships, where he provides a clear guide to the types and methods of construction of the vessels of the period, and brings to prominence the often neglected maritime aspects of the Hundred Years War. Finally – death the final portal – Brian Kemp reviews English church monuments of the period based upon the wide range of surviving examples, outlining the variety of design but emphasising that 'military' effigies were not the exclusive preserve of those who actually served in the war.

As each paper reflects the thoughts and researches of scholars working in specific areas where they themselves have expertise, there has been no attempt to integrate the papers or to make them conform to any kind of pattern. Indeed the interpretations found in one paper may seem to be contradicted or challenged in another. This is a useful reminder that in this kind of historical and archaeological research, nothing can be deemed cut and dried. This does not prevent, of course, the possibility of advances in our knowledge and our perception. It is to be hoped that these essays will show how active research on aspects of the Hundred Years War now is, as well as what work is still to be done on this exciting and significant period of military action.

It remains only to thank Trevor Rowley, Maggie Herdman and the staff of Rewley House for helping to make the initial conference such an enjoyable and succesful occasion, Nick Instone for drawing most of the figures, Mrs Elizabeth Berry and Mrs Carol Mackay of the Department of History, University of Reading, for typing several of the manuscripts, and finally Richard Barber and the staff of Boydell and Brewer for seeing it through the press.

ACKNOWLEDGMENTS

Plates I–III, Anne Curry; Plates IV, VI, VII, VIII, XIII–XVII, Michael Hughes; Plate V, Public Record Office, reproduced by permission of the Controller of Her Majesty's Stationery Office; Plates IX–XII, Michael Jones; Plates XVIII and XIX, Andrew Saunders; Plates XX–XXIII, Reproduced by permission of the Trustees of the Royal Armouries; Plates XXIV and XXV, By permission of the British Library; Plate XXVI, Bibliothèque Nationale, Paris; Plate XXVII, Bibliothèque Royale, Brussels; Plates XXVIII and XXIX, Robert Hardy; Plates XXX, XXXI, XXXIII and XXXIV, Simon Eager; Plates XXXII, XXXV–XXXVIII, Brian Kemp.

ABBREVIATIONS

AN	Archives Nationales, Paris
BIHR	*Bulletin of the Institute of Historical Research*
BL	British Library
BN	Bibliothèque Nationale, Paris
CCR	Calendar of Close Rolls
CIM	Calendar of Inquisitions Miscellaneous
CIPM	Calendar of Inquisitions Post Mortem
Complete Peerage	*The Complete Peerage of England, Scotland, Ireland and the United Kingdom*, ed. G.E. Cockayne *et al* (London, 1910–59)
CPR	Calendar of Patent Rolls
EHR	*English Historical Review*
EcHR	*Economic History Review*
PRO	Public Record Office
Rot.Parl.	Rotuli Parliamentorum
TRHS	*Transactions of the Royal Historical Society*

1

The Development of Battle Tactics in the Hundred Years War

MATTHEW BENNETT

IT IS A COMMON aphorism that the history of war is too important to be left to military historians. They tend to be seen as obsessed with battle with no further interest or wider understanding of the warring societies.[1] In truth, they have done themselves no favours in the past by emphasising 'decisive' victories. This over-values the long-term impact of even the most significant battle and distorts by undervaluing the other, far more common, activities of raid, attrition, fortification and siege in the warfare of any period.

By their very nature battles are ephemeral events, and historians have to rely upon largely subjective accounts in reconstructing them. Some consider this an uncongenial or even inappropriate task for their profession. 'Real' history is to be found in the study of 'real' information, such as can be found in the administrative records of governments: musters lists, tax records, accounts, diplomatic correspon-dence, building records and so on. Biased and 'journalistic' reportage of chroni-clers and government propagandists or the partial and often confused recollection of participants scarcely qualifies as history. Furthermore, the study of battles has tended to be conducted by soldiers.

There may seem nothing wrong with this, but it has led to them drawing upon their own military experience of modern warfare without making due allowance for the differences of another place and time. Just as the historians might benefit from some practical experience of, for example, 'living in the field', the soldier historians' often impressionistic accounts need more historical rigour. They tend to be critical of medieval commanders and their forces on grounds that are simply not valid for their times. This is true of Lt-Col. A.H. Burne, still the most well-known military historian of the Hundred Years' War.[2]

He deserves credit for the work he did in exploring battlefields and his

---

[1] Hence the growth of the 'War and Society' school of history, in which the study of warfare is 'legitimised' by reference to its social context. Unfortunately, and all too frequently, war often drops out of what become simply administrative studies.

[2] A.H. Burne, *The Crécy War* (London, 1955) and *The Agincourt War* (London, 1956). This two volume work was republished as recently as 1991, but with no cautionary preface taking into account the extensive researches over the last half-century.

observations may be perceptive. But he was guilty of missing the point about how medieval warfare was conducted, by concentrating on battles alone. He was even capable of saying of the period 1369–1396 (when the bulk of the English king's continental possessions fell into the hands of his French rival) that: 'The war (was) lacking in military interest, for there was remarkably little actual fighting'.[3] When the fortresses which guarded Aquitaine were being lost this is nonsense! As a result historians have tended to see the study of battles as a field for cranks and 'enthusiasts'. Since understanding a battle requires study of the tactics employed by the protagonists, tactics have been tarred with the same brush. Surely they cannot be important in comparison to the great moving forces of history exemplified by economic, demographic, medical, governmental and ideological factors?

Yet if it is valid to study the impact of religious reform movements in the later middle ages, then it should be acceptable to look at tactics, since both were important areas of intellectual concern. The former has a higher status, because intellectual religiosity has a long literary tradition and so it can be studied. In contrast, military theorising was part of an oral, vernacular and secular culture, which rarely survives in writing. In fact, from the early fifteenth century there is written evidence that military commanders were capable of innovating, experimenting and setting down how warfare should be conducted and how battles should be fought.[4] Above all they were capable of learning from experience, a talent which is almost never ascribed to the medieval military mind.

So tactics were important. They were important because failure to employ correct tactics could have a profound political impact, in a period when national leaders fought in the front rank of battle. In this context, clearly, time and intellectual energy were spent in discussing and attempting to put into effect, tactical variation. Attempting, for the medieval host was an unwieldly instrument for innovation. This not because it was made up solely of part-time soldiers; the hunting classes and their retainers at war, although there was always an element of that. In England, especially, many men made war their trade, and by the mid-fourteenth century there were substantial groups of men-at-arms and archers who might be considered professionals: they fought for pay and made their careers in the military service of the state. The indenture system promoted this situation. (That is to say a system of raising troops by contracts with individuals and their followings, from simple squires to men of high noble rank.) Fighting together over a season or over years such men learnt how to deploy tactically, both quickly and efficiently, and how to combine horse, foot and missile weapons to best effect. This is what made the English and their (chiefly) Gascon allies such good soldiers during the Hundred Years War. The French and their allies rarely achieved the same level of battlefield efficiency, even after Charles VII's reforms of the 1440s.[5]

---

[3] Burne, *The Agincourt War*, p. 20.
[4] See M. Vale, *War and Chivalry* (Oxford, 1981), pp. 30–2.
[5] The success of the reforms should not be over-rated, if we can believe the scornful comments of Philippe de Commynes about the battle of Montlhéry, 1465, in his *Memoirs: The Reign of Louis XI 1461 83*, trans. Michael Jones (London, 1972), pp. 68–80.

It is important to identify what tactics are. A recent, most widely read and otherwise excellent textbook on the Hundred Years' War confuses tactics with strategy. The chevauchée is explained in terms of 'Fabian tactics', which is to say: a policy of defeating an opponent without the risks of battle.[6] But the chevauchée (literally a 'ride') was a raiding *strategy*, inflicting economic damage and so weakening an enemy's political and moral authority in the ravaged region. The misuse of the word tactics in the strict sense means that they are not discussed as an important factor. As a result, the French reaction to English tactics which was a continuing development from the 1340s to the 1450s – the duration of the war – is not considered.

A further definition of the various levels of military activity should help to make the role of tactics clearer.

1. The level of diplomacy, of political manoeuvering.
2. The organisation of forces, how they were raised and paid for.
3. Logistics, that is the movement and supply of these forces.
4. Strategy, both overall and specific to theatre.
5. Operational or campaign strategy involving chevauchée, sieges and battle-seeking or avoiding courses of action.
6. Tactics, or close-range manoeuvre and use of troops and their weapons.
7. Individual acts of bravery (the aspect usually celebrated by a chronicler like Froissart).

So, in relation to the campaign of 1346, Edward III: claims the French Crown (diplomacy); raises forces by indenture (organisation); moves them across the Channel to Normandy (logistics); sacks Caen and advances to Paris (raiding strategy); then falls back to Crécy (operational decision); deploys his host defensively to ambush the pursuing French (tactics); and Edward, Prince of Wales, 'wins his spurs' in the ensuing encounter (heroics).

This is intended to be no more than a crude outline, but it does put tactics into perspective. If the study of tactics is now despised, it is because A.H. Burne and Sir Charles Oman raised them above these other aspects of warfare as the decisive factor – which it sometimes was and more often was not.[7] Their views are coloured more than a little by an anachronistic nationalism and affected by their belief in the superiority of English firepower 'throughout the ages'. So Burne the Gunner sees English archery as a sort of battlefield artillery (which to an extent it was, but the parallel should not be over-stressed). Sir Charles Oman is clearly influenced in his interpretation by his reading of the Peninsular War. This is the now generally accepted (though recently criticised) view that British musketry in line was inevitably superior to French column attacks, because of the number of weapons that

---

[6] C.T. Allmand, *The Hundred Years War: England and France at War, c.1300–c.1450* (Cambridge, 1988).
[7] Sir C. Oman, *A History of the Art of War in the Middle Ages*, 2 vols, vol. 2, 1279–1485 (First pub. 1898, revised and enlarged 1924). This work has also been reprinted recently (1991), although it badly needs updating.

could be brought to bear. The English archer formations flanking their men-at-
arms in Burne's reconstruction perform the same role. This serves to confirm the
eternal British-French stereotypes as well. The 'Brits' phlegmatic and well-
disciplined; the 'Frogs' excitable and uncontrolled; as it seemed to Victorian
English gentlemen at least![8]

A brief survey of archery tactics in the 'English' tradition may help to set the
subject in context. The archers' role at Hastings in 1066, is well known, although
the description of plunging 'fire' late in the day is only found two generations later
in Henry of Huntingdon's chronicle.[9] A detailed account of the Battle of the
Standard, fought between a northern English host and invading Scots near Northal-
lerton in 1138, places alternating bow and spearmen in the English line. This was
enough to shoot down and hurl back the impetuous Scottish charges; the day being
won by a counter-charge of the English cavalry reserve.[10] At Falkirk, in 1298, faced
with stationary Scottish schiltrons of massed pikemen, Edward I's archers 'shot-in'
their heavy cavalry. Perhaps this was also the plan on the second day of Bannockburn, sixteen years later. But the 'Hammer of the Scots' had been succeeded by his
ineffectual son, who mishandled his archers. Moving into a flanking position on
the main Scottish, they fell into disorder crossing a stream and were then counter-
charged and scattered by Robert the Bruce's well-used cavalry reserve.[11] As J.E.
Morris has shown, Edward I built up his missile arm by recruiting large numbers
of Welsh and English archers.[12] Under his grandson they were to make English
arms the most feared in Europe. How did this come about?

The most important short-term influences were probably the battle of Boroughbridge in 1322 and Dupplin Moor in 1332. On the first occasion, Thomas, Duke of
Lancaster was in rebellion against Edward II and retreating northwards. Sir
Andrew Harclay led the Royalist forces and defended the line of the river Ure with
a combination of dismounted men-at-arms and archers. Lancaster needed to break
through. He attacked the bridge with dismounted men and the ford with cavalry,
but both attacks were routed by the archery of the defenders. T.F. Tout, who
'discovered' this battle, believed that the archers were interspersed amongst the
men-at-arms.[13]

Ten years later, an opportunist expeditionary force led by Edward Baliol,

---

[8] P. Griffiths, *Forward into Battle* (Chichester, 1981), esp. ch. 3, The Alleged Firepower of
Wellington's Infantry.

[9] Henry of Huntingdon, *Historia Anglorum*, ed. T.A. Arnold, Rolls Series 74, VI, 28, pp. 203–4,
stresses the role of the archers at Hastings.

[10] J. Beeler, *Warfare in England 1066–1189* (New York, 1966), pp. 86–92 analyses the sources for
the battle in describing the likely English formation.

[11] See G.W.S. Barrow, *Robert Bruce and the Community of the Realm of Scotland* (London, 1965)
pp. 138–46 (Falkirk), 290–332 (Bannockburn); a more recent account of Bannockburn with several
detailed maps may be found in R.M. Scott, *Robert the Bruce, King of Scots* (Edinburgh, 1993) esp.
pp. 150–1.

[12] J.E. Morris, *The Welsh Wars of Edward I* (Oxford, 1901).

[13] T.F. Tout, 'The Tactics of the Battles of Boroughbridge and Morlaix', *Collected Papers*, 2 (1934),
pp. 221–25.

claimant to the throne of Scotland, similarly thrashed a much larger host of Scots by defending a defile with archers on the flanks (fig. 1.1).[14] In the following year, Edward III repeated the medicine at Halidon Hill. His three 'battles' were apparently each flanked by archers. The Scots under Sir Archibald Douglas had unwisely committed themselves to raising the siege of Berwick by a certain day. Their attack, uphill, in the now traditional, close-packed 'schiltroms' of spearmen, was bogged down in heavy ground (the area is still called Heavyside today), shot to pieces by the English archery and then massacred by a counter-attack of English cavalry (fig. 1.2). This was the model for English tactics throughout the Hundred Years' War.[14]

Its first application in France was at Morlaix in Brittany in 1342 (fig. 1.3). The earl of Northampton was supporting the Montfort candidate to the duchy. After initial successes in Montfortian areas he bit off more than he could chew by besieging Morlaix. Charles of Blois, the French candidate, led a much larger force (perhaps 3,000 men-at-arms and 1,500 Genoese mercenaries) against him. Northampton fell back to a defensive position a few miles north. He had a wood at his back, into which he put his baggage and horses, and a stream on one flank, adding a concealed ditch to his front. Charles attacked in three 'battles', one after the other. First came native Bretons, on foot and probably quite lightly armoured. They were shot down and hurled back onto the men-at-arms. The second battle charged on horseback, but fell into the ditch. The few who managed to get through were captured. After a delay a third French attack was launched but Northampton had already drawn back his forces – by now running out of arrows – into the wood. Hampered by the desertion of their Genoese crossbowmen the French were unable to break into the thickets and drew off. Northampton's men were short of food (and endured a siege of uncertain duration, perhaps for several days) before they charged out and broke through the encircling French lines.[15]

This was no great victory, although the English were greatly outnumbered, but it prefigured in several ways their successes at Crécy and Poitiers, respectively four and fourteen years later. As Burne points out, Northampton commanded the left wing at Crécy, and his presence may have influenced the tactics on that day. Personal experience and the passing on of information between contemporaries and even down the generations was crucial in the development of tactics.

The next encounter where English tactics proved superior, was, of course, at Crécy in 1346. Perhaps the story is well known. Edward III was in Normandy attempting to bring the French king to battle. He had twice failed to draw Philip into a fight in Flanders half-a-dozen years earlier, and the cost of that expedition, involving as it did an ambitious political alliance against France, had beggared the English government. The stand-off at Buironfosse (1339), as it was called, should not be forgotten because Philip chose to create a sort of fortified camp, which

---

[14] See R. Nicholson, *Edward III and the Scots* (Oxford, 1965), pp. 132–8.
[15] Morlaix, after Burne, *Crécy War*, p. 38 and Tout, 'Tactics'.

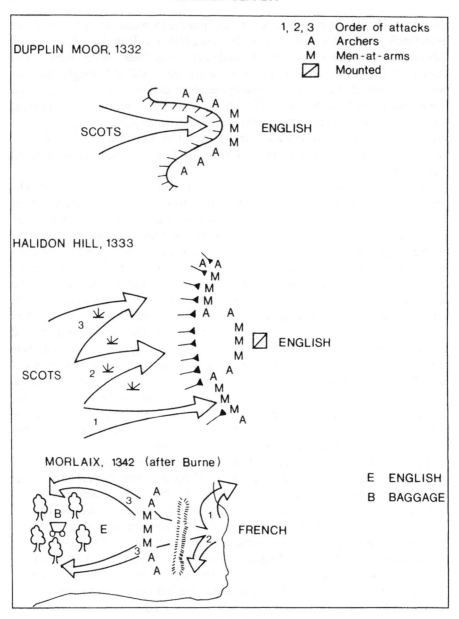

Fig. 1.1   (top) Dupplin Moor, 1332.
Fig. 1.2   (centre) Halidon Hill, 1333.
Fig. 1.3   (bottom) Morlaix, 1342.

Edward dare not attack.[16] So French commanders did not always opt for all out attack.

The situation was different in 1346. Edward had landed in western Normandy and chevauchéed to Caen, which he took and sacked. He then advanced toward Paris. It is not clear if he intended to bring the French on to him. He may have misjudged the vigour of Philip's response. Faced by much larger forces Edward began to withdraw north east to the Somme. The English fought their way across the ford at Blanchetacque, near the mouth of the river, and withdrew to a strong hilltop position at Crécy in Ponthieu. This was in territory well known to Edward. A recent paper suggests that the site had been carefully prepared beforehand, as regards supplies and ammunition. In addition, the field was apparently sown with pits, on the flanks at least, where the archers stood.[17]

This is perhaps the time to take a look at the old chestnut of how the English archers were deployed. Almost a century ago the pages of the English Historical Review were filled with debate on this subject. Froissart's description of the English at Crécy laid out 'à manière d'une herce' has caused much controversy as to what he actually meant. It could be interpreted as referring to the branches of a candlestick, a harrow (the most popular choice) or possibly, by reference to 'herrisson' a spiky fence (like a hedgehog). The one which has found most favour is that the archers were deployed on the flanks of each battle of men-at-arms and sloping slightly forward in order to provide a crossfire in front of the main battle line.[18] This has been elaborated by Burne into a formation with projecting 'teeth' of hollow wedges where two battles joined (fig. 1.4). There is a problem with this idea as it actually produces weak points in the English line, where, if contacted by heavily equipped men-at-arms, the archers would have been hard-pressed to defend themselves. In answer to this criticism proponents of Burne's idea suggest that the impact of the English archery would be to drive off attackers and funnel them into positions opposite their own men-at-arms, against whom, for reasons of social status opposing the men-at-arms preferred to fight.[19] I am not convinced by this argument.

It seems that on most occasions the English took care to protect their front with ditches or potholes, suggesting that they did not trust to hold off an enemy by

16 Comparison with warfare in the same area of Flanders in the eighteenth century is instructive, especially the campaign and battle of Malplaquet, 1709; see D. Chandler, *Marlborough as Military Commander* (London, 1973), esp. p. 253ff for the construction of an abbatis in wooded ground.

17 K.A. Fowler, 'News from the Front: Letters and Despatches of the Fourteenth Century', in *Guerre et Société en France, en Angleterre et en Bourgogne xive–xve siècle* (Lille, 1991), ed. P. Contamine, C. Giry-Deloison and M.H. Keen, pp. 63–92, esp. Document II, PRO, C 81/314/17803.

18 For the *EHR* debate, see E.M. Lloyd, 'The "Herse" of Archers at Crécy', July 1895, pp. 538–41; H.B. George, 'The Archers at Crécy', October 1895, pp. 733–38. J.E. Morris, 'The Archers at Crécy' July 1897, pp. 427–36 was the most influential. To him the 'herce' was a wedge-shaped formation. Yet surely he nods when translating 'deux battailes d'archiers à deux costés en la manière d'un escut' as describing shield-shaped formations and hence wedges?

19 See J. Keegan, *Face of Battle* (London, 1982), ch. 3 (Agincourt), esp. p. 100, for the supposed funnelling of the French men-at-arms.

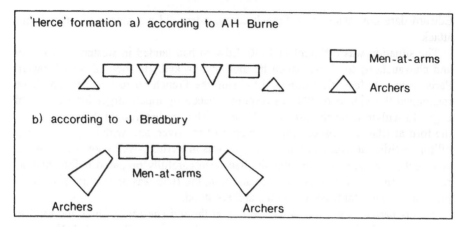

Fig. 1.4   'Herce' formation according to A.H. Burne and J. Bradbury.

'firepower' alone. This at least until they learned to use portable stakes as an obstacle. My theory is further reinforced by the advice of Jean de Bueil, in his treatise on warfare known as 'Le Jouvencel' (The Youth). This was written following personal experience in warfare, around 1466, and draws together the military lessons of the Hundred Years War. De Bueil advises deploying archers on the flanks of the main body, but protecting them by placing men-at-arms at either end of these wings ('aux deux bouts'). In fact, this description, and my interpretation of previous deployments, is close to a sixteenth-century layout of a core of close-order fighting men flanked with 'sleeves' of shot (although studying the 1890s debate I found that I was not the first to see the parallel).[20]

So, to return to Crécy. Edward seems to have formed his three 'battles' in the formation shown in fig. 1.5, although this is open to dispute. A recently published monumental work on the Hundred Years War to 1347, has the archers on the flanks surrounded by wagons for protection. I think that this is a misreading of Edward's use of wagons to protect his flanks and rear from encirclement, an ancient device used successfully against French cavalry as recently as 1304, at Mons-en-Pévèle by Flemish forces.[21] The English archers had to be more mobile than this if they were to perform effectively. For as J.E. Morris pointed out, they were not 'animated dummies'. Viollet-le-Duc's comparison with Napoleonic 'tirailleurs' is a telling one.[22] These musketry skirmishers formed a screen across the battalions' front, disrupting an enemy's formation and chain of command with their sniping fire. Similarly the archers could have started in front of the men-at-arms before falling

---

[20] Jean de Bueil, *Le Jouvencel*, ed. C. Favre & L. Lecestre, 2 vols (SHF, Paris, 1887–9) vol. 2, p. 37. See E.M. Lloyd, 'The "Herse" of Archers', pp. 539–40 for sixteenth-century parallels.
[21] J. Sumption, *The Hundred Years' War: Trial by Battle* (London, 1990), pp. 526–8; *Annales Gandenses*, ed. and trans. H. Johnson (London, 1951), pp. 66, 68–9.
[22] See the *EHR* debate, note 18.

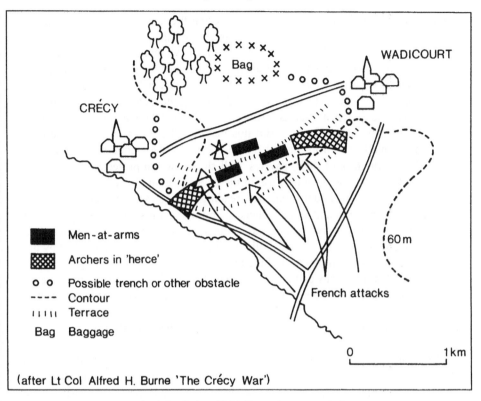

CRÉCY

WADICOURT

Bag

■ Men-at-arms

▨ Archers in 'herce'

o o Possible trench or other obstacle

---- Contour

ı ı ı ı ı Terrace

Bag Baggage

French attacks

60 m

0   1 km

(after Lt Col Alfred H. Burne 'The Crécy War')

Fig. 1.5 Crécy, 1346 (Burne's topography).

back to the flanks as an enemy approached. They could even have skipped between any pot-holes which had been dug while cavalry were brought down by them.[23]

At Crécy then, the archers seem to have been deployed forward and on the flanks. Their crossfire may have only covered the front of their own battle, although they may have been able to shoot over the heads of their men-at-arms owing to the terraced nature of the hillside.[24] Whatever was the case, the French attack failed through lack of coordination. Philip VI is rarely given any credit for generalship. But it is worth pointing out that he had successfully defeated a Flemish force at Cassel in 1328 with a well-judged cavalry flank attack. Further, his avoidance of battle at Buironfosse in 1339, and the following year at Bouvines, had proved masterstrokes in that Edward's campaigns collapsed as a result. Such a policy took some nerve to carry through, though, as it meant accepting the

[23] Geoffrey le Baker describes potholes one foot square and one deep (R. Barber, *The Life and Campaigns of the Black Prince* (London, 1979), p. 44) but according to H. de Wailly, *Crécy 1346: Anatomy of a Battle* (Poole, 1987), 51, 72–74, there is no indication from aerial photographs of any such defence.

[24] De Wailly, *Crécy*, pp. 72–3, n. 2 & 3 mentions a terrace upon which Edward's reserve 'battle' was positioned, but doubts that Prince Edward's 'battle' had the same advantage.

ravaging of his lands without reply, and enduring the taunts of chivalrous young nobles that this was the behaviour of the fox and not the lion. When Philip came upon Edward's army on 26 August, 1346, he may have thought that he finally had the English at a disadvantage (or that the humiliation outside Paris was too much to bear). I doubt also that he was the same man as at Cassel eighteen years earlier.[25]

His dispositions, if he had any, involved deploying the Genoese crossbowman in front, while mounted men-at-arms formed the traditional three battles in the centre, with any infantry on the flanks.[26] But this may be all too neat a description of a force hastily deploying from line of march. Certainly the Genoese crossbowmen suffered from the lack of their 'pavises' (tall shields which protected them whilst they reloaded), as these were on carts in the baggage train. They have been much reviled and hence misunderstood. My reading of Froissart suggests that they formed up under command and advanced with three great shouts to keep them in formation. That they were outshot was a function of their smaller numbers and more rapid shooting of the archers, both of which might have been remedied by the pavises. But it was the impatience of the French chivalry to be at the English which was the real disaster. Many and uncoordinated charges, delivered frontally, were no solution to the tactical problem, although apparently there was some breakthrough of the English archers of the Prince of Wales' battle. Philip had no control over the action and was only involved in the fighting when the English mounted for the pursuit.

Crécy proved the superiority of the English tactical system. What attempts did the French make to counter it? Already outside St Omer in 1340, a flank attack had been used to turn the position of forces commanded by Robert of Artois. But the troops who ran away that day were his inexperienced Flemish allies, and Robert won the day (on that field at least) with a determined counter-attack to his front, combining archers and dismounted men-at-arms.[27] In Tout's collected papers, he draws attention to 'Some neglected fights between Crécy and Poitiers'.[28] At Lunalonge, 'somewhere in Poitou' in 1349, an English force led by the Captal de Buch, was attacked by Jean de Lisle, seneschal of Poitou and Jean de Boucicault (fig. 1.6). The French sent part of their mounted force against the dismounted English, while another body galloped around the English rear to capture their horses. Unfortunately for the French their forces were defeated in detail, but they did drive off the English horses, forcing the victors to retire on foot during the night to a nearby fortress.

In 1351, on 6 April, near Taillebourg in the Saintonge, Guy de Nesle, marshal of France, chose to dismount most of his men-at-arms, except for two groups which he kept mounted on either flank of his main battle (fig. 1.7). It should be said that he still lost, and was captured, Tout surmising that the mounted flanks were still no

---

[25] See J. Sumption, *Trial by Battle*, p. 288, for accusations of 'reynarderie' made by young nobles against Philip VI in 1339.
[26] Ibid., pp. 528, on Philip VI's dispositions.
[27] Ibid., pp. 341–3 on St Omer.
[28] T.F. Tout, *Collected Papers*, 2 (1934), pp. 227–31.

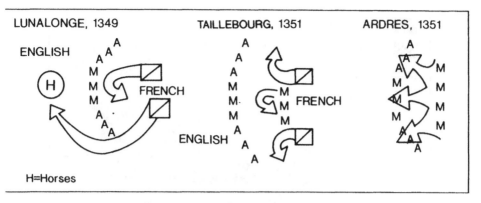

Fig. 1.6 Lunalonge, 1349.　　**Fig. 1.7** Taillebourg, 1351.　　**Fig. 1.8** Ardres, 1351.

counter to flanks of archers. In the same year, just two months later, in the northern theatre near Ardres, the lord of Beaujeu dismounted all his force to attack John of Beauchamp, captain of Calais, who was conducting a chevauchée (fig. 1.8). Beaujeu died, but the French triumphed taking Beauchamp with estimated English losses of 700 killed and captured. (We are not told who advanced to the attack although this might have been crucial, according to Jean de Bueil, below).

The following year, at Mauron in Brittany, there was a much larger battle between Guy de Nesle's forces and those under the command of Sir Walter Bentley. The standard English formation was countered by retaining one 'battle' of 700 men-at-arms on horseback. These were successful in driving off the archers who opposed them. But in the centre and on the other flank the dismounted attack, although pushing Bentley's line back as far as the cover to its rear, was defeated and de Nesle was killed. So the English had the victory, although the mounted French division was able to draw off unmolested. Bentley was so enraged by the failure of his right flank archers that he had thirty of them beheaded for cowardice ('pour encourager les autres' presumably; Burne believes this indicates that only thirty fled!).

The lesson of these encounters is that the French were thinking tactically, that they were experimenting, and that these experiments were carried out all over France. Guy de Nesle was a royal official as was de Lisle, so this looks like an official policy to seek a battle-winning tactic, not just inspired improvisation at local level. That it was not universally successful may be because, to paraphrase Jean de Bueil: 'A dismounted force which attacks another dismounted force is beaten.'[29] So much for the benefits of hindsight; but the difficulty in maintaining formation was a real one, and disorder the main factor in defeat.

If King John had devised a plan to disrupt the English formation, he was unable

---

[29] Jean de Bueil, *Le Jouvencel*, vol. 1, p. 153. His full remark is: 'Everywhere and on all occasions that footsoldiers march against their enemy face to face, those who march lose and those who remain standing still and holding firm win.' (This translation is from P. Contamine, *War in the Middle Ages*, trans. M. Jones (Oxford, 1984) p. 231.)

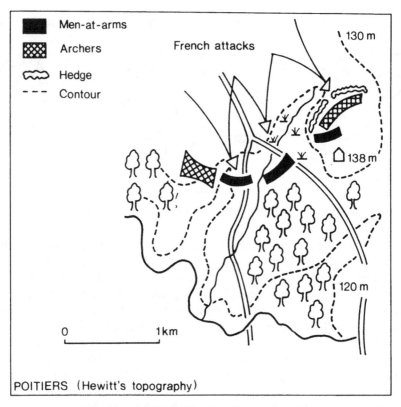

Men-at-arms

Archers

Hedge

Contour

French attacks

130 m

138 m

120 m

0   1 km

POITIERS (Hewitt's topography)

Fig. 1.9 Poitiers, 1356 (Hewitt's topography).

to put it into effect at Poitiers, in 1356. His much larger force had caught up with Edward, Prince of Wales' chevauchée a few miles south of the city, where the English were trying to get their heavily-laden waggons of booty over the River Moisson. All accounts of the battle are very confusing. It seems to have been what would later be called 'a scrambling fight'. Edward certainly intended that this should be the case. For he brought his forces into an area of broken ground so unlike most of the plains surrounding Poitiers (fig. 1.9). The map is only one guess as to the dispositions, which were probably fluid during the battle anyway. The Prince's three 'battles' (one of which may have been south of the river when the action began) were defending a position protected by hedges, trees and marshy land. The French, in much greater numbers, seem to have had only two avenues of approach.

After a day's delay for negotiation, the French attacked. Edward may have been trying to slip away when this happened, which is why Warwick's left 'battle' may have been across the river. But if it was, it soon returned to play an important part in the action. First, the French tried surprise, a rapid cavalry charge led by the marshals Clermont and Audrehem but this foundered due to the terrain and the English archery. Then the Dauphin's vanguard battle attacked on foot, to be driven back after a hard fight. The defeat of this force seems to have caused the second 'battle' under Orléans, to flee. This suggests that it was mounted. But the third and largest battle, commanded by the king, arrived after some delay and also walked into the attack. The main problem for the French seems to have been the lack of coordination between their attacks, as well as the terrain which made it difficult for them to bring their greater numbers to bear. As it turned out, it was the exhausted English who took the initiative, Edward mounting some, or all of his men, to counter-attack. The crucial factor was the flanking movement led by Jean de Grailly, Captal de Buch, who led his mounted force into (probably) the left rear of the French force. The shout which his men gave when they launched their attack was crucial in breaking the French morale. Although it is likely that they still out-numbered the Anglo-Gascon force, they crumpled under the two-pronged attack, leaving King John and most of his upper nobility prisoners in Edward's hands.[30]

Poitiers was decided by one side having and keeping the tactical initiative. Valiant French attempts to wrest this from Edward failed because their forces were not flexible enough to cope with the situation which was presented. Once again French missilemen are notable by their absence, only featuring in the description of the final fight. While the English system could combine missile-power and shock, the product of good discipline, it could not be beaten. The result was that, for a generation, in France at least, the French went back to the successful strategy of avoiding battle. The battle of Auray in Brittany, in 1364, was an exception. Here Bertrand du Guesclin, the Breton mercenary who was to become one of chivalry's greatest heroes, was in command. He tried the tactic of advancing his men-at-arms on foot behind pavises, in order to reduce casualties and disorder from the English arrows. Although it succeeded in this, the French still lost the hand-to-hand fight and Du Guesclin was captured. This fate was to befall him again three years later at Najera, in Spain, where he faced the Prince of Wales's army fighting on the other side of the Castillian succession dispute. Du Guesclin's caution, learned by hard experience, could not be impressed upon his allies, and once more the English tactical system was triumphant.

The battle of Aljubarrota in 1385, provides us with detailed information of how a defensive position was prepared to give a killing ground for the archers. To my knowledge, Crécy has never been excavated, so the field defences are unknown, but in the late 1950s an archaeological dig at Aljubarrota produced remarkable results (fig. 1.10). This shows the left wing of the position and possibly the centre too. Note the ditch, 'not so deep that a dismounted man could not leap it' (Froissart), and the V-shaped field of potholes about a foot square and deep, some 200 yards wide by 100 yards in depth, in rows roughly a yard apart. The Portuguese dispositions placed the English archers in two wings in front of the men-at-arms. They seem also to have been to the flanks, as Froissart describes them as shooting from there. The first attack was made by dismounted knights,

---

[30] For the most detailed map and description, see J.J. Hewitt, *The Black Prince's Expedition of 1355–57* (Manchester, 1958), pp. 110–39, map p. 115.

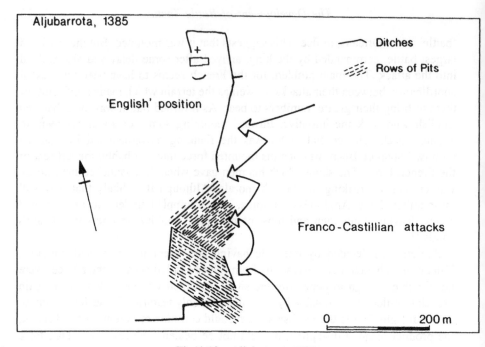

Fig. 1.10 Aljubarrota, 1385.

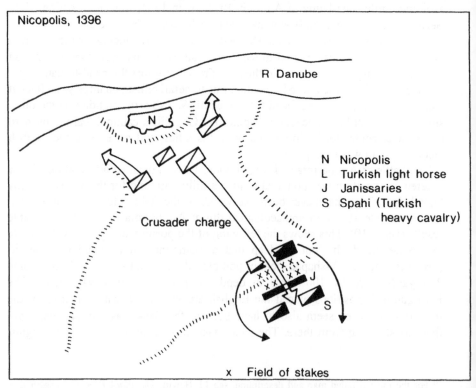

Fig. 1.11 Nicopolis, 1396.

who crossed the ditch, but having done so were attacked in the rear by lightly-armed troops, presumably swarming around them, and to the front by the defending men-at-arms. The result was a massacre of the supposedly 4,000 strong vanguard. When the Castillians arrived and delivered a mounted charge they were quickly repelled and the defenders mounted up to counter-attack in pursuit. What can be seen at Aljubarrota must have been reproduced on the many battlefields which are no longer visible.[31]

The next phase of tactical development concerns the Burgundian experience, in which the battle of Nicopolis was crucial.[32] Nicopolis (in modern Bulgaria) was the place where the largely Burgundian and French crusaders of 1396 were totally defeated by the Ottoman sultan Bayezit (fig. 1.11). The battle map is taken from A. Attiya's book on the subject and the best description comes from the 'Book of the Deeds and Sayings of Marshal Boucicault'. Disdaining to take the advice of their Hungarian allies the crusaders attacked a defensive position. They were unaware that a light cavalry screen masked a field of stakes 'a bowshot deep' filled with Janissary foot archers. Brought to a halt by the obstacle, the crusader men-at-arms either tried to force their horses amongst the stakes, dismounted and tried to remove them, or just dismounted and pushed on up the hill. Eventually most seem to have chosen the last option. Contacting the lightly armoured Turkish foot they routed them. But breasting the rise after this victory they found themselves horseless and exhausted, faced by the cream of the Ottoman heavy cavalry. After some resistance there was a general surrender.[33]

The importance of this battle relates to the role of the stakes. This is the first reference, as far as I am aware, to such a defence. What is more Froissart describes it as in the form of a 'herce'. There is an alternative explanation for 'harrow' interpretation mentioned earlier – that it represents the spacing of men in the same way as the spikes of a harrow, that is to say alternately and not one-behind-the-other. If this is what Froissart meant all along, then it is not formation and not deployment which is important. It implies a loosely-spaced group of archers, all able to pick targets and shoot without obstruction, several ranks deep. The stakes add a further refinement in that the archers have a defensive belt within which they can manoeuvre or retreat to its cover. It is almost impenetrable to mounted men and can only be neutralised by the strenuous efforts of dismounted men whilst in close archery range. It was a mobile version of the woods and hedges which the English archers had previously sought on the battlefield.

[31] A. do Paço, 'The Battle of Aljubarrota', *Antiquity*, 27, 1963, pp. 264–69 and pls. 38 & 39a. The pits are variable in length, depth and distance apart laterally, but might have been drawn up on the rule of thumb of a yard long, half-a-yard wide and a foot deep. Certainly, the rows seem to have been consistently ten feet apart. (I understand that a more recent report on the battlefield was produced, in Portuguese, in 1993, but this had not come to hand at time of publication.)
[32] B. Schnerb, 'La bataille rangée dans la tactique des armées bourguignonnes au début du 15e siècle: essai de synthèse', in *Annales de Bourgogne*, 71, 1989, pp. 5–32.
[33] A. Attiya, *The Crusade of Nicopolis* (London, 1934), pp. 82–97; *Le livre des fais du bon messire Jehan Le Maingre, dit Bouciquaut*, ed. D. Lalande (Geneva, 1985).

According to the *Gesta Henrici Quinti* this is how Henry ordered his archers to prepare stakes.

> As a result of information divulged by some prisoners, a rumour went round the army that enemy commanders had assigned certain bodies of knights, many hundreds strong and mounted on barded horses, to break the formation and resistance of our archers when they engaged us in battle. The King, therefore, ordered that every archer, throughout the army, was to prepare for himself a stake or staff, either square or round, but six feet long, of sufficient thickness and sharpened at both ends. And he commanded that whenever the French approached to give battle and break their ranks with such bodies of horsemen, all the archers were to drive their stakes in front of them in a line and some behind them and in between the positions of the front rank, one being driven into the ground pointing towards themselves, the other end pointing towards the enemy at waist-height. So that the cavalry, when their charge had brought them close and in sight of the stakes, would either withdraw in great fear or, reckless of their own safety, run the risk of having both horses and riders impaled.[34]

It seems likely that Henry had heard of the success of this device at Nicopolis two decades earlier. If this is true then there is a delicate irony here. Marshal Boucicault owed his defeat and capture at Nicopolis to the tactical use of archery. At Agincourt he suffered the same fate. How did Henry learn the trick? Doubtless it circulated orally, but it was also 'published' (in the medieval sense of the word) in the book celebrating Boucicault's career in 1411, just four years before Agincourt. What deepens the irony is that Boucicault had refined some tactics to defeat the English and intended to use them for the Agincourt campaign. Dr Christopher Philpotts only recently discovered this battle plan in a damaged Cottonian manuscript in the British Library.[35]

Bertrand Schnerb points out that at Othée in 1408, John the Fearless defeated the Hainaulters with a tactical plan that mimicked the English system. His main battle, dismounted, was flanked by 2,000 archers who poured arrows upon the surprised Flemings, meanwhile 400 men-at-arms and 1,000 'gros valets' (more lightly equipped) remained mounted to sweep in on the flanks and rear. We have seen that this was a standard counter to English dismounted dispositions since the 1350s. Boucicault was attempting something similar, as fig. 1.12 shows.

Dr Philpotts showed in his article that this was the plan, however ineptly performed, for Agincourt. It proposed cavalry charges upon the flanks and rear of the English with troops of more lightly armoured horse, while the heavy men-at-arms slogged it out in the main battle, on foot. But everything went horribly wrong for the French at Agincourt (fig. 1.13). The flank charges were undermanned and cramped for room and were effectively neutralised by the defensive stakes; their

---

[34] *Gesta Henrici Quinti*, ed. and trans. F. Taylor and J.S. Roskell (Oxford, 1975), pp. 68–71, slightly modified.

[35] C. Philpotts, 'The French plan of battle during the Agincourt campaign', *EHR*, 30, 1984, pp. 59–68. For a translation and explanation of this document see M. Bennett, *Agincourt: Triumph against the Odds* (London, 1991) pp. 62–6.

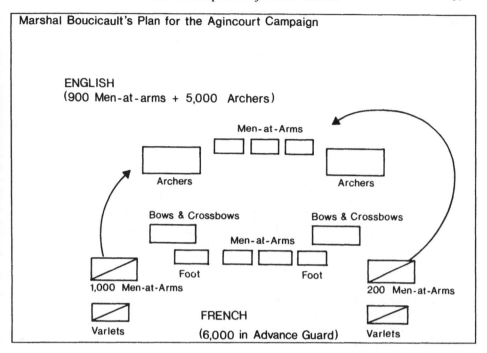

Fig. 1.12   Marshal Boucicault's plan for the Agincourt campaign.

missilemen were not utilised but were rather pushed behind the vanguard of men-at-arms whom they should have been supporting. The attacks on foot were swept by archery, blunted by the mud (with the resultant exhaustion of the men-at-arms) and repulsed by the relatively fresh English men-at-arms. To cap it all the English archers proved nimble, deadly opponents in the boggy ground, swinging leaden mallets which they used for driving in the stakes. National stereotypes dominate again!

It appears from the foregoing that chivalrous types learnt nothing; but they did. The Burgundian Ordinance for John the Fearless' advance on Paris in 1417 shows how. This was first published by J.F. Verbruggen in 1959 (and later translated by Richard Vaughan in his book on the duke). It is well known, but Schnerb does not make the connection between the two plans clear, although he cites them both.[36] Duke John lost a brother and numerous other relatives and vassals at Agincourt. He must have pondered on what went wrong. So his plan stresses (Clauses 9 & 10) that there must be sufficient space to deploy the main battle so that it does not crowd the van or neutralise the bowmen, as happened at Agincourt. Furthermore,

---

[36] J.F. Verbruggen, 'Un plan de bataille du duc de Bourgogne (14 septembre 1417) et le tactique de l'époque', in *Revue internationale d'histoire militaire*, 20, 1959, pp. 443–51. This is translated by R. Vaughan, *John the Fearless* (London, 1966), pp. 148–50, although he omits clause 2 and confuses the issue by re-numbering the document's clauses. Schnerb, 'La bataille', p. 32, mentions Nicopolis but does not understand the significance of the battle.

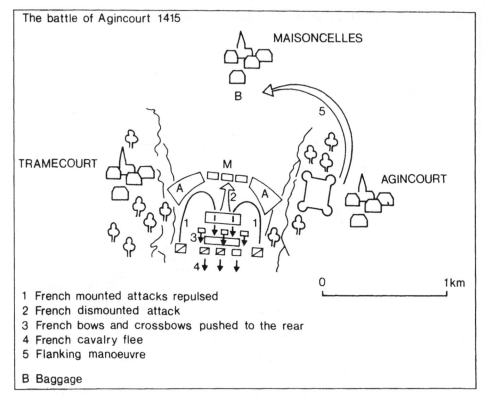

Fig. 1.13   The battle of Agincourt, 1415.

during his advance on Paris he practised his army in drawing up in this formation, in order that his men should be able to do it in the presence of the enemy. Monstrelet draws attention to the fact that John threatened strict punishments for anyone withdrawing from the battle. Clause 2 '. . . Everyone, of whatever rank, must keep to his standard or banner in battle, with no excuses to leave it. And, on the day of battle no-one, on pain of losing his life and possessions (sur peine de perdre corps et biens), shall flee . . . And (the duke) wishes anyone who discovers those in flight shall kill them and cut them into pieces and shall gain their possessions. And, if by chance they should not be captured, the duke calls them traitors, evil men and committers of the crime of "lèse majesté" ' (fig. 1.14).[37]

This had been the case at Agincourt, when the third, mounted division, melted away; it had been the case at Poitiers and it was the medieval general's greatest problem. What John demanded was discipline. Vaughan does not realise the significance of the disciplinary clause, which he omits from his translation; but battlefield discipline is crucial to success, upon it rests the proper execution of a tactical plan. Hence the Burgundian requirements of the creation of units with clearly distinguished standards and the requirement to keep to them. These new

37 J.F. Verbruggen, 'Un plan de bataille', pp. 444–5.

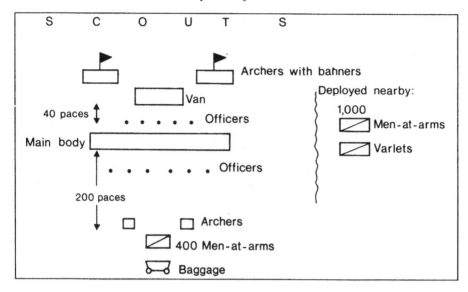

Fig. 1.14 John the Fearless' *Ordinance* of 1417.

instructions gave the Burgundian – potentially at least – an effective battlefield weapon.[38]

The Burgundian encounter with the Armagnacs at St-Rémy-sur-Plain in 1422, saw them deployed with 1,200 dismounted men-at-arms, supported by 500 missilemen flanking them and 2,400 mounted 'valet d'armes'. The formation resembled nothing so much as the sixteenth-century disposition of a main body with 'sleeves' of shot, mentioned above. The Ordinance dictates small banners for missilemen (in order that they might operate separately in what were later called 'commanded' bodies of shot). A waggon-fort protected the rear of this formation; an old tactic and a good one. When the enemy's mounted charge was repelled the Burgundians counter-attacked with a loud shout. Co-ordinated shouting was another aspect of English tactics instanced at Poitiers and elsewhere. So when Burgundians and the English combined at Cravant to force the river crossing they were playing the same game. At Verneuil in 1424, the French flank attacks were neutralised by English stakes (although some fell down in the hard ground). The tactical debate was carried on both on and off the battlefield.

The English had a successful system and stuck to it. When it failed in the last two big battles of the war, at Formigny and Castillon, it was not because artillery blew the archers away, but because Kyriell and Talbot failed to employ the tactics properly. But artillery was beginning to make an impact in the field. When the Burgundians used it against the Barrois in 1430 they combined the shooting with a

---

[38] See M. Vale, *War and Chivalry*, pp. 148–9, on the importance of units and flags. The Burgundian failures against the Swiss are not relevant here!

great shout. Many of the enemy, 'went to ground' (in modern parlance) terror-
stricken by the impact of the noise and blast.[39]

So, in conclusion, there is a link to be made between the English archery of the
Hundred Years' War and British musketry of the Napoleonic Wars. But it is not
solely 'firepower' that matters; it is the combination of missile fire and the shout –
the first to shake the enemy, the second to let him know that you are still confident
enough to close with him, which often decided the day. Nor should this be seen as
a specific national characteristic, as nineteenth-century English historians saw it –
three rousing British cheers to see off the excitable lesser breeds! It was a game to
which anyone could learn the rules, if they were prepared to submit to the necessary discipline and to practise. Tactics were a transferable skill and central to the
conduct of one aspect of medieval warfare.

[39] Schnerb, 'La bataille', p. 31.

2

English Armies in the Fourteenth Century

ANDREW AYTON

ON 12 APRIL, the Sunday after Easter, 1360, an English army led by Edward III stood fully arrayed for battle outside Paris.[1] After two decades of intermittent war, the stage was set for a decisive confrontation between Plantagenet and Valois. The gauntlet had been thrown down, but much to Edward's chagrin the dauphin declined to take up the challenge. Despite the anticlimactic turn of events, the spectacle of an English army before Paris, with several columns marching, like Joshua's host, 'close under the faubourgs from sunrise till midday', would linger long in the memories of those who were there. Sir Thomas Gray harked back to these events in his military memoirs.[2] Many of the deponents in the Court of Chivalry cases of the 1380s recalled that they had been participants in what the deposition of that old veteran Sir Adam de Everingham described as the 'great voyage when the late king and his army had been before Paris'.[3] To have been arrayed with their king in this display of military might outside the French capital was clearly a source of lasting pride – and it is easy to understand why, for this particular army was indeed a formidable fighting machine. An excellent set of pay accounts suggests that its effective strength at the start of the campaign was approaching 10,000 men.[4] This would make it one of the largest English armies fielded during the Hundred Years War, surpassed in size during the fourteenth-century phase of the war only by the hosts assembled for the Normandy campaign of 1346 and for the subsequent siege of Calais in 1347. But Edward III's army in 1359–60 was formidable in more ways than just its size. It was exceptionally well equipped; and it was led by a glittering array of military talent, headed by the king's most trusted lieutenants, including the Prince of Wales, Henry, duke of Lancaster, the earls of Northampton and Warwick and Sir Walter Mauny: men who had been responsible for many of the English military successes of the preceding two decades. In the autumn of 1359, as this army landed in France, the reputation

---

[1] *The Anonimalle Chronicle, 1333 to 1381*, ed. V.H. Galbraith (Manchester, 1927), p. 46. All documents cited in the footnotes are in the custody of the Public Record Office, London. I am grateful to my colleague Dr J.J.N. Palmer for comments on a draft of this paper.
[2] *Scalacronica*, ed. and trans. Sir H. Maxwell (Glasgow, 1907), pp. 156–7.
[3] *The Scrope-Grosvenor Controversy*, ed. N.H. Nicolas (2 vols, London, 1932), i. pp. 240–1.
[4] E101/393/11 fos. 79–116v. The total excludes non-combatants, as well as the contingents of continental men-at-arms, Welsh infantry and others who left the king's pay during the first few days of the campaign.

of English arms was as high as it had ever been. In the view of the Liègeois chronicler, Jean le Bel, the English were 'les plus nobles et les plus frisques combastans qu'on sache'.[5] The transformation since the dark days of Edward II's reign, since the débâcle of Bannockburn in 1314 and the series of dismal campaigns in Scotland and Gascony during the following decade, had indeed been astonishing. At the heart of England's rise as a front-rank military power in the middle decades of the fourteenth century were changes in military organisation, in the composition of armies and in the conduct of war: changes which, when taken as a whole, amount to a major overhaul of the military machine at the disposal of the English crown. Some historians, indeed, have called it a 'military revolution'.[6]

It has become customary in discussing the Edwardian military revolution to focus particular attention on changes in methods of recruitment and forms of remuneration: in short, on the emergence of paid, contract armies. The provision of pay on a large scale has been seen as a catalyst for wider developments, with the 'indenture system', the raising of armies by means of short-term, written contracts between the king and his captains, as the most effective way in which paid armies could be put in the field. In broad brush-stroke terms, the feudal host, based upon the compulsory, unpaid provision of companies of men-at-arms by tenants-in-chief in fulfilment of their military obligations, had been superseded by contract armies, consisting of paid volunteers. Seen from the perspective of the later fourteenth century, a radical change in recruitment practice had taken place, but the transformation occurred only gradually and the seeds of change had long been sown. English kings had been employing paid contingents for several centuries prior to the Edwardian period. What we see in the first half of the fourteenth century is the establishment of *wholly* paid armies. Hitherto, complexity of recruitment practice had prevailed. A typical royal army of Edward I's reign, such as that which fought the Caerlaverock campaign in 1300, consisted of a mixture of feudal, voluntary unpaid and paid elements. Magnates, concerned that their retinues should properly reflect their status, supplemented their shrunken feudal quotas with additional men-at-arms and met the extra expense themselves. Even when pay was available, some magnates, like Thomas, earl of Lancaster, resolutely refused to accept it for their men. Turning to those who did receive the king's pay, we should not imagine them all to be volunteers. Many had been pressured into the performance of military service. In the case of the aristocracy, this pressure might involve a personal – though non-feudal – summons, or a general invitation addressed to those possessed of a particular level of landed wealth (in 1300, £40 *per annum* landholders). For lowly foot-soldiers, the pressure would come from the operation of commissions of array: the high rates of desertion from the shire levies during Edward I's Scottish campaigns suggest that many of those arrayed were anything but enthusiastic volunteers. Armies including both paid and unpaid elements persisted into the 1320s. Troops serving in fulfilment of the feudal obligations of

---

5   *Chronique de Jean Le Bel*, ed. J. Viard and E. Déprez (2 vols, Paris, 1905), i. p. 156.
6   M. Prestwich, *The Three Edwards: War and State in England, 1272–1377* (London, 1980), p. 62.

tenants in chief were still in evidence in the hosts raised in 1322 and 1327.[7] By the time of Edward III's campaigns in Scotland in the mid 1330s, royal armies were wholly paid, even though, for the moment at least, many captains bringing contingents did so in response to individual mandatory – though non-feudal – summons from the crown. Paid service, then, was not necessarily voluntary service. Even when we find captains contracting freely with the crown, as many did during the Hundred Years War, we may be sure that *they* would often need to turn the screws of obligation and exploit ties with local communities when recruiting their retinues, calling upon the services of indentured retainers, tenants and members of a wider affinity. English armies were held together, albeit loosely, by threads of obligation; wholly freelance sub-contractors provided only a proportion of the manpower of a contract army.

It is usual to speak of 'paid armies', but it is important to remember that for the rank and file of these armies pay was very often only one element in a 'package' of terms of service, involving both benefits and obligations. One benefit *not* related to the receipt of pay was the letter of protection: a document, issued by Chancery, which gave the recipient security from a wide range of legal actions for the duration of a specified period of service. A man knowing that court proceedings were pending at the time of his departure for war could secure a letter of protection and thereby halt the process of law until he had returned to England; but it is likely that most letters of protection were obtained as precautionary measures, to deal with unexpected legal actions. Since the traditional warrior class was also the landowning class, with a great deal to lose at the hands of litigious neighbours and rivals, it is not surprising to find that often at least a third, and sometimes as many as a half, of the men-at-arms serving in a mid fourteenth-century army secured the issue and enrolment of protections before leaving the kingdom. In a very real sense, the availability of protections, along with the development of enfeoffment to use, allowed the aristocracy a degree of freedom to perform, if only intermittently, their traditional martial function at a time of regular, heavy recruiting demands. Mention should also be made at this point of charters of pardon, granted as reward for spells of service in the king's armies, since the government used them as an even more blatant recruiting device. Here was a means of securing legal redemption, of wiping the slate clean, and many criminals seized the opportunity with both hands. During the Scottish and French wars large numbers of war-service pardons were issued (including, for example, several thousand during and after the Crécy-Calais campaign in 1346–47), the great majority to non-aristocratic combatants.

The issue of pardons was not connected specifically to the receipt of pay (indeed, for some campaigns, those seeking a pardon were obliged to serve 'at their own expense'); but the other terms of service which affected, in particular, men-at-arms were all related in one way or another to the receipt of the king's wages.

---

[7] N. Fryde, *The Tyranny and Fall of Edward II, 1321–1326* (Cambridge, 1979), chapter 9; N.B. Lewis, 'The Summons of the English Feudal Levy, 5 April 1327', *Essays in Medieval History Presented to Bertie Wilkinson*, ed. T.A. Sandquist and M.R. Powicke (Toronto, 1969), pp. 236–49.

Firstly, there was the bonus payment known as *regard*. This was introduced for continental expeditions in the mid-1340s and appears to have been intended as a supplement to men-at-arms' pay to help cover the ever growing cost of plate armour. At the usual rates, paid as a lump sum to captains, *regard* represented a supplementary payment of about 6d. per day for each man-at-arms. This was a significant bonus, since the usual daily rates of pay – 2s. for knights and 1s. for ordinary men-at-arms – remained unchanged right through the fourteenth century. A man-at-arms receiving the king's pay for continental campaigns would also benefit from the appraisal of his principal war-horse, so that, in the event of its loss, he would be able to claim from the crown an appropriate cash payment as compensation (*restauratio equorum*). The sums involved were not insignificant, since a man-at-arms' war-horse was his most expensive item of equipment. Drawing on the evidence of surviving appraisal lists, we can see that the average value of war-horses taken by Englishmen to France at the start of the Hundred Years War was about £15; with esquires of modest means often being content with £5 mounts and great captains, like the earl of Northampton, serving with magnificent *destriers* valued at £100. To put these figures in perspective, a knight serving in the king's army for one year would receive, in theory at least, about £45 in pay and *regard*. Horse appraisal and compensation was, therefore, a most welcome dimension of paid service. It was a privilege for those taking the king's pay, but also, in the earlier fourteenth century at least, a prerequisite of receiving pay. From the crown's point of view, the horse appraisal process was an integral part of muster and review, a means of checking that men-at-arms were serving with horseflesh of respectable quality. This, at the start of the Hundred Years War, meant horses worth at least 100s.

The last element in the standard package of terms of service accepted by men entering the king's pay concerns the division of the spoils of war. In taking the king's pay, a man accepted that he owed the crown a proportion of the profits, from booty and ransoms, which he might accumulate whilst on campaign. In practice, men-at-arms and archers would deliver this portion of their winnings to their captain, and he in turn would render the same proportion of his overall takings to the crown. The long-established view has been that the king's portion was a third;[8] but recent research has established that until the early 1370s, provided the full package of benefits was on offer – normal rates of pay and *regard*, and horse appraisal – then the senior contracting party would expect to receive *half* of the value of his subordinates' profits. As with most aspects of military organisation during this era of war, the package of terms of service was by no means fixed in granite. There were occasional experiments and, in the early 1370s, a major and permanent reform. The records for the campaigns of 1372 and 1373 reveal the nature of the changes that were made.[9] Horse appraisal was abandoned and to compensate for this, *regard* was paid at double the former usual rate and the king's

[8]   D. Hay, 'The Division of the Spoils of War in Fourteenth-Century England', *TRHS*, 5th ser., 4 (1954), pp. 91–109.
[9]   For example, E101/68/4 nos. 92–94; E101/32/26 mm. 3–4.

portion of the winnings of war was reduced from a half to a third. Horse appraisal was administratively expensive, but cost-cutting was probably not the only motive behind the reforms; the government appears also to have been aiming to provide more favourable terms of service. In this they achieved a measure of success: the typical man-at-arms *was* likely to be better-off under the new arrangements. The mechanism for horse compensation had always been an imperfect method for covering campaign costs. Only one of a knight's several war-horses would be appraised and thus eligible for compensation at any one time; and horse compensation payments were often hopelessly in arrears. Moreover, with war-horse quality declining perceptibly as the century progressed, the need for appraisal and compensation may have seemed less pressing than before; and, under the reformed package of terms, double *regard* offered a larger assured lump-sum payment to cover the costs of campaign preparations.

Paid military service, then, was actually service which involved a range of benefits and obligations. These terms of service are perhaps most readily seen in indentures of war, but the package of terms would operate perfectly well when no written contracts were employed. Bearing in mind the prominence accorded to the 'indenture system' in many discussions of the Edwardian military revolution, it is worth emphasising that indentures of war were scarcely employed at all for the major expeditions led personally by Edward III during the first phase of the Hundred Years War.[10] Take, for example, the army with whose parade outside the walls of Paris in April 1360 this chapter began. Its personnel were certainly subject to the normal terms of service. The pay-rolls reveal the operation of most elements of the package; and, as we shall see shortly, this army was not at all backward-looking in its structure and composition. Yet, as with the army which fought the Crécy-Calais campaign, no formal written contracts between the king and his English captains were deemed necessary, for both of these armies were led personally by the king and administered directly by the royal household's financial department, the Wardrobe. The army of 1359–60 was still, as it had been in Edward I's day, 'the household in arms', although the household division – the companies brought by royal household bannerets and knights, which under Edward I might provide a third or more of paid heavy cavalry – was smaller by the mid to late fourteenth century, contributing about a sixth of men-at-arms in 1359 and a similar proportion to armies later in the century.[11]

The 'indenture system', then, was a mechanism designed to fill the administrative vacuum which appeared when the king was not leading the army in person and the clerical staff of the royal household were not on hand to supervise the distribution of wages and deal with related matters, such as horse appraisal. Indentures of war had shown their potential in this respect during the reigns of the first

[10] The use of contracts for a cancelled expedition in 1341 was necessitated by the crown's reliance on wool assignments to finance recruitment: M. Prestwich, 'English Armies in the Early Stages of the Hundred Years War: A Scheme of 1341', *BIHR*, 56 (1983), pp. 102–113.

[11] C. Given-Wilson, *The Royal Household and the King's Affinity. Service, Politics and Finance, 1360–1413* (New Haven and London, 1986), pp. 63–4.

two Edwards, when they had been used to recruit troops for garrison service and for spells of duty on the Scottish border and in Gascony. In the early summer of 1337, on the eve of the continental war, about 500 men-at-arms were raised by contract for a Scottish expedition which the king did not intend to lead in person.[12] Indentures of war emerged as a distinctive feature of the first phase of the Hundred Years War because the struggle was fought simultaneously on several fronts, with most of the expeditionary forces being led, not by the king himself, but by his lieutenants. For example, in the spring of 1345, as the king contemplated a campaign in northern France, Henry of Grosmont, earl of Derby contracted to take 2,000 men to Gascony, whilst the earl of Northampton agreed to serve with about 500 men in Brittany.[13] The 'indenture system', with captains accounting for their periods of service directly at the Exchequer, became the invariable method of raising armies during the second phase of the war, from 1369, because the king, increasingly inactive during the 1370s, was no longer directly involved in the struggle. By the time of the Agincourt campaign in 1415, all armies, whether or not they were to be led by the king in person, were raised by means of indentures of war.

The establishment of wholly paid armies, whether recruited by means of informal agreements between king and captains or formal written indentures of war, greatly enhanced the quality and effectiveness of the military resources at the disposal of the English crown. The size of armies and the duration of their service could be pre-determined and adjusted to suit particular military requirements; and appropriate budgeting and administrative provisions could be made. Numbers of personnel and quality of equipment could be checked by regular muster and review. It would not be true to say that 'control was lax' in the fourteenth century; a great many pay accounts, muster rolls and other documents confirm the regularity of personnel checks. With paid, contract armies, a king had at his disposal the means of waging war on an ambitious scale, of executing coordinated strategic plans, such as the multi-pronged attacks on France in the 1340s and 1350s, when expeditionary forces operated simultaneously in Brittany, Gascony and northern France. A strategy of this kind, depending as it did upon the work of a team of lieutenants, offered great opportunities to the militarily talented members of the aristocracy, whether from the higher nobility – like Henry, duke of Lancaster and William de Bohun, earl of Northampton – or of more modest gentry stock, like Sir Thomas Dagworth and Sir Walter Bentley. The captains relieved the crown of much of the burden of recruitment and military administration, and at the same time acquired considerable influence in the direction of the war. These responsibilities were potentially costly; indeed, the functioning of the military machine *depended* upon contracting captains making full use of their own financial and manpower resources. The mobilisation of feed retainers speeded up the process of

---

[12] N.B. Lewis, 'The Recruitment and Organisation of a Contract Army, May to November 1337', *BIHR*, 37 (1964), pp. 1–19.
[13] K. Fowler, *The King's Lieutenant: Henry of Grosmont, First Duke of Lancaster, 1310–1361* (London, 1969), pp. 230–2; E101/68/4 no. 72.

recruitment, as well bringing a degree of stability to a contract army. Magnate money eased the cash-flow problems with which military expeditions were invariably beset. Timely injections of a captain's own cash would help to get expeditions underway, keep them moving and hold them together. Of course, privatisation of the war effort also brought opportunities for gain. Apart from those princely ransoms much-discussed by historians, some captains found that 'margins of profit' could be secured by recruiting men at pay rates below those offered by the crown. Perhaps most important as an attraction, if as elusive in fulfilment as ransom-hunting, was the prospect of enhanced political influence and personal honour which successful war leadership could bring. But profits of whatever kind could not be relied upon. Altogether more certain was that war leadership would eat into a noble captain's personal resources. Dependence on the wealth and social authority of the nobility ensured that command of major field armies was rarely given to the 'professional' captains, but remained in the hands of senior members of the titled nobility. For example, of the major expeditions from 1369 to 1380, four were led by one or more of Edward III's sons, whilst the only non-noble captain to be an army commander during this period, Sir Robert Knolles in 1370, found it difficult to exercise authority over his lieutenants. This is not to suggest that the 'professional' captains were of little value to the English war effort, for they certainly performed an invaluable service as independent commanders in *secondary* theatres of war. For example, maintaining the sometimes precarious English foothold in Brittany, often with no more than a handful of paid troops, was the responsibility of a series of experienced, resourceful soldiers of gentry stock: men like Sir Thomas Dagworth, Sir John Hardreshull and Sir Walter Bentley.[14]

Paid service, and particularly the 'indenture system', did much more than merely enable a group of captains to advance their ambitions in the king's war; it also created an environment which allowed the latent military potential of the whole aristocracy to be harnessed more effectively. Baronial suspicion had first to be overcome: some magnates under Edward I found the subordinate status which receipt of the king's pay implied intolerable. But given the cost of campaigning in Scotland, this reluctance was unlikely to endure and paid service became firmly established as the norm during the course of the Scottish wars. By the start of the French war, the aristocracy had been eased into a new way of thinking; war, a social responsibility, an 'honourable obligation', but costly and sometimes bitterly resented, had become paid, contract work. Pay, along with letters of protection and enfeoffment to use, had made it easier for the aristocracy to fulfil their military potential, to perform their function as a warrior élite; and, from the king's point of view, a major continental war had become a realistic proposition. Yet, accepting the king's wages was one thing; being willing to serve overseas was quite another. It is important to remember that the English aristocracy's enthusiasm for the French war at the time of the great expedition of 1359–60 represented a complete transformation of outlook from their lukewarm, sometimes downright hostile, attitude to

---

[14] M. Jones, 'Edward III's Captains in Brittany', *England in the Fourteenth Century*, ed. W.M. Ormrod (Woodbridge, 1986), pp. 99–118.

overseas military service during the reigns of the John, Henry III and the first two Edwards. The knightly class in England, it was said, 'did not give a bean for all of France'. It is hardly surprising, then, that the government considered it necessary to offer pay at double the usual rates for the early campaigns of the continental war (1338–40) and to employ foreign mercenaries in large numbers. Yet within a few years there had been a major shift in attitudes and a marked increase in the level of military participation within the English aristocracy. How had this change come about? Part of the explanation is to found in the eagerness of the nobility, following the political crisis of 1341, to be reconciled with the king;[15] but the aristocracy needed a push in the right direction if it was to be induced to take up the sword *en masse*. That there may have been as many as 4,000 (and possibly more) English men-at-arms at the siege of Calais in 1347[16] was largely the result of heavy royal pressure exercised through a new military assessment based on landed wealth. This experiment met with opposition in the Commons and was soon abandoned; but it had forced the secular landowning community to face-up to their traditional military responsibilities and it had involved many of them, either directly or by substitution, in an enterprise which led to the triumphs at Crécy and Calais. The process of aristocratic 're-militarisation' had, then, required a kick-start; but campaign successes, exploited by royal propaganda and consolidated by the encouragement of chivalric *esprit de corps* through such inspired *coups* as the appropriation of the soldier martyr St George as patron of the Order of the Garter, kept up the momentum. The army which Edward III assembled in the autumn of 1359 included more than 3,000 English men-at-arms[17] (of whom, over 700 were bannerets and knights). This was a most impressive figure for post-plague England, an aristocratic recruitment level which, apart from the siege of Calais, had probably not been attained since the battle of Falkirk in 1298. Although a proportion of these men would have been professional soldiers, men like John Hawkwood, whose origins were less than aristocratic, the great majority would have been drawn from the gentry – that is, from about 9,000 to 10,000 families.[18] In fact, the pool of potential men-at-arms for the French war in 1359 was rather smaller than this, since by no means all of the English nobility and gentry were available for continental service. England was a patchwork of local military communities and those of the northernmost shires and of the 'maritime land' of southern coastal counties were often preoccupied with defence responsibilities, a preoccupation which extended to the whole kingdom in 1359 in the face of a serious threat of invasion. All things considered, the 'military participation ratio' of the aristocracy at the time of the show of force outside Paris in April 1360 was indeed impressive.

15 W.M. Ormrod, *The Reign of Edward III* (New Haven and London, 1990), pp. 100–103.
16 On the interpretative difficulties of the 'Calais Roll', see A. Ayton, 'The English Army and the Normandy Campaign of 1346', *England and Normandy in the Middle Ages*, ed. D. Bates and A. Curry (London, 1994), pp. 253–68.
17 The earl of Arundel's retinue, which included 2 bannerets, 25 knights and 108 esquires, didn't sail (E101/393/11 fo. 80): these men would bring the overall total near to 3,500 men-at-arms.
18 C. Given-Wilson, *The English Nobility in the Late Middle Ages* (London, 1987), pp. 69–83.

If pressed for a view on Edward III's continental enterprise, the great majority would no doubt have echoed the Garter motto: 'shamed be he who thinks ill of it'. Small wonder that the king in 1359 could afford to turn away many of the foreign mercenaries who had flocked to join his army, for 'he had brought enough men from his own country to complete his task'.[19]

The recruitment level of 1359–60 represents a landmark in the English aristocracy's new-found appetite for continental campaigning. The scale of the gentry's response in 1359 was not repeated until Richard II's campaign in Scotland in 1385, the next expedition to be led by the king in person.[20] The field armies during the period 1369–80 were of more conventional size, numbering from 4,000 to 6,000 fighting men, with proportionately scaled down, but still substantial, numbers of men-at-arms: several of the armies fielded more than 2,000 of them, which suggests an enduring aristocratic commitment to the war in France. But the 're-militarisation' of the gentle-born was not to be long-lasting, not least because campaigning opportunities thinned out significantly at the end of the century. Nor, for some, had it ever been particularly profound. Among the knights and esquires who accompanied their king to France in 1359 were many for whom this would have been the highlight of an intermittent career in arms: intermittent because of their commitments in England, the management of their estates and the governmental and judicial responsibilities which arose from the possession of land. This is not to suggest that such 'occasional' soldiers contributed little to the functioning of the English war machine. If the king was periodically to mount large-scale expeditions, such as those of 1346 and 1359, and yet to avoid dependence upon foreign mercenaries, the service of large numbers of 'occasional' soldiers was essential. Moreover, a strategy which relied primarily upon the employment of short-service contract armies actually made optimum use of the native aristocracy's military potential. For heads of gentry families and others with domestic commitments in England, long periods of service were effectively ruled out. As the century progressed and the French war entered a particularly intensive phase (1369–89), the numbers of county knights taking up their swords, even for short expeditions, diminished steadily. Captains contracting with the king had difficulty finding the numbers of knights stipulated in their indentures. To some extent the smaller proportion of *strenui milites* in later fourteenth-century armies mirrored a general decline in the numbers of knights in society: a fall from perhaps 1,500 in 1300 to well under 1,000 in 1400, as knighthood became a more burdensome estate, administratively and financially; but the numbers of *fighting* knights may have declined at a more rapid rate. By the 1370s and '80s, typically, fewer than 10% of

---

[19] *Chroniques de Jean Froissart*. ed. S. Luce et al. 15 vols, Société de l'Histoire de France (Paris, 1869–1975), v. p. 197.

[20] There were perhaps as many as 4,500 men-at-arms in this army: N.B. Lewis, 'The Last Medieval Summons of the English Feudal Levy, 13 June 1385', *EHR*, 73 (1958), pp. 5–6. Cf. A.L. Brown, 'The English Campaign in Scotland, 1400', in *British Government and Administration. Studies Presented to S.B. Chrimes*, ed. H. Hearder and H.R. Loyn (Cardiff, 1974), pp. 40–54.

an army's men-at-arms would be knights, as compared with about 20% or more for armies of comparable size earlier in the French war; and the shrinkage in the numbers of *strenui milites* continued further during Henry V's reign.

In spite of diminishing numbers of militarily-active knights, the English military community in the mid to late fourteenth century did not suffer from a shortage of men-at-arms. On the one hand, there were expanding numbers of non-aristocratic professional soldiers, men drawn to war by the prospect of profit rather than by birth (to whom we shall return later). On the other, there were men of gentle blood with time on their hands: men awaiting inheritances or younger sons expecting to inherit very little, perhaps reconciled to the fact that a military career was their best chance of making their way in the world. Many of them never advanced beyond the status of esquire. Some specialised in garrison service, such as the military professionals involved in the protracted defence of Aquitaine during the last decades of the century, many of whom were from Cheshire or Lancashire. Some were fortunate in finding regular service with one of the more bellicose members of the higher nobility, such as Edward, Prince of Wales or the two dukes of Lancaster, Henry of Grosmont and John of Gaunt – magnates whose military responsibilities necessitated the maintenance of a permanent retinue of reliable men. Feed retainers, together with the men in their companies, provided a nucleus around which the less stable, more transitory elements in a magnate's war *comitiva* could be assembled. Important as such retainers were in providing a backbone to a contract army, probably far larger numbers of men in the pool of regularly serving personnel had no such permanent commitment to a single magnate. They enlisted for one expedition after another in a variety of theatres of war under a series of different captains. Their restlessness certainly contributed to that unsettled appearance which English armies exhibited during this period; but, in effect, an old, muchused pack of cards was simply being reshuffled. The Nottinghamshire knight Sir Nicholas de Goushill illustrates well the life of the committed, yet restless soldier. During an eventful career, which began with the battle of Halidon Hill in 1333 and lasted thirty-five years, he served in Scotland with William, Lord Deyncourt, in Ireland with William of Windsor, in several parts of France with Henry, earl of Derby, two earls of Salisbury and Sir Robert de Herle, ending with service in William, Lord Latimer's retinue on John of Gaunt's *chevauchée* in 1369. The intensity with which Goushill followed a life in arms appears to have been prompted by the extraordinary longevity of his parents, who lived into their eighties; he didn't inherit his family's property until he was an old man. William de Thweyt's problem was that, as a younger son of a minor Norfolk gentry family, he stood to inherit very little. His response was a career which spanned exactly the same period as Goushill's, though in his case he combined involvement in the great expeditions – he was at Halidon Hill, Sluys and Crécy – with several spells of garrison duty, at Corfe castle in Dorset and in Ireland. Men like Goushill and Thweyt formed the seasoned, dependable backbone of the Edwardian military community. For such veterans as these, lacking prospects at home and drawn by birth to the martial life, regular paid service in a war with many dimensions represented perfect employment. They, just like Dagworth, Bentley, Chandos and the rest of the notable captains were beneficiaries, and products, of the Edwardian military revolution.

Historians considering the transformation of the English war machine during the second and third quarters of the fourteenth century have devoted a good deal of attention to the emergence of paid armies and the 'indenture system'; but in addition to these developments, and in part bound up with them, the years separating the battle of Bannockburn from Edward III's expedition to France in 1359–60 also witnessed profound changes in the structure and general character of English armies. The host which Edward II led to the relief of Stirling castle in 1314 and which was heavily defeated by the Scots at Bannockburn, probably consisted of about 2,500 men-at-arms serving in companies of various sizes and 15,000 infantry, raised in the shires by commissions of array. The two sections of the army – the men-at-arms and the foot soldiers – were numerically unbalanced, they were recruited separately and they fought separately. The contrast with the army with which Edward III embarked upon the march to Reims in 1359 is striking indeed. This consisted, as we have seen, of nearly 10,000 men, of whom the most important elements were about 4,000 men-at-arms (including perhaps 700 continental mercenaries) and over 5,000 mounted archers. This was a large army by the standards of the French war (logistical constraints usually restricted armies to half this size), but it was also notable for the predominance of mounted troops and the rough equality between the numbers of men-at-arms and mounted archers – a balance which was, moreover, reflected in the composition of individual retinues making up the bulk of the army's strength. Those retinues were very varied in size: one thing that the Edwardian military revolution did *not* bring about was the establishment of military units of uniform size, such as we find, for example, in the standing armies of some continental states in the fifteenth century. The retinues in an English field army were temporary establishments, their size usually reflecting, in broad terms, the rank and social status of their captains. In 1359 the Prince of Wales landed in France with a retinue which had the proportions of a small army: the pay-rolls suggest that it was nearly 1,500 men strong. At the other end of the scale, King Edward's army in 1359 also contained dozens of very small companies led by knightly captains. Sir Richard Pembridge, for example, was accompanied by no more than nine fighting men. Between these extremes, a typical knight banneret might have a retinue consisting of sixty to seventy men; and an earl would usually have several hundred men in his. But whether large or small, the retinues in the army of 1359–60 were often composed of roughly equal numbers of men-at-arms and mounted archers. The earl of Warwick, for example, served with a retinue consisting of 120 men-at-arms and 120 mounted archers, whilst the banneret Sir Robert de Morley was accompanied until his death by thirty men-at-arms and thirty horse archers.

The structure of the army which arrayed outside Paris in April 1360 highlights, therefore, two of the crucial developments in the transformation of the English fighting machine in the mid-fourteenth century: the emergence of the mounted (or 'horse') archer; and the establishment of the 'mixed' retinue, consisting of men-at-arms and mounted archers. The transformation of the military machine, as witnessed by the army raised in 1359, was only gradually achieved. There had been a number of unsuccessful experiments following Bannockburn and only after the battle of Halidon Hill in 1333 is it possible to see lasting changes in the character and organisation of English armies. The mounted archer appears for the first time in significant numbers in the surviving records in 1334. In the summer of 1335, there were about 3,350 of them in the army of rather more than 13,000 men which Edward III led to Scotland. Yet of these mounted archers, only about a third were serving with men-at-arms in mixed retinues and the greater part of the king's army in the summer of 1335 was still being raised in the shires by commissions of array.[21] The onset of the war with France gave added impetus to the process of change in English military organisation, to the rise of the mixed retinue and the declining contribution of shire levies. The transformation was admittedly not achieved overnight. County and urban levies continue to figure prominently in the pay-rolls of some English armies until at least 1360 – as witnessed, for example, by the major contribution of arrayed infantry to Edward III's army at Crécy and the siege of Calais. But the direction of change is unequivocal. Particular stimulus was given to this movement by the 'indenture system'; but the process of change can be seen equally well in those armies which were not raised by means of formal written contracts. Take, for example, the army which conducted the campaign in Brittany in 1342–43.[22] The main body of this army, which arrived in the Duchy with the king in the autumn of 1342, appears from the pay-rolls to have included 1,700 foot soldiers raised by commissions of array. But these men served for only a short period and some infantry contingents never actually arrived in Brittany. So, the effective strength of the king's army was formed by about 1,800 men-at-arms and 1,800 mounted archers, with the great majority of retinues being composed of balanced numbers of each. Seen in this light, then, the army of 1342–43 begins to appear a smaller version of the great army of 1359; indeed, it is not dissimilar in overall proportions to those armies, now raised almost exclusively by indentures of war, which fought in France after the resumption of hostilities in 1369. The English expeditionary forces during the years from 1369 to 1380 were dominated by mixed retinues, very often composed of roughly equal numbers of men-at-arms and mounted archers. A planning document headed *Pur le viage de Portugale*, showing the contingents expected to comprise Edmund, earl of Cambridge's expeditionary force of 1381, lists ten retinues, ranging in size from 40 to 1,000 men, each with exact parity of men-at-arms and archers.[23] This one to one ratio may well have represented the perfect balance of complementary personnel; but if it was the optimum arrangement, it had but a brief heyday. In the last years of the fourteenth century, as the numbers of fighting knights declined, so we also find a larger proportion of archers in royal armies. At 6d. per day, mounted archers were relatively inexpensive (and, given their tactical importance, very cost effective), but their increased numbers *vis-à-vis* men-at-arms also no doubt reflected the growing

---

[21] R. Nicholson, *Edward III and the Scots* (Oxford, 1965), pp. 199–200.
[22] For the pay-roll, see E36/204 fos. 105v–10v.
[23] C47/2/49 m. 2.

prosperity of the yeoman farmer in the decades following the Black Death. Archers outnumbered men-at-arms by 2 or 3 to 1 in many of the retinues in Richard II's army of 1385 and by the time of the Agincourt campaign in 1415, the optimum ratio of archers to men-at-arms was deemed to be 3 to 1.

The emergence of the mounted archer as associate of the man-at-arms in mixed retinues brought about a significant shift in the social composition of the military community. Compared with the poor-quality infantry of Edward I's armies, the mounted archers of the mid to late fourteenth century were more expensively equipped and, consequently, drawn from a wealthier social group; they were men of yeoman stock, 'men of some standing in local society'. So, with the diminished role for infantry and the rise of the mounted archer, military service in the king's armies was now becoming the preserve of a smaller section of society; the military community had a narrower social base. Moreover, the gap between the chivalrous and non-chivalrous of the military community had also narrowed, for just as the heraldic separation of knights and esquires was becoming blurred during the fourteenth century, so the social and economic distinctions between archer and man-at-arms were also becoming less pronounced. This process may have been more marked in some parts of England than others. In Cheshire, for example, as Philip Morgan has shown, there were many archers 'whose standing, within the confines of county society, was analogous to that of men-at-arms raised elsewhere in England'.[24] A single family might contribute both men-at-arms and archers to a royal army; a man might serve in both capacities during the course of his career, perhaps as a consequence of a change in fortune. Social mobility was possible; the opportunities for enrichment and social advancement were frequently mentioned by contemporary writers. Admittedly, the extent of Sir Robert Knolles' rise from archer to wealthy knight was not often emulated, but there must have been many amongst the swelled numbers of English men-at-arms in the later fourteenth century, serving in royal armies and garrisons, as freebooters, mercenaries or crusaders, who had not been born into the chivalric class. It is clear that Sir Thomas Gray, a product of an old northern family and thoroughly imbued with traditional values, did not entirely approve. At one point in his *Scalacronica* he draws attention to the swarms of young men from all over England who descended upon France in the 1350s: 'young fellows who hitherto had been of but small account, who became exceedingly rich and skilful in this [kind of] war . . . many of them beginning as archers and then becoming knights, some captains'.[25]

The emphasis on mounted troops and recruitment on the basis of individual retinues consisting of roughly equal numbers of men-at-arms and archers greatly enhanced the effectiveness of the English fighting machine under Edward III. Mounted expeditionary forces could operate with speed and flexibility. The *chevauchée*, the destructive, mounted raid, which was used so frequently in the war in France, had been influenced by the experience of the protracted Scottish wars, in

---

[24] P. Morgan, *War and Society in Medieval Cheshire, 1277-1403* (Manchester, 1987), p. 109.
[25] *Scalacronica*, pp. 131, 134.

which both sides had recognised the importance of mobility. In 1336, on the eve of the French war, Edward III himself led a small-scale raid into the Scottish High-lands and gained first-hand experience of the effectiveness of a wholly mounted force of men-at-arms and archers. The *chevauchées* in France were often on a larger scale, audacious challenges to the authority of the Valois kings and some-times, as with the Prince of Wales' raids in 1355–56, spectacularly successful. If brought to battle, an English army consisting of balanced numbers of men-at-arms and archers could offer an effective and flexible tactical response. In a series of hard-fought battles during the first phase of the French war – Morlaix (1342), Crécy (1346), Mauron (1352), Poitiers (1356) to name only the most notable – dismounted men-at-arms and archers combined in defensive formation to repulse the attacks of numerically superior opponents. The massed hitting-power of the archers thinned-out the enemy at a distance, blunting their impetus, thereby giving the English men-at-arms, fighting shoulder to shoulder in disciplined formations, the edge in the hard-fought mêlées which these battles invariably involved. As with the development of the *chevauchée*, the origins of the distinctive English tactics of the Hundred Years War can be traced to the Anglo-Scottish wars earlier in the fourteenth century. Although large numbers of foot archers had been recruited in Edward I's reign, they were not well equipped, nor well disciplined; nor were they yet employed in a coordinated fashion. The real tactical turning point was not the battle of Falkirk (1298), but the battle of Bannockburn, when the flower of English chivalry, fighting in the traditional fashion on war-horses, were routed by a Scottish army consisting in the main of pikemen. It was this humiliating defeat which seems to have brought about a major shift in tactical thinking in England. A combination of dismounted men-at-arms and archers in defensive formations remi-niscent of Scottish schiltroms was the basis of Sir Andrew Harcla's success at Boroughbridge in 1322 and was later employed to devastating effect against the Scots at Dupplin Moor in 1332 and Halidon Hill in 1333. It was entirely natural that these tactics should also be used in France where numerical inferiority usually obliged the English to adopt a defensive posture. Occasionally, of course, we do find the English launching a mounted charge, as at Auberoche in 1345; but even when the tactical situation required that an offensive stance be adopted, the attack was as likely to be conducted by men-at-arms and archers on foot, as for example at La Roche Derrien in 1347. To appreciate the completeness of the tactical revolution, the extent to which the English aristocracy had abandoned fighting on horseback, we should focus attention not so much on the comparatively few major battles of the period, but rather on those numerous small-scale encounters which abound in the pages of the narrative sources: minor skirmishes in which we find the English showing great consistency in their tactical methods. In the Scottish border country, as well as France, the English dismounted to fight as a matter of course; whilst by the early 1360s, Englishmen serving in the White Company had introduced their distinctive tactical methods into Italian warfare as well.

The tactical revolution affected the character of English armies in several ways. The aristocracy's abandonment of mounted combat in favour of fighting on foot had a number of practical consequences. The man-at-arms' equipment had to be modified to allow for maximum mobility out of the saddle. Plate armour was developed to accommodate combat on foot and the flowing surcoat was replaced by the short jupon. The lance, the cavalry weapon par excellence, was used by dismounted men-at-arms as a pike in bristling 'hedgehog' formations.[26] More intriguingly, the relegation of the war-horse to a secondary battlefield role (pursuit or flight) appears to have had a significant effect on the quality of horseflesh taken on campaign. The average value of appraised English war-horses dropped from £16 for the first major campaign of the French war in 1338–39 to about £9 for the 1359–60 expedition. The effect of the tactical revolution on the collective mentality of the English aristocracy cannot be measured in such precise terms, yet the blow to the aristocratic sense of identity can easily be appreciated. The war-horse had been, after all, the *sine qua non* of chivalrous combat. It was, as much as anything, what distinguished a man-at-arms at muster from his social and military inferiors. In commenting on how the English at Halidon Hill 'fought on foot, contrary to the old habits of their fathers', the chronicler, Geoffrey le Baker,[27] would have been expressing the thoughts of many of the knights and esquires in Edward III's army. In fact, the English aristocratic warrior appears to have reconciled himself to the tactical revolution rather quickly and a clear distinction soon emerged in English military circles between deeds of chivalry, which were most appropriately performed on horseback amongst his peers – on the tournament field and in those individual combats and small-scale encounters which often occurred on campaign – and the practical business of battlefield fighting which was most effectively done on foot in disciplined tactical formations, in combination with archers. But the rise of the archer, his tactical importance underlined in the later fourteenth century by his numerical predominance, undoubtedly left the aristocratic combatant with a greatly altered military status. No sooner had the provision of pay and a major continental war provided him with an opportunity to convert the ideal of a warrior class into a functioning reality, than he found himself no longer the only really important component of the military community. If not exactly a mere supporting battlefield player (as he has sometimes been portrayed), the aristocratic fighter had become the partner of the bowman in a tactical system which depended upon them both. Moreover, he was now increasingly likely to find himself fighting shoulder to shoulder with *parvenu* men-at-arms, men who were certainly not of gentle blood. War was no longer an activity which set the minor aristocrat apart from his social inferiors. The fading of the gentry's interest in war, which is only too evident during the fifteenth-century phase of the Hundred Years War, may well be as much connected with this change in military status, as with the heavier demands of shire administration and local justice.

These, then, were the principal developments in English military institutions in the fourteenth century: the emergence of wholly paid armies and the 'indenture system'; the restructuring of armies around wholly mounted retinues of men-at-

---

[26] See Sir Thomas Gray's description of the battle of Lunalonge: *Scalacronica*, pp. 136–7. Cf. T.F. Tout, 'Some neglected fights between Crécy and Poitiers', *EHR*, 20 (1905), pp. 727–8.
[27] *Chronicon Galfridi le Baker de Swynebroke*, ed. E.M. Thompson (Oxford, 1889), p. 51.

arms and archers recruited by a re-invigorated class of aristocratic captains; and the narrowing of the social base providing manpower for the military community. These developments, combined with the changes in strategy and tactics which stemmed from them, contributed in no small degree to the dramatically improved performance, and correspondingly enhanced reputation, of English arms on the continent in the mid-fourteenth century. Underpinning this overhaul of the military machine, fuelling the more effective mobilisation of the realm's manpower, was the exploitation of the kingdom's economic resources through national taxation; the revenues from direct taxation of the laity and clergy and from customs duties on exported wool were the lifeblood of the contract armies which conducted the war in France.

All this may well amount to a 'military revolution', but we should not be blind to the limits of the transformation that had occurred. There were no centrally planned, highly structured institutional reforms to compare with the *ordonnances* of the Valois kings of France and the dukes of Burgundy. What fourteenth-century England experienced was a 'quiet revolution', involving institutional evolution, gradual development with occasional bursts of rapid change, frequently as much a consequence of the interplay of circumstances as of royal planning. The military institutions which emerged were not without faults and limitations. Contract armies were well-suited to a strategy of free-moving *chevauchées*, but there was more to the French war than *chevauchées*. 'Siege warfare', as Anthony Goodman has noted, 'was not an English military speciality; English forces were more at ease on *chevauchée*, unencumbered by elaborate siege trains'.[28] The fourteenth-century phase of the Hundred Years War was punctuated with unsuccessful sieges: Tournai (1340), Vannes (1342–43), Rennes (1356–57), Reims (1359), St-Mâlo (1378). The ultimately successful investment of Calais, 1346–47, was a triumph of endurance rather than ingenuity or superior military technology. Although gunpowder weapons made their first appearance during the period under review – primitive cannon were employed at Crécy – they did not contribute significantly to English military enterprises until the reign of Henry V. Nor was a military machine based upon short-service contract armies particularly well-suited to those strategic commitments which required long-term occupation, garrisons rather than flying columns. In the fourteenth century, such commitments stretched England's financial and manpower resources to their limits. In Aquitaine, the English relied heavily on the Gascon nobility.[29] In Brittany, and indeed elsewhere in France, the English 'presence' was more often based upon private enterprise, garrisons living off the country, than upon royal pay – with all the disciplinary problems which inevitably resulted from such an unsatisfactory arrangement. The Lancastrian conquest of northern France would in due course necessitate the adaptation of the 'indenture system' to meet the demands presented by a strategy of steady territorial expansion

---

[28] A. Goodman, *John of Gaunt. The Exercise of Princely Power in Fourteenth-Century Europe* (Harlow, 1992), p. 235.
[29] See, for example, M. Vale, *The Angevin Legacy and the Hundred Years War*, 1250–1340 (Oxford, 1990), p. 262.

and long-term occupation. But already in the later fourteenth century a proportion of military expenditure had become a permanent commitment: the security of Aquitaine, Ireland, the Scottish Marches and Calais were accepted financial responsibilities in peace as well as war. As John Gillingham has observed, the Calais garrison was 'the nearest most English kings ever came to having a standing army'.[30]

Further Reading

On English armies in the early fourteenth century, see M. Prestwich, *War, Politics and Finance under Edward I* (London, 1972); idem, 'Cavalry Service in Early Fourteenth-Century England', *War and Government in the Middle Ages*, ed. J. Gillingham and J.C. Holt (Woodbridge, 1984); and the same author's monumental *Edward I* (London, 1988). The pioneering work on the armies of Edward III's reign was done by Albert Prince. Still useful are his articles: 'The Indenture System under Edward III', *Historical Essays in Honour of James Tait*, ed. J.G. Edwards et al. (Manchester, 1933); 'The Strength of English Armies in the Reign of Edward III', *EHR*, 46 (1931); and 'The Payment of Army Wages in Edward III's Reign', *Speculum*, 19 (1944). More recently, important work has been done on Edward III's armies in Scotland by R. Nicholson and N.B. Lewis (see notes 7, 12 and 21). On the English armies in France under Edward III and Richard II, see the articles by M. Prestwich and A. Ayton (cited in notes 10 and 16); and by J. Sherborne: 'Indentured Retinues and English Expeditions to France, 1369–1380', *EHR*, 79 (1964); idem, 'John of Gaunt, Edward III's Retinue and the French Campaign of 1369', *Kings and Nobles in the Later Middle Ages*, ed. R.A. Griffiths and J. Sherborne (Gloucester, 1986). The major biographies of Henry of Grosmont by K. Fowler (see note 13) and John of Gaunt by A. Goodman (note 28) include much important material on war leadership and military organisation. Invaluable insights into the workings of the 'indenture system' are offered by A. Goodman, 'The Military Subcontracts of Sir Hugh Hastings, 1380', *EHR*, 95 (1980); and S. Walker, 'Profit and Loss in the Hundred Years War: The Subcontracts of Sir John Strother, 1374', *BIHR*, 58 (1985). H.J. Hewitt's *The Organization of War under Edward III* (Manchester, 1966) remains a rewarding study of many dimensions of the war effort. On the English aristocracy and the French war, K.B. MacFarlane, *The Nobility of Later Medieval England* (Oxford, 1973) is an essential work; A. Ayton offers a sketch in 'War and the English Gentry under Edward III', *History Today*, 42 (March 1992) and a longer study in *Knights and Warhorses: Military Service and the English Aristocracy under Edward III* (forthcoming). For stimulating investigations of a regional military community, see P. Morgan, *War and*

---

[30] J. Gillingham, 'Crisis or Continuity? The Structure of Royal Authority in England, 1369–1422', *Das spätmittelalterliche Königtum im europäischen Vergleich*, ed. R. Schneider (Sigmaringen, 1987), p. 67; and see p. 74.

Society in Medieval Cheshire, 1277–1403 (Manchester, 1987) and M.J. Bennett, *Community, Class and Careerism: Cheshire and Lancashire Society in the Age of Sir Gawain and the Green Knight* (Cambridge, 1983). Other aspects of the English military community are explored in M. Jones, 'Edward III's Captains in Brittany' (see note 14); N. Saul, *Knights and Esquires: The Gloucestershire Gentry in the Fourteenth Century* (Oxford, 1981); S. Walker, *The Lancastrian Affinity, 1361– 1399* (Oxford, 1990); and J. Barker, *The Tournament in England, 1100–1400* (Woodbridge, 1986).

3

English Armies in the Fifteenth Century

ANNE CURRY

SPLENDID AS Shakespeare's *Henry V* is on stage or screen, it is misleading. Whilst it rightly emphasises that the siege of Harfleur and the battle of Agincourt were hard fought by troops who were both 'happy' and 'few', it wrongly implies that these victories of Henry's first French expedition led directly and smoothly to the sealing of the treaty of Troyes in 1420. Shakespeare fails to kill off John, duke of Burgundy, whose murder at the hands of the Dauphinist party at Montereau on 10 September 1419 removed any chance of a united front against Henry. More significantly, he omits Henry's second campaign completely. Yet in both political and military terms it was this campaign, having as its initial objective the conquest of Normandy, which transformed the English position in France. Whilst we could debate Newhall's judgement that Normandy could have been conquered from 1417 even if Agincourt had never been fought, it is more difficult to deny another of his observations, that Henry's second campaign marks a step forward in the military art.[1] To conquer territory required a systematic and continuous campaign of siege warfare; to retain it securely thenceforward necessitated the installation and maintenance of garrisons. Earlier English involvement in France can furnish examples both of sieges and of garrisoning, but there is nothing which truly compares with the comprehensive nature of Henry's campaign of conquest and occupation. Commencing with a landing at Touques on 1 August 1417 and continuing without remission until the Troyes settlement was agreed in principle, it formed the longest uninterrupted action of the Hundred Years War to date.

Henry persisted in conquering vein even when the duchy was effectively his in the wake of the surrender of Rouen in January 1419. He began to advance into the upper Seine and Oise valleys towards Paris, an area which his clerks were subsequently to call the 'pays de conquête'. The treaty of Troyes of May 1420 made Henry heir and regent of the kingdom of France and gave him control of areas under Burgundian allegiance, which included Paris. This peace settlement may have modified the grounds upon which he justified his military activities but it did not remove the need for further campaigns of conquest. Indeed the treaty committed him to reduce those areas which persisted in their loyalty to the disinherited Dauphin Charles (later Charles VII) and the Armagnac party. The remainder of

---

[1] R.A. Newhall, *The English Conquest of Normandy, 1416–1424* (New Haven, 1924), p. xiii.

Henry's reign and the first seven years of that of his son saw the persistence of this policy of conquest: in mopping up campaigns around Paris; in the enforcing of Anglo-Burgundian rule in Champagne and Brie: in repeated attempts to secure the last outpost of Valois Normandy, Mont-St-Michel: and in southward campaigns into Maine, Anjou and towards the Loire, the latter culminating in the fateful siege of Orléans in 1428–9. When Joan of Arc raised the siege and defeated the retreating army at Patay, the death knell of English expansion was sounded. Thenceforward, defence became the keynote of English military policy in northern France. Even so, the need for offensive action persisted, although now in the form of *reconquest* rather than conquest.

Conquest and defence had differing implications for military organisation, but both placed a heavy burden on the English, as also on the inhabitants of the northern French territories occupied during this fifteenth-century phase of the Hundred Years War. The aims of this essay are to provide a basic outline of, and to make some effort to quantify, English military provision in this period. Space does not permit a complete survey of English military organisation in all its aspects or in all its geographical locations. The approach is descriptive rather than analytical, and the bias is towards Normandy and the 'pays de conquête' for which sources are rich and plentiful,[2] but even these areas are not dealt with comprehensively. Important aspects such as war finance, strategy and tactics, fortifications, armaments, victualling and so on will scarcely be touched upon.

For ease of discussion, English military organisation will be considered under three headings: expeditionary armies recruited in and sent from England; the maintenance of garrisons in Normandy and the 'pays de conquête'; and the raising and deployment of field armies in these same areas. As will become apparent, however, these forms of organisation need to be viewed in tandem rather than in isolation. There was a constant need for coordination of military effort between the English in England and the English (and their native supporters) in France. The expeditionary armies rarely operated in a vacuum but were intended to be supplemented by, and coordinated with, the military structures established within the conquered territories, a point which English political and military historians have sometimes overlooked. This level of coordination, whilst not unique to this period of the war, was arguably on a larger scale than in earlier stages of the Anglo-French conflict. Moreover, the English had never before maintained royal garrisons in Valois France on such an extensive scale for such a long period. Save for Calais, the garrisons of the reigns of Edward III and Richard II had been short-lived, geographically dispersed and lacking in overall central organisation, and in neither the fourteenth nor fifteenth century were large numbers maintained at royal expense in Gascony.[3] Likewise, although the English had exploited the military obligations of landholders, both native and planted, in Ireland, Gascony and

---

[2] This essay is based largely upon my doctoral thesis, 'Military Organization in Lancastrian Normandy, 1422–1450', CNAA/Teesside Polytechnic, 1985. See also C.T. Allmand, *Lancastrian Normandy 1415–1450. The History of a Medieval Occupation* (Oxford, 1983), chapter 7.

[3] Between October 1452 and October 1453, however, large numbers of men were distributed

Scotland, there is no real equivalent in terms of scale or policy to the Lancastrian land settlement of Normandy whereby Henry and his successors distributed holdings in the conquered territories to their own soldiers and administrators in return for offensive and defensive military service. The overall drift of Henry V's policy is clear. He had landed in Normandy in 1417 with every intention of staying there. To this end he posed as its rightful duke (a title which he used at least in the early stages of the second campaign), seeking to exploit (or more properly, perhaps, to revive or even to invent) native traditions to enhance his legitimacy and his military position.[4] Both the garrison structure and the exploitation of 'feudal' service remained in place until the expulsion of the English in 1450. Here, as in so many other aspects of military organisation and political attitudes, the English maintained practices laid down in the very first days of Henry V's conquest.

Our first topic of scrutiny, the organisation of the expeditionary armies sent from England, has an even longer pedigree. Fifteenth-century expeditionary armies were organised on much the same lines as those of the previous century, especially those raised since the war reopened in 1369. Once captains had indented with the crown,[5] the Exchequer was instructed to make payment, usually giving the captain half the wages due for his intended company immediately with the remainder being handed over at embarkation. It is thus through authorisations to the Exchequer to issue pay (the Writs and Warrants for Issue, PRO E404), and the accounts of the payments themselves (in the Issue Rolls, E403), that details of the armies can be ascertained. Displaying their customary concern for authentication of payment, Exchequer officials checked that the captain's troops had materialised by taking a muster before embarkation. The surviving musters as well as the indentures have been placed in one of the PRO's artificial classes, E101 (Accounts Various), in which can also be found subsidiary financial documentation concerning the expeditions, including some accounts filed by captains upon their return from service.[6] Much of the authenticatory material, including, regrettably, many indentures and musters, is no longer extant, probably because it was regarded as redundant once accounts had been terminated.

Indentures provide details of the proposed numbers and composition (in this

---

between 17 different garrisons in Gascony (M.G.A. Vale, *English Gascony 1399–1453* (Oxford, 1970), pp. 240–1). Fronsac was regularly maintained at the expense of the English Exchequer.

[4] C.T. Allmand, *Henry V* (London, 1992), chapter 7; A. Curry, 'Lancastrian Normandy. The Jewel in the Crown?', in *England and Normandy in the Middle Ages*, ed. D. Bates and A. Curry (London, 1994), pp. 235–52.

[5] A statute of 5 Richard II c.10 obliged indentures to be put into writing and one of the parts to be sent to the Exchequer so that they might be made available when returning captains came to submit their accounts. There is a useful summary of procedures in J.H. Wylie and W.T. Waugh, *The Reign of Henry V* (3 vols, Cambridge, 1914–29), 1, p. 464.

[6] A particularly good example is to be found in the accounts filed by the executors of John, earl of Arundel, for his service in the coronation campaign of 1430–1 (PRO, E101/52/23). Here, as in other examples, it seems to have taken many years for the final account to be settled. Documents in E101 are listed in *PRO Lists and Indexes No. XXXV* (London, 1912), and its various supplements. Some accounts concerning the war are to be found in PRO, E364 (Foreign Accounts), listed in *PRO Lists and Indexes No. XI* (London, 1900). The Warrants for Issue and indentures are indexed in *Lists and Indexes, Supplementary Series No. IX* (London, 1964).

period largely comprising mounted men-at-arms, otherwise described as 'lances', and mounted archers) of the company with which a captain contracted to serve, noting also the length of intended service, date and place of muster, and outlining conditions regarding pay, gains of war, disciplinary control and so on. By 1415 the indenture format was well established as were the conditions of service. Rates of pay and regard for service in France were identical to those of the late fourteenth century,[7] and the clauses on gains followed the rule of thirds. Most campaigns were intended to last six months in the first instance, although there are some variations here. The indentures for the 1415 and 1417 campaigns required a year's service, as did those of the 'coronation' campaign launched in May 1430 and John Beaufort, duke of Somerset's expedition of July 1443. Some captains even indented for two years' service in 1435, and indentures of only a few months duration are found in 1424 and 1449. These variations give some guide to the intended nature and seriousness of each enterprise. Given the tendency towards administrative stand-ardisation in indenture terms, deviations in conditions of service are also signifi-cant. They too can reveal much about the crown's anticipation of its military needs and the financial constraints under which it operated. When money was short in 1449, for instance, Sir Robert de Vere had to agree, in an indenture for six-months service with 100 men-at-arms and 300 archers, to receive only six weeks pay at the outset, half the usual advance, with a similar payment being accorded at the point of muster and the rest to be paid in instalments during the campaign.[8] Variations in indenture terms also suggest that captains were keen and able to negotiate advant-ageous arrangements.[9] Other sources can reveal further aspects of how the crown persuaded the nobility to participate in campaigns. The price paid for the service in 1436 of the Neville brothers, Richard, earl of Salisbury and William, Lord Faucon-berg, came in the form of favourable replies to petitions presented by them shortly after their indentures had been sealed. The king agreed to pay arrears for previous service on the northern borders 'considering the good will of his cousin, Richard, earl of Salisbury, to do him service in France'.[10] Further concessions were won concerning the Neville inheritance, which Salisbury disputed with the senior branch of the family, Fauconberg was permitted to enfeoff the manor of Marske, and his brother was granted lands in Normandy which had previously been held by Lord Ferrers.[11] Such 'perks' were by no means unusual, but the crown's willingness to allow them was much influenced on this occasion by its desire to send a large army, indeed the second largest of the reign, to recover the large expanse of Upper Normandy which had fallen to the French over the previous six months.

---

[7] Lower rates applied in Gascony and for service within the British Isles.

[8] PRO, E404/65/225 (indenture of 20 August 1449).

[9] See, for instance, the conditions negotiated by John Beaufort, duke of Somerset in 1443, discussed in M. Jones, 'John Beaufort, duke of Somerset and the French expedition of 1443', in *Patronage, the Crown and the Provinces in Later Medieval England*, ed. R.A. Griffiths (Gloucester, 1981), pp. 79–102.

[10] PRO, E28 (Council and Privy Seal) 56/36.

[11] Ibid., 56/32, 36; *Proceedings and Ordinances of the Privy Council of England, 1386–1542*, ed. N.H. Nicolas (7 vols, London, 1834–7), 4, p. 336; E28/57/89.

Variations can also be seen in the pattern of indenting. In some cases, the crown entered into only one 'great' indenture, usually with a leading nobleman, for all of the troops intended to make up the expeditionary army. On other occasions, the crown indented with many individuals who promised to bring companies of varying sizes which together made up the army. It may have been for the crown's administrative ease that organisation and recruitment were delegated to one individual – 'privatised', perhaps, to use modern parlance. The first example of this is Thomas Montagu, earl of Salisbury's 1428 expedition, where unusual indenture terms also made the earl largely independent of the authority of the duke of Bedford as Regent of France. This experiment in organisation, a failure given the earl's early demise and the French raising of the sige of Orléans, was not tried again until after Bedford's death, but seems to have become an increasingly popular ploy in the 1440s where all expeditions were organised in this fashion. There is, it seems, a size factor too. When the king wished to cross in person with a very large army, as in 1415, 1417 and 1430, the net had to be cast very widely indeed: the coronation expedition saw 114 separate companies indenting directly with the crown, although we must remember that these ranged from the couple of archers brought along by a minor household official to the several hundred troops in a company headed by a peer.[12] On some campaigns, including those which were royal-led, indentures were sealed over several weeks as men were induced to serve, which produced the effect of a multi-companied army. Whether the variety of procedures made much difference in practice is difficult to tell; it is clear that when there was only one great indenture, the single captain entered into sub-indentures[13] with men who in the 'multi-company' form of organisation might well have indented directly with the crown. There were some implications for recruitment, however. Where many individuals indented directly with the crown it is much more likely that the numbers they promised were a realistic reflection of what they knew they could bring. A single great indenture was much more speculative, and was probably a rough estimate on the part of the captain, 'talked up' by the king or royal officials. On several occasions when a single indenture was used, there was a shortfall in total numbers or else in the category of men-at-arms. It is interesting to note that Salisbury's indenture in 1428 allowed him to recruit archers if he could not find enough men-at-arms, implying that he did not have at the outset a firm idea of whom he might attract to his service. On the whole, however, the mechanics of recruitment remain rather a grey area. This period of the war saw far less use of pardoned criminals than the previous century, but all other types of recruitment are evidenced – family members, tenants, neighbours, annuitants. By no means all men, however, can be shown to have an identifiable link with the captain

---

[12] There is a detailed discussion of this army in H. Ratcliffe, 'The Military Expenditure of the English Crown, 1422–35', unpub. M.Litt. thesis, University of Oxford, 1979, chapter 2.

[13] In the case of the 1428 expedition we have both Salisbury's great indenture of 27 March 1428 (PRO, E101/71/825), printed in *Letters and Papers Illustrative of the Wars of the English in France during the reign of Henry the Sixth, King of England*, ed. J. Stevenson (2 vols in 3, Rolls Series, London, 1861–4), 1, pp. 404–14, and 45 of his sub-indentures in PRO, E101/71/2/826–868B, probably delivered to the Exchequer by the earl's executors when his account was settled.

under whom they served. Indeed the frequency with which armies were despatched, and the enhanced opportunities for military employment within the conquered terrritories made it highly likely – more likely than in the fourteenth century perhaps – that men would serve under a wide range of captains. A case study at the end of this chapter will reinforce this point.

As already noted, the survival of the indentures is not complete, but their loss is compensated to some degree by the large number of Warrants for Issue which summarise the indenture terms, and by the good run of Issue Rolls. The lacunae in musters is more unfortunate because for they provide the only full record of names of soldiers. The muster rolls for 1415 and 1417 are incomplete, and only one other muster is extant for the reign of Henry V, that of 1421 where all 4,100 soldiers are listed. For the period after Henry's death, rolls are extant only for five expeditions in the 1440s. Plate V is taken from the muster of Richard, duke of York's army at Portsdown on 26 March 1441.[14] As with fourteenth-century armies we can ascertain the names of some men who served on other expeditions by examining grants of protections or letters of attorney enrolled in the French Rolls (PRO, C76, also known as the Treaty Rolls),[15] but care must be exercised here. A much smaller percentage seem to have received such grants compared with their counterparts in the previous century. Of the 1,025 men-at-arms in the 1421 muster, for instance,[16] only 28 are found taking out protections or letters of attorney. Moreover, the French Rolls do not give an indication of military rank nor can we be certain that those receiving protections were intending to cross as soldiers in a captain's retinue or in another capacity, perhaps as servants, victuallers or craftsmen.

Even with such limitations in source survival, it is possible to discover much about the expeditionary armies of the period. Between 1415 and the signing of the truce of Tours in May 1444 scarcely a year went by when an expedition was not launched from England to northern France, in some years more than one. This was in addition, of course, to the continued sending of troops to Gascony, admittedly in relatively small numbers and much less frequently,[17] and to the major expedition of approximately 7,675 sent under Humphrey, duke of Gloucester in 1436 to save Calais.[18] If we chart the armies sent to Northern France between 1415 and 1450 (fig. 3.1), some interesting observations can be advanced. Although armies were despatched with considerable frequency, certainly more intensively than at any stage in the fourteenth-century wars, they were, save on a few notable occasions, generally of a small size. The largest expeditions were, as in the fourteenth century, those which the kings headed in person in 1415, 1417 and 1430. Yet only the expeditions

---

[14] PRO, E101/53/33.

[15] For the reigns of Henry V and VI these are calendared in the *Annual Reports of the Deputy Keeper of the Public Records*, 44 (London, 1883), Appendix pp. 545–638, and 48 (London, 1887), Appendix pp. 217–450. For a discussion of this source for the study of fourteenth-century armies see Ayton, *supra*, p. 23.

[16] PRO, E101/50/1.

[17] The only major expedition to Gascony before the crisis of the early 1450s was in 1439 when 2,300 were despatched (Vale, *English Gascony*, p. 112).

[18] R.A. Griffiths, *The Reign of King Henry VI* (London, 1981), pp. 203–5.

Date	Size	Ratio	Date	Size	Ratio
1415	10435	1 : 3	1433	1110	1 : 4
1417	10809	1 : 3.5	1434	920	1 : 5.6
1418	2000	1 : 3	1434	1168	1 : 4
1420	1275	1 : 3.5	1435	1987	1 : 6
1421	4100	1 : 3	1436	1745	1 : 5.5
1422	1079	1 : 3	1436	1981	1 : 4
1423	1520	1 : 3	1436	4200	1 : 4
1424	568	1 : 3	1437	2076	1 : 6
1424	1641	1 : 3	1438	1646	1 : 3.8
1425	1396	1 : 3	1439	963	1 : 3
1426	800	1 : 3	1440	2081	1 : 20
1427	1200	1 : 3	1441	3798	1 : 3.7
1428	2694	1 : 5	1442	2500	1 : 11.5
1429	800	1 : 7	1443	4549	1 : 6.6
1429	1000	1 : 19	1444	400	1 : 3
1430	3199	1 : 12	1448	1000(?)	?
1430	4792	1 : 3	1449	563	1 : 9
1431	2649	1 : 4	1449	400	1 : 3
1431	799	1 : 3	1450	2635	1 : 9
1432	1220	1 : 5	1450	400	1 : 3

Fig. 3.1 Expeditionary armies crossing to northern France, 1415–1450; total sizes and ratios of men-at-arms to archers.

of 1415 and 1417 can compare favourably in size with the major campaigns of Edward III. Under Henry VI few armies exceeded 2,000 men. Those which did fall into two main categories: first, as a manifestation of a new, offensive initiative, such as Salisbury's advance to the Loire in 1428, the opening of York's second period of office as lieutenant-general in 1441, and the *chevauchée*-style campaign of John Beaufort into Maine and Anjou in 1443; and secondly, at moments of crisis, in 1430–31 when there was a need for both a prestigious showing at the French coronation of Henry VI and a response to recent French military successes, again in 1436–7, following the disasters of 1435 and the loss of Paris, and in 1450 when the very survival of Lancastrian Normandy was in jeopardy.

Yet raw numbers by themselves can be rather misleading. Armies might be similar in size, as for instance those of 1430 and 1443, or 1428 and 1450, but their composition was quite different. The principal difference lies in the ratio of men-at-arms to archers. By the time of the expedition launched under Thomas, duke of Clarence in 1412, the prefered ratio for an English expeditionary army seems to have been 1:3, in contrast to the 1:1 commonly found in the armies of the later fourteenth century. As fig. 3.1 reveals, all of the campaigns of Henry V and those of the early part of his son's reign were organised on a 1:3 basis, but as the years passed, the proportion of archers was often greater, sometimes considerably so. Michael Powicke has argued that this move away from the 1:3 ratio was indicative of a growing disinterest in the war which made recruitment of men-at-arms, the military representatives of 'politically significant' society, increasingly difficult.[19] As further evidence of this ebbing of enthusiasm, Powicke points to a contemporaneous decline in knightly and aristocratic involvement in expeditionary armies. There is not space here to discuss these arguments in detail, but two observations can be advanced. First, ratios were less fixed than might appear. A comparison of the indentures and Warrants for Issue with the Issue Rolls reveals that the number indented was not always the number which crossed, so that quite frequently the intended ratio was not the ratio which actually materialised. Some examples of this are given in fig. 3.2. The earl of Salisbury's army of 1428, for instance, was intended to have a ratio of 1:3 but the earl took advantage of a clause in his indenture which permitted him to substitute 200 of his men-at-arms with 600 archers.[20] This implies that archers were easier to recruit, that is, that there was a more extensive pool from which to recruit. A study of the time needed to raise armies suggests that those with larger proportions of archers were recruited more quickly, and thus were more conveniently launched in response to emergencies, as in 1429 and 1449.[21] Where a larger proportion of archers was envisaged even at the point of indenture, cost may have been a dictating factor; as archers were paid only a half of the daily rate of pay of a mounted man-at-arms (i.e. 6d. as opposed to 12d.), twice as many could be raised for the same expenditure, an important consideration at times of financial crisis such as in the 1440s when the cumulative burden of high military expenditure since 1415 began to overwhelm the English government. If a large show was what was paramount, if sieges or their raising were the predominant military needs, then archers could prove just as useful as men-at-arms. It is dangerous, therefore, to assume as Powicke did that armies with larger percentages of archers were necessarily 'second best'. Rather we should see changes in ratio at worst as cost-cutting measures, and at best as examples of military experimentation. After all, Henry V's successes in 1415 and 1417 were won with armies which had twice the proportion of archers of Edward III's force of 1359.

Secondly, what of Powicke's arguments on declining aristocratic and knightly involvement? It is true that their participation declined over the period, although one must bear in mind that the glittering military arrays of 1415, 1417 and 1430, all royal-led, were so atypical of fifteenth-century armies that there is considerable danger in using them as yardsticks. Again, however, a comparison of the indentures

[19] M. Powicke, 'Lancastrian Captains', *Essays in Medieval History presented to Bertie Wilkinson*, ed. T.A. Sandquist and M. Powicke (Toronto, 1969), pp. 371–82.
[20] In the event he raised only 450 archers in lieu of 156 men-at-arms. Note that his indenture allowed payment only for the substituted 200 men-at-arms, which would have covered the costs of 400, not 600, archers.
[21] Details of the length of time between initial planning and final embarkation are given in Curry, 'Military Organization', pp. 32–4.

Date	d	e	b	kt	m-at-a	archers	Total	Ratio
1428	–	(1)	–	(30)	(600)	(1800)	(2400)	(1:3)
		1		**2**	**444**	**2250**	**2694**	**1:5**
1437	–	(1)	(1)	(11)	(320)	(1790)	(2110)	(1:5.6)
		1	**1**	**9**	**299**	**1777**	**2076**	**1:6**
1441	(1)	(2)	(4)	(36)	(900)	(2700)	(3600)	(1:3)
	1	**2**	**4**	**13**	**801**	**2997**	**3698**	**1:3.7**
1443	(1)	–	(4)	(30)	(800)	(3400)	(4200)	(1:4.3)
	1	–	–	**7**	**600**	**3949**	**4549**	**1:6.6**
1449	(–)	(–)	(–)	(1)	(100)	(1200)	(1300)	(1:12)
	–	–	–	**1**	**55**	**508**	**563**	**1:9**
1450	(–)	(–)	(–)	(1)	(315)	(2780)	(3095)	(1:8.8)
	–	–	–	**1**	**255**	**2380**	**2635**	**1:9**

Key d = duke, e = earl, b = baron or knight banneret, kt = knight bachelor,
m-at-a = men-at-arms, ratio = ratio of men-at-arms to archers.

Fig. 3.2 Some examples of variations between numbers and composition of troops indented (in parenthesis) and actually crossing (in bold) in expeditionary armies.

and Warrants for Issue with the Issue Rolls is instructive for it shows that shortfalls in knightly recruitment were particularly common (see fig. 3.2). But to take this as indicative of a falling-off of military standards is dangerous. Powicke ignored the participation of knights in garrison command in northern France and that the smaller armies of this period required fewer officers. Moreover, knights and peers had no distinctive military status, mustering as men-at-arms alongside esquires yet costing more because pay was boosted by social rank. The fact that English military needs were from 1417 well-nigh continuous had certain implications. Not only did this offer unparalleled opportunities to the professional soldier below the rank of knight but it also made participation in the French wars less attractive to men with commitments in England. It is clear that aristocratic and knightly participation was affected by the increasingly troubled politics of the reign of Henry VI, and by the attitude to the war of the decidely 'stay-at-home' king himself. But the whole question needs to approached on a much wider dimension. It is clear, for instance, that the number of active knights had been in constant decline since the heyday of Edward III, but this has more to do, perhaps, with differences in the way distraint of knighthood was used and to the fact that the status of esquire or gentleman was increasingly acceptable in the military sphere.[22]

Let us return to the armies themselves. The surviving Exchequer materials allow us to study the armies from the initial indenture to their transportation overseas. On the last point, the shipping accounts, often appended to the Issue Rolls, are of

[22] For a recent discussion see P.R. Coss, *The Knight in Medieval England, 1000–1400* (Gloucester, 1993), pp. 133–4, and chapter 5 *passim*.

particular value. Tracing the service of the expeditionary armies in France is more problematic. The indentures give the place and purpose of service in unspecific terms, often simply 'pour nous servir en notre royaume de France ou ordonne . . . seroit'. Sometimes other Exchequer sources, such as musters taken on campaign and accounts filed by captains on return, are of assistance, as are random references in privy council materials and petitions. Chronicle accounts are also useful although imprecise in their chronology. Expeditionary armies were financed by the English Exchequer, so do not feature in the financial records of France and Normandy save under certain circumstances – where they were to join with field armies raised in the occupied territories, or where they were used to reinforce vulnerable garrisons. Let us take the example of the 963-strong army which mustered under Sir Richard Woodville, Sir William Peyto and Sir William Chamberlain at Winchelsea in late June 1439, crossing, probably to Honfleur, towards the end of the next month. Upon landing, Woodville and at least part of the army were detailed to the rescue of Meaux. By September 300 men were ordered to serve in the defence of Pontoise until their indentures expired at the end of the year, but replacements soon had to be recruited locally, suggesting that some of the troops from England had been wounded, killed or had deserted.[23]

This leads us neatly to our second topic, the organisation of garrisons within the conquered territories. Their study cannot be entirely divorced from that of the expeditionary armies. In the early stages of Henry V's invasions, these armies formed the sole source of troops for garrisoning towns and castles as they surrendered, and they continued to be significant for garrison recruitment throughout the occupation as men chose to stay on, often in the garrison which they had initially reinforced. Others crossed from England to join a garrison independently, either at their own initiative or by arrangement with the garrison captain. Another important source of recruits was provided by the 'pool' of ex-servicemen which soon developed within the conquered territories, some of whom are also worthy of the description 'settlers' for they aquired land either by royal grant, rent or purchase, sometimes followed civilian occupations and even married locally. They moved in and out of paid royal service as they desired and as military needs dictated. For example, many who gave up garrison service once the victory at Verneuil in 1424 had reduced the need for the intensive defence of Normandy seem to have joined up again during the crisis of 1429.

These conclusions on recruitment are made possible by a computer-assisted study of muster rolls, both for the expeditionary armies and for the garrisons themselves.[24] Given the nature of Henry V's conquest, it is not surprising that we should have a large amount of documentary evidence for the garrisons. The Norman Rolls (PRO C64) of the English Chancery, deliberately initiated from the landing on 1 August 1417, give details of appointments to captaincies up to the

[23] PRO, E28/61; Rouen, Archives Départementales de la Seine Maritime, Fonds Danquin XI/147; BN, pièces originales 3050 Wideville 22; AN K65/1/31 and 31bis.
[24] I am grateful to the British Academy and University of Reading for funding my compilation of a computer database, and to Jane Medcalf, Johnnie Harris and Janine Iveson for data entry.

death of Henry V.[25] It is more difficult, however, to know the numbers and composition of the garrisons of his reign because relatively few musters survíve and the accounts of Henry's *trésorier-général*, returned to the English Exchequer, only give the total cost of the garrisons. Calculations based upon this evidence suggest that over 3,000 troops had been placed in garrison by the end of 1418, perhaps equivalent to 25% of the English force then in the duchy, and that the garrison establishment increased to 4,000 over the next two years.[26]

We are on firmer ground from 1421 once the garrisons were funded exclusively from local rather than English funds and hence accounted within Normandy. Henry V's separate Norman *chambre des comptes* was abolished in 1424 and the financial organisation of all English-held lands was transfered to the *chambre* in Paris. When the English lost the capital to Charles VII in 1436 a new Norman *chambre* was established at Rouen. At the expulsion of the English in 1450 the records of their rule were left behind in France. Over subsequent centuries they have experienced many vicissitudes; poor storage, transfer from one place to another, destruction by fire and revolution, and dispersal by theft and sale.[27] Only in the 1830s did some materials come to England, when collections amassed by French antiquarians came onto the market and were bought by the Trustees of the British Museum. Some have gone even further afield to the USA and Canada, whilst others have found their way into French national and departmental collections. A rough calculation suggests that 40–50% of the original archive of Lancastrian France survives, although weighted heavily towards Normandy and the 'pays de conquête'. But it has been so much dispersed and rearranged that it is very difficult to reconstruct how it was originally compiled. Witness, for instance, the fate of the muster rolls of the Caen garrison in the last months of 1437. That for October is now in the Bibliothèque Nationale, that for November forms part of the Fonds Danquin at the Archives Départmentales du Calvados at Caen. The December muster is also in Caen but in the Collection Mancel of the Musée des Beaux Arts.[28] The troubled history of the archive also makes it difficult to know whether lacunae are due to the ravages of time or to English maladministration in the period itself. What is one to make, for instance, of the fact that only 11 Norman garrison musters survive for the period after Michaelmas 1448? Did the system of mustering break down or have documents of the last years of the occupation merely suffered disproportionately from the ravages of time? Even before 1448 there is an uneven survival rate both chronologically and geographically. The preservation of full account books for 1423–24, 1425 and 1428–29 provides a fairly comprehensive

---

25 PRO, C64, calendared in *Rotuli Normanniae* (Record Commission, London, 1835), pp. 145–385 and in the *Annual Reports of the Deputy Keeper of the Public Records*, 41 (London, 1880), Appendix 1, pp. 671–810, and 42 (London, 1881), Appendix, pp. 313–472.

26 Allmand, *Henry V*, pp. 213–14, based mainly on Newhall, *English Conquest*, ch. 5.

27 M. Nortier, 'Le sort des archives dispersés de la *chambre des comptes*', *Bibliothèque de l'école des chartes*, 123 (1965), pp. 460–537. See also C.T. Allmand, 'The Collection of Dom Lenoir and the English Occupation of Normandy in the Fifteenth Century', *Archives*, 6 (1964), pp. 202–10.

28 Respectively, BN, manuscrit français (ms fr) 25774/1259; Caen, Archives Départmentales du Calvados, Fonds Danquin F 1354; Caen, Musée des Beaux Arts, Collection Mancel XVI/43.

picture of garrisons and field armies in these highly significant years, but that of 1448–49, now in the British Library, is lacking its first 107 folios where details of the garrisons would have been enrolled.[29]

Even with so many archival problems there is much to go on. Lancastrian military organisation in northern France was highly bureaucratic: the level of control exercised there by financial officials was no less great than that exercised by the English Exchequer in the case of expeditionary armies. As Newhall showed, garrison administration became increasingly rigorous as the 1420s progressed, partly in response to native demands for greater control of the behaviour of men in garrison.[30] In its fully-fledged form the system of control, which Newhall dubbed 'muster and review' from the principal methods of inspection used, necessitated at least 19 documents per garrison per year to effect payment of the troops therein: an annual indenture laying down the duties of the captain, usually issued at Michaelmas, the beginning of the accounting year; two orders, to the *trésorier* and the *receveur-général*, to allow payment; quarterly orders to muster; quarterly musters taken on a specific day, which were backed up from 1429 onwards by 'counter rolls' recording the activities and war gains of the troops over the previous three months; and finally quarterly 'quittances', whereby the captain acknowledged payment of the money for his men.[31] (Save for a brief experimentation in 1430–1 in paying soldiers individually, the garrison captains received all the pay for disbursement to their men. This paralleled the practice in the expeditionary armies, but whilst captains there received pay in advance of service, the garrison captains were paid quarterly in arrears.) The whole system was aimed at preventing fraud by captains and their men, and as a bureaucratic system it can only serve to impress. One wonders, however, whether it did not sometimes prove too complex for its own good. We can sense the frustration of captains such as John, Lord Talbot, who was refused full pay until he had provided firm evidence that he really did have three men called John Browne in his garrisons at Harfleur and Montivilliers.[32] A further complication was that when detachments from garrisons were called out for field service, they received pay directly from the officials of the *chambre des comptes*, usually in fortnightly chunks. These payments had to be deducted from the wages due to the garrison captain when these were paid at the end of the quarter. Deductions also had to be made for unoffical absences from garrison, and for the royal share in gains of war made by the soldiers during the quarter, both matters being recorded by the garrison controllers on their 'counter rolls'.

An administrative nightmare even before one starts to consider the personalities involved! Yet whilst it might have been hell for the administrators and commanders of the time, the historian has good reason to rejoice, for despite the many documentary gaps this is an exceptionally rich source. On five occasions we have

[29] Respectively, BN, ms fr 4485, 4491, 4488, and BL, Additional Manuscript 11,509.
[30] R.A. Newhall, *Muster and Review. A Problem of English Military Administration, 1420–1440* (Cambridge, Mass. 1940), and his *English Conquest of Normandy*, ch. 5.
[31] Newhall, *Muster and Review*, pp. 158–9.
[32] BN, Clairambault 134/128 (27 Feb. 1441).

Date	Garrisons with data	Total evidenced	Total projected
Mich 1422/3	37	3029	4000/4500
Mich 1423/4	48	4055	4500
Mich 1424/5	37	2787	3000/3200
Mich 1425/6	17	722	nd
Mich 1426/7	18	762	nd
Mich 1427/8	16	675	nd
Mich 1428/9	25	1192	1600/2000
Mich 1429/30	39	3240	3500
Mich 1430/1	35	2743	3500/4000
Mich 1431/2	36	2594	3600
Mich 1432/3	26	1873	3600
Mich 1433/4	29	1999	3500
List 1433/4	37	2936	3400
Mich 1434/5	42	2603	3000*
List Oct 1434	43	4276	4400
Mich 1435/6	38	3926	4500/5000
List Mch–July 1436	36	5884	5884
List June–Oct 1436	35	5309	5309
Mich 1436/7	33	4248	4800
Mich 1437/8	32	3296	4000/4200
Mich 1438/9	38	4031	4200
Mich 1439/40	29	2825	3700/3900
Mich 1440/1	27	2511	3500/3700
Mich 1441/2	33	3036	3500
Mich 1442/3	29	2117	3000/3300
Mich 1443/4	18	1472	nd
List 1444/5	35	2266	2500
Mich 1445/6	36	2196	2500
Mich 1446/7	30	1714	2400
Mich 1447/8	33	1886	2100

The year is taken as beginning and ending at Michaelmas. Mich 1422/3 signifies, therefore, the period from 29 September 1422 to 28 September 1423.

nd – inadequate data.

* – excluding companies for the field, which are included in the Oct 1434 list.

Fig. 3.3 Total annual size of regular garrison establishment, 1422–1448.

official or semi-official lists surveying all the garrisons of Normandy and the 'pays de conquête'.[33] Otherwise we must piece together much dispersed documentary evidence. Some idea of the total size of the garrison establishment can thus be gained (fig. 3.3), and changes in numbers and distribution, occasioned by strategic needs, can be charted. In comparing 1423–4 (fig. 3.4) and 1424–5 (fig. 3.5), for example, we can see how secure the English felt themselves to be in the wake of their victory in battle at Verneuil. Not only was the garrison establishment reduced by a third, but also the frontier garrisons to the south and east, as well as the key strongholds of Rouen and Harfleur, were much reduced in size. French successes in 1429, however, obliged the refortification of the Seine garrisons (fig. 3.6), although not quite to 1423-4 levels. The list of all garrisons in the summer of 1436 (fig. 3.7) reveals the impact of the disasters of the previous six months or so – the loss of Harfleur, Dieppe and other places in the pays de Caux, and the considerable reinforcing of all the remaining garrisons. By contrast, the sealing of the truce of Tours in May 1444 prompted a reduction in all garrisons (fig. 3.8). As there is little evidence of major change after the truce, it can be suggested that Charles VII was able to take advantage of this weak defensive position when he invaded Normandy in 1449–50. It is interesting to note, however, in the light of our discussion of ratios in the expeditionary armies, that the garrisons retained throughout the period a predominant ratio of one man-at-arms to three archers. The distribution of mounted and foot was determined by location; the garrisons of the coast and heartlands comprised mainly foot, but the frontier garrisons were considerably more 'mobile'.

About 45 places, the major towns and castles, were regularly garrisoned in Normandy and the 'pays de conquête' between 1422 and 1450 (fig. 3.9).[34] In the early days of the conquest Henry V had installed English troops in many of the smaller places of the duchy too, but such places were soon given to the leading members of his army as part of the Lancastrian land settlement.[35] This policy of granting out lands was of advantage to the crown in both military and financial terms for it transferred the responsibility and cost of maintaining and garrisoning fortifications to the landholders themselves – another example of medieval 'privatisation'. Estate accounts can show expenditure on fortifications by landholders, and occasionally the size and composition of the (usually small) garrison can also be ascertained.[36] Some land grants also obliged recipients to send troops at their

---

[33] 1433–34, London, Lambeth Palace Library, Ms 506, fols 16v–20r, printed in *Letters and Papers Illustrative of the Wars*, 2, pt 2, pp. 540–6; October 1434, London, College of Arms, Arundel Ms XLVIII, fols 274r–276v; 30 March–1 July 1436, BN, ms fr 25773/1071; 29 June–1 October 1436, BN ms fr 25773/1112; 1444–45, Lambeth Palace Library, Ms 506, fols 28r–30r, printed in the *Journal des Savants de Normandie* (1844), pp. 45–9.

[34] For contemporary garrisons in Paris see G.L. Thompson, *Paris and its People under English Rule. The Anglo-Burgundian Regime 1420–1436* (Oxford, 1991), chapter 4.

[35] See Allmand, *Lancastrian Normandy*, chapter 3, and R.A. Massey, 'The Land Settlement in Lancastrian Normandy' in *Property and Politics. Essays in Later Medieval English History*, ed. A.J. Pollard (Gloucester, 1984), pp. 76–96.

[36] See, for instance, those for Tancarville, where there was an important castle held by the Grey family (Rouen, Archives Départmentales de la Seine Maritime, serie E, unclassified).

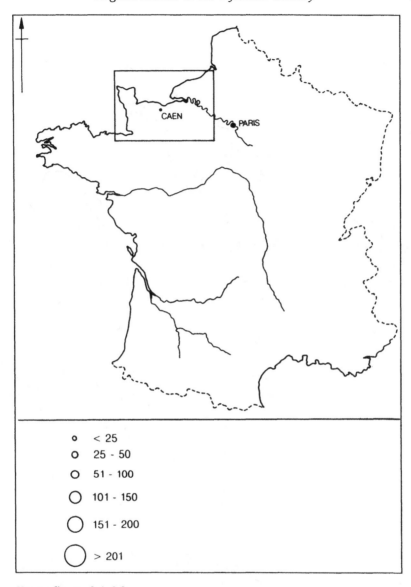

Key to figures 3.4–3.8

own expense to reinforce a neighbouring royal castle in times of emergency and, in addition, holders of urban property, both native and planted, and the villagers of the surrounding countryside were obliged to pay watch (*guet et garde*). Such arrangements were intended to reduce the crown's defensive burden both in financial and organisational respects and to generate a vested interest in the occupation on the part of English and Norman alike. They are difficult to quantify in terms of manpower and it must also be admitted that neither the land settlement nor the exploitation of *guet et garde* were devoid of problems and shortcomings. This is

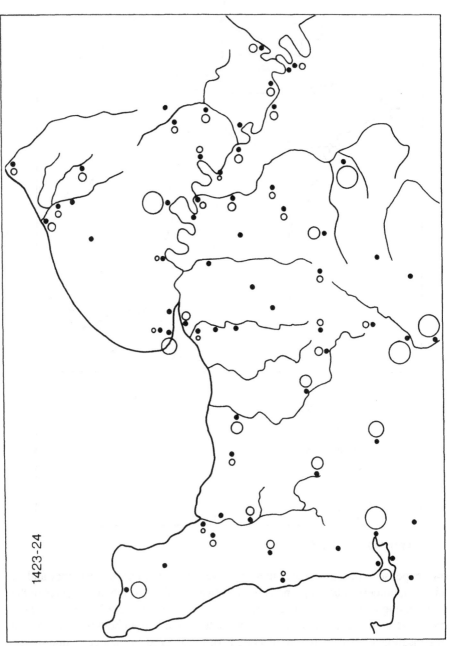

1423-24

Fig. 3.4 Distribution of garrison troops in Normandy and the 'pays de conquête', 1423–24.

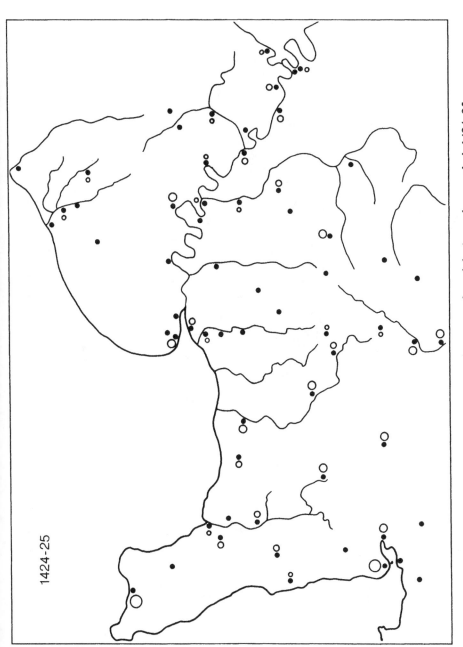

1424-25

Fig. 3.5   Distribution of garrison troops in Normandy and the 'pays de conquête', 1424–25.

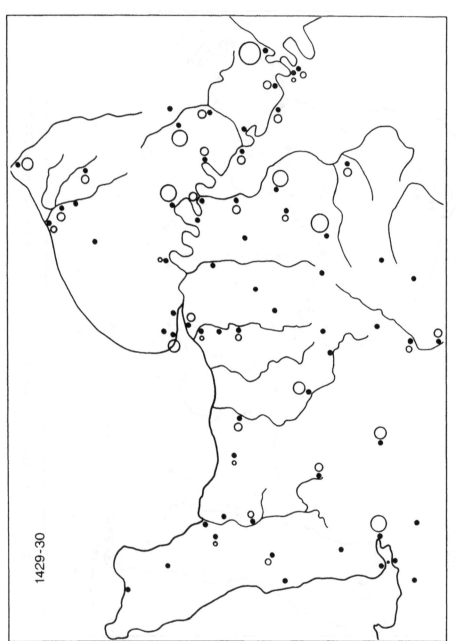

Fig. 3.6 Distribution of garrison troops in Normandy and the 'pays de conquête', 1429–30.

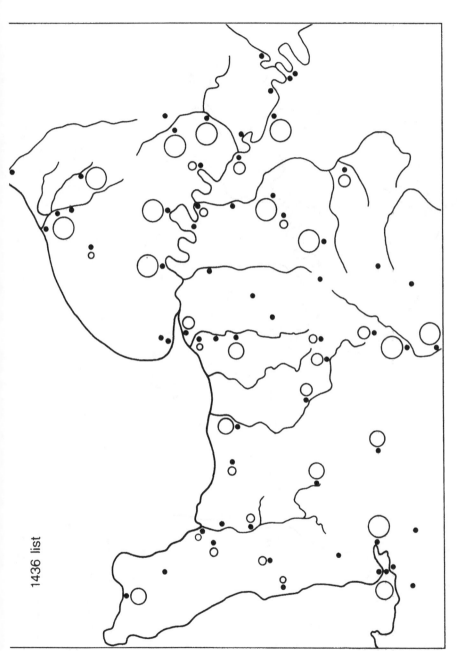

1436 list

Fig. 3.7 Distribution of garrison troops in Normandy and the 'pays de conquête', March–July 1436.

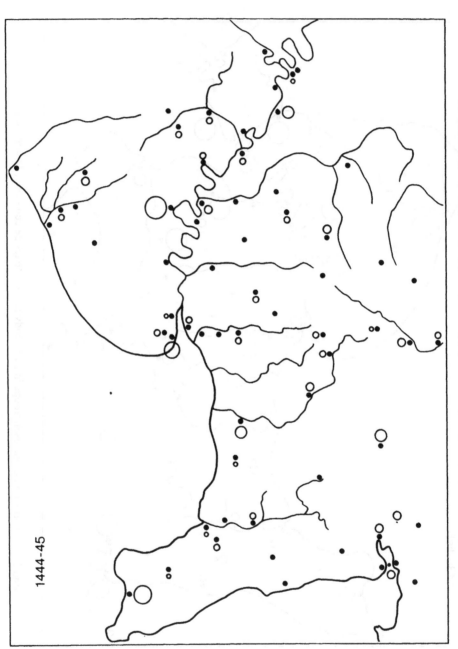

1444-45

Fig. 3.8 Distribution of garrison troops in Normandy and the 'pays de conquête', 1444–45.

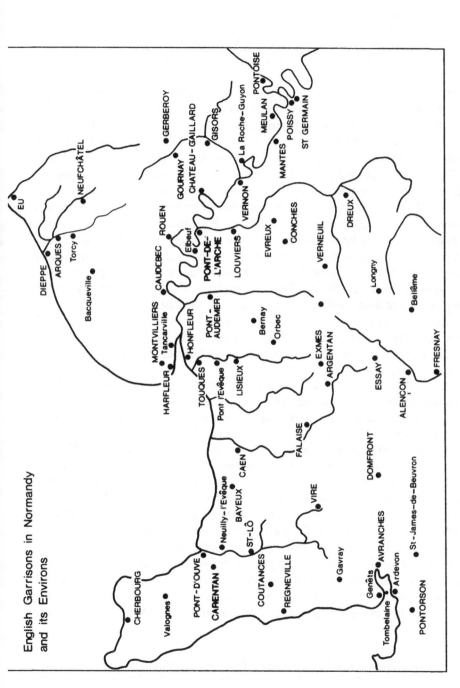

Fig. 3.9 English garrisons in Normandy and its environs, 1417–50 (regular garrisons in capitals).

best illustrated, perhaps, by the events of 1449–50 where private fortifications seem to have been unable to offer any resistance to French attack and where several places are known to have been betrayed by disgruntled natives on watch duty.[37] None the less, these forms of provision must not be ignored when looking at the defence of English-held Normandy.

Let us now consider the third topic, the raising of field armies within the duchy. As we have seen, expeditionary armies always provided an important source of troops for field campaigns in France, but once the occupation became established, other ways of raising men for such activities could be, and indeed had to be, exploited. If the English were to be able to respond to emergencies in a quick and efficient fashion, then they could scarcely wait for an expedition to be planned and despatched. On the other hand, field campaigns were often specific in their objectives and of fairly short duration, so that it would have been uneconomical to have maintained a standing army for the field within France. Thus forms of military organisation had to be developed within the conquered lands which would facilitate the speedy provision of field troops as and when necessary. Three mechanisms can be detected and will be discussed in further detail in due course; the use of non-garrison retinues; the detailing of detachments from the garrisons; and the exploitation of feudal and communal obligation. This last category, as we shall see, raises several difficulties of analysis because the troops serving 'by obligation' did not normally receive royal pay. Troops raised by the first two means are more easily studied because they were paid and thus feature, like the garrisons, in the records of the *chambre des comptes*.

It is difficult to generalise about field armies. Sizes varied enormously from a few hundred to a few thousand depending upon the nature of the proposed action and upon whether expeditionary troops were also intended to be used. Moreover, like the garrisons, field armies were reduced or boosted as necessity demanded. After two months at the siege of Pontorson in 1427, for instance, the 200 or so serving under Sir John Fastolf saw half of their number detailed to another siege at Malicorne on the Marne.[38] Some troops might serve for periods as short as fifteen days if their duty was simply to ensure that foodstuffs got through to threatened places, as in early June 1438 when Thomas Gerard, captain of Gisors, commanded 400 men, partly drawn from the garrisons of Gisors, Gournay and Conches for the revictualling of Montargis, an outpost in enemy territory to the north-east of Orléans, although some of this company, including Gerard himself, may have gone on to join Lord Talbot in his attempts to reinforce Pontoise towards the end of the month.[39] Other field armies might be kept in action for several months if a siege was being laid or the enemy were active in an area. To cite Montargis again, when

[37] A. Curry, 'Towns at War: Relations between the Towns of Normandy and their English Rulers, 1417–50', in *Towns and Townspeople in the Fifteenth Century*, ed. J.A.F. Thomson (Gloucester, 1988), pp. 155–6.
[38] BN, nouvelles acquisitions françaises (naf) 1482/47. For musters of the company at the siege on 14 March 1427 and 10 April see BN, ms fr 25767/216 and 25768/225 respectively.
[39] BN, ms fr 25775/1407 and 1408, 26066/3826, and BN, Clairambault 220/15.

the English laid siege in 1427, they did so with 2,000 or so troops from mid-June to 5 September. On this date, according to Waurin, up to half met their deaths at the hands of a French relieving army.[40]

The English army at the siege of Montargis seems to have been made up not only of expeditionary troops but also of non-garrison companies raised in France. The latter formed an important source for field armies. In the 1410s, 20s and early 30s at least, it seems that there were several nobles, knights and esquires in English France not based in garrison but who held a retinue, or perhaps the core of one which could be boosted in times of emergency. For the most part these seem to have been connected with the King's household up to the death of Henry V, and thenceforward that of the duke of Bedford. Such companies are frequently seen in field armies, most notably perhaps in the 2,400 strong army which Bedford organised in July and August 1429 to protect Paris and its environs against Joan of Arc's army fresh from its successes at Orléans and Patay. Here, the retinues varied considerably in size from less than 20 to (in the cases of Matthew Gough, Richard Guethin and Thomas Gower) 160 men.[41] The organisation of these retinues remains unclear, as indeed does the whole question of Bedford's military household with which many of these retinue holders were associated. We know that Bedford had a bodyguard of 100 men-at-arms and 300 archers which he kept at Paris or else at his favoured residences at Mantes and Vernon when they were not accompanying him on his peregrinations. After 1429 the retinue was normally resident with him at Rouen, and was reduced to 300 men as a cost-cutting measure in 1434. Unfortunately the retinue is poorly documented, because it seems to lie outside the regular system of muster and review, although parts of it can be seen detailed to field actions, as for instance in the summer of 1424 when 15 men-at-arms and 45 archers 'de lostel de monsieur le Regent' were sent under the command of two of his household knights, Sir John Handford and Sir Ralph Neville, to assist Lord Scales at the siege of Gaillon.[42] Similar conclusions can be reached about the military households of those entrusted with the command of English interests after Bedford's death. Thus York held 200-250 men in his first period of office and Warwick 180 in his.[43] When York crossed to take up his second lieutenant-generalship in 1441 he had a company of 110 men-at-arms and 330 archers, but in the next year he is found in the field with only 38 men-at-arms (including 5 knights) and 126 archers.[44] The size of Edmund Beaufort's retinue as lieutenant-general is not known precisely, but all indications suggest that it was much smaller

[40] BN, ms fr 4484 f. 45v and following; 26050/807; Jean de Waurin, *Receuil des croniques et anchiennes istories de la Grant Bretagne a present nomme Engleterre*, ed. W. and E. Hardy (Rolls Series, London, 1868–84), 3, pp. 216–17, although note that he puts the English army's original size at 3,000. He also comments that Montargis 'sied en assez fort lieu'.

[41] BN, ms fr 4488, pp. 541–9.

[42] BN, ms fr 4485, p. 283.

[43] York, BN, ms fr 26062/3085, 26063/3212, 26064/3421; Warwick, BN, Clairambault 139/13 and 112.

[44] PRO, E101/53/33, BN, Clairambault 170/72.

than those of his predecessors and needed supplementing by garrison detachments.[45]

By the mid-1430s there seem to be fewer of the non-garrison companies in evidence. This may be due, perhaps, to Bedford's reforms in October 1434 which set up permanent field companies attached to specific garrisons, and to the changes incumbent upon the 'annus horribilis' of 1435, after which Bedford's affinity began to return home to England, and the English fell back upon an increasingly defensive position in Normandy. Some important points of continuity can be stressed, however, regarding the non-garrison retinues and their role in field provision. Already in the late 1410s and 1420s, regional field commanders held companies under their direct authority, forming a kind of headquarters staff which was able to assist in the mustering and deployment of armies in the field. From the early 1430s this seems to have become more formalised so that leading commanders, such as the earl of Arundel and Lords Talbot and Willoughby, held personal retinues of 20 men-at-arms and 60 archers. At the death of Bedford, or perhaps shortly before, the company of 20 + 60 ceased to be associated exclusively with regional field commands but became the permanent feature of a magnate involved in the war, resident with him whether in field or garrison. This standard retinue could be enlarged as necessary for major campaigns (when John Beaufort held a wider authority as 'lieutenant general sur le fait de la guerre' in 1440 his personal retinue was increased to 30 + 90),[46] or parts could be detailed to serve as detachments elsewhere.[47]

In the case of Talbot as marshal and Scales as seneschal, these retinues were also associated with the conduct of their (largely honorific) offices. Other office holders held permanent companies which were often detailed to service in the field, the most important being the retinues of the *baillis*. As under French rule, the *baillis* were responsible for local administration and justice, but during the English occupation they acquired an enhanced military function. From Michaelmas 1426, their retinues, primarily intended to assist and protect the *bailli* in his civilian duties, were standardized at two men-at-arms and 24 archers, but were then boosted in size, often by the addition of garrison detachments, when employed in field campaigns. (A cautionary tale here. A further 120 men under John Ap Ris and Edmund Darduf were ordered to the *bailli* of Caux late in 1435 after Dieppe had fallen 'pour faire guerre aux adversaires du roy occupans Dieppe et leur tenir frontiere'.[48] The quasi-commando nature of these additional troops, probably recruited from those who did not have permanent garrison postings, is suggested by the fact that 18 months later Ap Ris and his men billeted themselves illegally upon the town of Orbec and had to be removed forcibly by Lord Scales.)[49] *Baillis* were

---

[45] M.K. Jones, 'The Beaufort Family and the War in France', unpub. Ph.D. thesis, University of Bristol, 1982, p. 218.

[46] AN, K 65/1/15, BN, Clairambault 200/88.

[47] A case study of the use and composition of Talbot's retinue can be found in A.J. Pollard, *John Talbot and the War in France, 1427–1453* (London, 1983), pp. 70–1, 83–95.

[48] AN, K 64/1/24.

[49] BN, ms fr 26062/3146.

often given temporary, small-scale regional commands and were frequently called upon to assemble and lead feudally-summoned troops. Another official frequently found in the field was the master of the ordnance. He held two retinues, the first a mounted escort of one man-at-arms and 17 (or slightly fewer) archers, and the second a group of around seven skilled craftsmen. When field action demanded, both his military escort and his specialist retinue could be increased in size, the latter on occasion to 50–60 men.[50] The financial administrators of the *chambre des comptes* also had small retinues of 10-15 men but in times of crisis or when they were escorting large quantities of money to pay troops in the field these too could be temporarily boosted to as many as 60.[51]

The last source of non-garrison troops for field service was the considerable pool of ex-soldiers living in English-held lands. There can be no doubt that these veterans, often described as 'living off the land and not in receipt of royal wages' ('gens vivans sur le pais sans gaiges'), constituted a problem in terms of discipline and the maintenance of good relations with the native population. But they retained their military value as they could be recruited and demobbed as necessary both for field service and garrison reinforcement. They were numerous enough to provide a regular source of replacements for shortfalls in garrison detachments and expeditionary companies. Moreover, encouraging (or forcing) them back into the regular army was one way of controlling their behaviour, at least for a short while. On some occasions, most notably in the late 1430s and 40s when many soldiers found themselves unemployed in the wake of reductions in the garrison establishment, such men constituted up to 40% of armies raised for particular field actions, and were usually placed under the command of experienced captains or *baillis*. After the truce of Tours, a more radical solution had to be found to rid Maine and Normandy of surplus soldiery; if places could not be found for them in garrisons, they were ordered to return to England.

The use of non-garrison companies for field service was paralleled by the calling-out of garrison detachments. The seriousness of any particular enterprise can be revealed by the numbers withdrawn and by the extent of the catchment area from which they were summoned.[52] Almost all of the garrisons of Normandy and the 'pays de conquête', for instance, sent companies in August 1424 in anticipation of the *journée* at Verneuil. For the various sieges of Mont-St-Michel, however, it was customary to restrict the call-out to the garrisons of the Cotentin. This area was largely immune from French attack, so there was no problem in garrisons having men absent for lengthy periods of time. In other scenarios and locations the withdrawal of garrison troops could be a risky busines. It was probably in response to this problem that Bedford reorganised the garrisons in October 1434. In at least 20 key locations he supplemented the regular garrisons by introducing mobile companies of between 40 and 200 men. These were ordered to reside in garrison

---

[50] C.T. Allmand, 'L'artillerie de l'armée anglaise et son organisation à l'époque de Jeanne d'Arc', *Jeanne d'Arc. Une époque, un rayonnement* (Paris, 1982), p. 77.

[51] Curry, 'Military Organization', p. 186.

[52] Ibid., Appendix X, for case studies.

but to be on permanent standby for field service. The scheme was probably overtaken by the events of 1435 and 1436. Garrison detachments continued to provide field troops after this date (31%, for instance, of the 2,000-strong army with which Edmund Beaufort lay siege to Harfleur in 1440 was drawn from 14 garrisons), but the increased need for vigilant garrison defence may have encouraged the use of 'gens vivans sur le pais' in the stead of garrison detachments. The problems inherent in using garrison detachments in the field came to a head in the final denouement of 1449-50. Not only did places from which troops had been withdrawn fall too easily but also defensive needs proved so overwhelming that it was too risky to raise a large field army by calling out detachments.

It is also interesting to note that the third form of raising field troops – the exploitation of feudal obligation – apparently was not used in 1449-50. Yet it had been one of the lynch-pins of military arrangments in Lancastrian Normandy. As we have seen, the land settlement had a strong defensive objective. In addition it was clearly intended to provide troops for the field.[53] Many of the land grants, and most particularly those of the highest value and extent, demanded the service of a certain number of men in the royal host 'during the current war' at the landholder's own expense.[54] Henry also sought to exploit the existing personal military obligations to the French crown of native nobles who accepted his rule. In both cases, troops were called out by a royal summons which resembled the traditional French semonce des nobles. Issuing his first summons as early as March 1418, Henry seems to have used it on at least three and possibly five subsequent occasions in Normandy before his death.[55] From 1422 to the truce of Tours, the summons was issued a further 50 or so times.

In theory, the use of the summons should have raised around 1,400 men. Assessing the actual military value of the land settlement is, however, exceptionally problematic. As the troops were to be sent at the landholder's own expense, they do not feature in the records of the chambre des comptes. An assessment of the response to a feudal summons can only be gauged on the few occasions when troops so raised were given royal pay. In April 1429, for instance, 639 men, largely natives under the command of Norman knights, were paid for escorting victuals to the English army besieging Orléans, perhaps because such escort service was not deemed to be included in their obligations.[56] In July and August of the same year, in the 2,400-strong army organised by Bedford for the safeguard of Paris, feudally-recruited troops seem to have provided about 200 men, of whom 53 can be shown to have been serving by virtue of the obligations of Norman nobles, the rest by those of English landholders.

It is possible, of course, that larger numbers were provided on other occasions at

---

53 See in general A. Curry, 'Le service féodal en Normandie pendant l'occupation anglaise (1417–1450)', La France Anglaise: Actes du 111e congrès national des sociétés savantes, Poitiers, 1986 (Paris, 1988), pp. 233–57.

54 Wylie and Waugh, Reign of Henry V, 3, p. 241.

55 Curry, 'Military Organization', Appendix IX.

56 For these figures and those cited subsequently see Curry, 'Le service féodal', pp. 252–3.

the landholders' expense. Indeed, the recurrent issue of a feudal summons may be taken to imply a continuing confidence that troops could be raised by such means. However, there is ample evidence that both the defensive and offensive obligations incumbent upon land holders proved difficult to enforce. Absenteeism of fief holders was already a major problem in the 1420s. There had been a drift of personnel back to England, the result of relative peace in Normandy and of the changing political circumstances at home consequent upon the death of Henry V. By November 1427 the situation was serious enough to merit an order from Bedford that landholders should take up personal residence in the very near future on pain of having their revenues sequestrated and spent by royal officials on defence of their fiefs, or, in the last resort, of losing their lands altogether.[57] The order explained that, because the grantees had not performed all the duties incumbent upon their tenure, the king had been obliged to send large expeditionary armies financed out of English revenues. Even if the order succeeded in bringing some landholders back to Normandy, this was not enough to prevent its reissue in August 1429 at the height of the military crisis, nor to reduce the need for future expeditions to be launched from England. In this respect, the military raison d'être of the land settlement must be viewed as only partially successful. It is noticeable, too, that the frequency of summons declined after 1436. By then many grantees had lost their lands to the French or else had found them devastated and of little value, and there could no longer be complete confidence in the loyalty of local nobility. The last point reminds us of the dangers of attempting to exploit the military obligations of a native population: it is also likely that attempts to draw on the military capacity of the rural population, by issuing an *arrière-ban*, misfired, contributing to the revolt in and loss of most of Upper Normandy in 1435–36.[58] Thus, whilst feudal and communal obligation did make some contribution to the English military position, it cannot be precisely quantified, and its efficacy fluctuated according to political as much as military circumstances.

So far the focus of this essay has been on administrative structures and aggregation of numbers, forgetting, perhaps, that these structures and numbers were in reality constituted by people, indeed by individuals. This is not the fault of the sources, for they allow us to study the military careers of even the rank and file in a way that is not possible for earlier periods of English military history. Let us conclude, therefore, by letting some individuals emerge from what has been, to this juncture, a rather faceless approach.

It is appropriate, perhaps, to take one of the men whose monumental effigy is illustrated and commented on elsewhere in this volume, that of Sir John Cressy (d.1445) at Dodford, Northamptonshire. Whilst we cannot know what Sir John actually looked like for his effigy is not intended as a portrait, we can reconstruct

---

[57] BN, ms fr 26050/797, repeated in England at the order of the Privy Council on 3 August 1429, *Proceedings and Ordinances*, iii, p. 349. The order to muster an English expeditionary force in March 1427 included the instruction that no one should be recruited if they held lands in France which obliged them to military service (*CPR 1422–29*, p. 404).

[58] Curry, 'Le service féodal', pp. 255–6.

his military career. It would be dangerous to accept Cressy's career as typical – all those involved in the war have an individually distinctive record of service – but it does bring out a pattern of experience which is not unique to him alone. What is most noticeable is the mix of expeditionary and garrison service. The first definite record of his involvement in English France is between April and August 1432 when he was serving as lieutenant to the earl of Arundel, captain of the town and bridge garrisons at Rouen under the general authority of the overall commander of Rouen, the duke of Bedford.[59] By then, Cressy was 25 years old; his father's inquisition *post mortem* tells us that he was born on 25 March 1407.[60] This date of birth makes it unlikely, therefore, that he was the John Cressy serving as a man-at-arms in the garrison of Domfront in 1420. Indeed, we do not know when Sir John first served in France nor when he was knighted. He was already 'Sir John' when he entered into a life indenture with Thomas, Lord Roos in November 1429,[61] and he may well have crossed in Roos's retinue in the coronation expedition of 1430, if not also with the same captain in the 1427 expedition. We do not know when the lieutenancy at Rouen began (Arundel had held the captaincy at least from November 1431 and possibly from late September 1430) but we do know that by December 1432 Sir John Arundel had replaced Cressy as lieutenant. Cressy's next appearance in the military records is when he led his own company of 28 men-at-arms and 90 archers in the expeditionary army of July 1435.[62] In December he reappears as a musterer of the English garrison of Le Crotoy, and in February 1436 he took up his first garrison command at Eu only to have the place soon fall to the French.[63] By the following November he was lieutenant to the duke of York at Caen, an office he held until December 1437.[64] There is no evidence of his serving overseas again until York's expedition of March 1441 when he headed a retinue of 19 men-at-arms and 118 archers, and found himself detailed with Sir Richard Woodville to assist in the defence of Pontoise.[65] When his six-month indenture expired in early September, he took up the captaincy of Gisors, where he seems to have remained until Michaelmas 1442.[66] By February 1444 he was captain of Orbec, Lisieux and Pont-l'Evêque, offices he held until his death. The inscription on his tomb states that he died on 3 March 1445 in Lorraine, but the exact location remains to be identified. If he was by this time counsellor of the King in France, as his tomb inscription suggests, he may have died at Toul whilst engaged in peace negotiations with the French. Whatever the case, he died shortly before his thirty-eighth birthday, having spent a good proportion of his maturity in military service.

From documentary evidence the names of 92 of his men-at-arms can be ascertained, of whom 18 appear in the muster of March 1441 (plate V). By searching for

---

59 BN, ms fr 25770/697, naf 1482/122.
60 *CIPM*, 3, p. 125.
61 *CPR, 1429–36*, p.330.
62 PRO, E101/71/3/882, E403/719.
63 *CPR, 1429–36*, p. 525; BN, ms fr 25772/938.
64 BN, ms fr 26061/2978, BL, Additional Charter 6905 and references to musters in note 28 above.
65 PRO, E101/53/33, BN, pièces originales 929 Cressy 3.
66 BN, loc. cit.

these 18 names in a database of men-at-arms derived from all known musters, counter rolls and protections, we can come to some conclusions on patterns of service. We must bear in mind, however, the impact of uneven source survival and the difficulties of personal identification. Any conclusions reached must be regarded as suggestive rather than definitive. Enough evidence does remain, however, to show that movement between captains and geographical locations was common.

Only one man-at-arms in the 1441 muster, John Cayne, can be proved to have served under Cressy on another occasion, namely in October and November 1437 during his lieutenancy of Caen.[67] William Cressy may have been related to Sir John, although it has not been possible to ascertain how: by November 1442 he was serving as foot in the garrison of Tancarville under the captaincy of John Matthew.[68] John Malory took out a protection to cross to France in 1444 under John Langton.[69] John Creke was a member of Sir Thomas Hoo's personal retinue in 1447.[70] Lowis ap Howell served in December 1437 in Talbot's garrison at Neufchâtel; William Langton was at Lisieux under John Stanlowe in 1439 and again at Alençon under Edmund Beaufort in 1440.[71] Richard Popelay joined the garrison of Pontoise, then captained by Sir Thomas Gargrave, when his expeditionary service under Cressy came to an end, a significant career move given that we know that Cressy's retinue, or at least part of it, had been detailed to the reinforcement of Pontoise during the 1441 campaign.[72]

Some members of Cressy's company in 1441 appear in the records more frequently, enabling us to gain a fuller impression of the pattern of military experience. Hugh Venables, for instance, was a mounted man-at-arms in the garrison of Harfleur in 1434–5 under William Minors. Although he crossed with Cressy in March 1441, he did not assist in the reinforcing of Pontoise but was detailed instead to the company of John Pemberton, mustering again with part of the expeditionary army at Harfleur in June. By 1449 he was in a company for the field based at Vernon under William, Lord Fauconberg.[73] Henry Blakbourne appears in garrison musters for Neufchâtel under Edmund Beaufort in 1429 and Sir Lewis Despoy in1436, and served in the 1443 expedition in the company of Sir Robert Vere.[74] John Bryan was serving under Robert, Lord Willoughby in 1431–2, first in his personal retinue at the siege of Louviers and then in his garrison at Pontoise. He helped Lord Talbot to reinforce Pontoise in 1439 and, like Popelay, joined the same garrison when his expeditionary service under Cressy ended.[75] Thomas

---

67 BN, ms fr 25774/1259; Archives Départementales du Calvados F 1354. He is not listed in the December muster.
68 BN, ms fr 25776/1593.
69 *Deputy Keepers Report*, 48, p. 391.
70 BN, ms fr 25777/1777, 1794.
71 BN, Clairambault 201/63; BN, ms fr 25775/1427 and AN, K 66/1/57.
72 AN, K 67/1/40.
73 BN, ms fr 25772/924, 934, PRO, E101/54/2, BN, ms fr 25778/1834, 1838.
74 BN, ms fr 25768/428, 25772/950, PRO, E101/54/5 m. 2.
75 BN, naf 8606/20, ms fr 25770/684, 721, Clairambault 202/6, AN, K 67/1/40.

Galant had served at the siege of Tancarville under Sir Thomas Griffin in September 1437, before moving on to the garrison of Mantes under Sir Thomas Hoo in June 1439 and as a reinforcement under John Wake at Rouen later in that same year.[76]

Tracing the careers of John Strelley, John Walsh and John Radcliffe is more problematic as there was clearly more than one man with each name. Another John Strelley, for instance, crossed in the 1441 army in the retinue of Sir Richard Woodville. Either there really were two men of this name, or else a fraud had been committed at the time of muster! Hugh Pauncefote, Pierres Starkey and John Raymonde do not appear in the database save for their 1441 entry. Nor does William Cavinvill unless he was the William Canvyle who crossed in Thomas, Lord Camoys' company in 1415 and Sir John Radcliffe's in 1417, or the William Cawvell under Willoughby at Pontoise in 1429.[77] This is not so incredible for some men certainly did have lengthy military careers, but we may have here an example of another frequent phenomenon amongst the soldiery of a son following his father into service.

As noted earlier, it has been impossible in this short survey to cover all aspects of the armies of this period. There can be no doubt of the considerable potential of the source material, even taking into account its lacunae. Nor can we deny that it reveals a massive investment of men, money and organisational activity on the part of Henry V and his successors in the pursuit of their French interests. Our brief review of military careers suggests that the 'investment level' of the soldiering classes was no less great. It is easy to see, therefore, that many must have returned to England at the final denouement of 1449–53 disappointed, disillusioned and disgruntled. Even Shakespeare could not deny that failure in France was to have catastrophic effects for the Lancastrian dynasty in England.

[76] BL, Add Ch 137, BN, ms fr 25775/1417, Clairambault 206/2.
[77] N.H. Nicolas, *The History of the Battle of Agincourt* (London, 1833), p. 342, PRO, E101/51/2, BN, ms fr 25768/434.

4

The War in Aquitaine

MALCOLM VALE

AT THE OUTBREAK OF the Hundred Years War in 1337, the oldest surviving continental territory of the English crown lay in South-West France. Since 1152, there had been a Plantagenet administration in the duchy of Aquitaine. The tendency among some French historians to speak of an 'English occupation' of the region has to be firmly resisted. Gascony (the linguistic or ethnic unit) or Aquitaine (the political unit) was an inheritance rightfully held by the kings of England as dukes of Aquitaine. The very phrases 'English Gascony' or the 'English administration of Aquitaine' can also be misleading, especially during the period before Edward III's assumption of his claim to the throne of France in 1340. 'Plantagenet' Aquitaine, which does not carry connotations of English colonialism or exploitation, would be preferable. We are therefore dealing with a region (or group of regions) in which the population, or its politically active members, did not consider itself to be 'occupied' by a 'foreign' power: the kings of England were the immediate and 'natural' lords of the area, and a certain long-standing loyalty to them was evident at every stage of the war. Of course it was cut across and undermined by other interests and by rival claimants to the fidelity of the Gascons, but that was a commonplace of most of the so-called princely states of later medieval France. In the last analysis, however, the very fact that it was by force of arms that the duchy was finally annexed to the French crown in 1451–3 may tell us much about Gascon loyalty and less about English military efforts to retain this long-standing continental possession.

There is, first of all, a historiographical point to be made: our knowledge of the course and nature of the war in South-West France is very incomplete. Although the issue of sovereignty over, and homage for, Aquitaine lay at the very root of the war's origins, the actual course of the fighting, and the military organisation and resources of the duchy have been relatively little studied. We now know almost as much about the military operations and effects of war in the 1290s and 1320s as at any stage of the greater conflict which broke out between England and France in 1337. There are some exceptions to this generalisation, of course: Kenneth Fowler's study of Henry of Grosmont's lieutenancy in Aquitaine during the 1340s and H.J. Hewitt's and Richard Barber's accounts of the Black Prince's expeditions of the mid-1350s and administration in the 1360s provide useful material for the

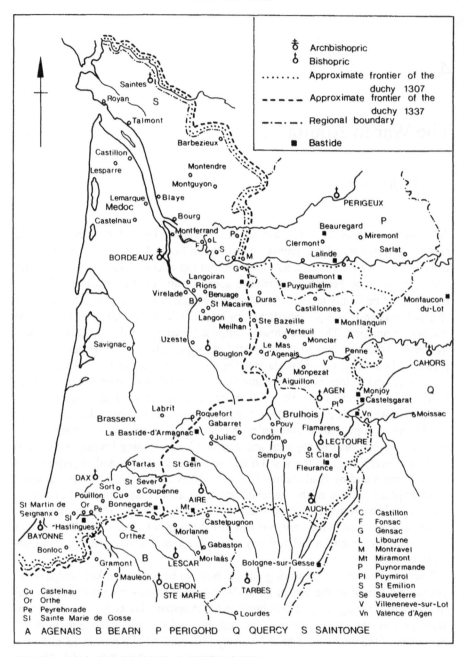

Fig. 4.1 The duchy of Aquitaine in 1307 and 1337.

course of war in the fourteenth century.[1] Kenneth Fowler's long-awaited book on the Free Companies will no doubt illuminate further aspects of fourteenth-century warfare in and around the duchy. Professor Tucoo-Chala has told the story of Gaston Fébus of Foix-Béarn's role in the conflict in the mid- and late-fourteenth century.[2] I have tried, in two books, to examine some aspects of the conflict at its very beginning, and during the fifteenth century, but there is still a great deal to be done, for both the fourteenth – and fifteenth – century phases of the war.[3] One reason, I think, for this problem lies in the availability of sources. After the death of Yves Renouard in 1965, a joint Anglo-French project to publish the Gascon Rolls was discontinued, leaving that great series of Chancery enrolments of all letters and many other documents relating to Gascon business unpublished after 1317. Publication of the Gascon Rolls, as *Rôles Gascons*, had initially been begun by Francisque Michel and Charles Bémont between 1885 and 1896 but had been stopped when they reached 1307.[4] Renouard's edition, checked and amplified by PRO staff such as Chaplais, Barnes and Latham, only took the sequence up to 1317.[5] From that date, until the cessation of the series in 1460, we have to fall back upon Rymer, Carte, Delpit and the other partial and sometimes inaccurate editions of documents concerning Gascon affairs.[6] This means that for the entire course of the Hundred Years War the major English archival source for events in Aquitaine is unpublished. We are otherwise left with the idiosyncratic and uneven writing of Froissart for the fourteenth century, and a near-complete absence of reliable narrative sources for the fifteenth, with the possible exception of the French chroniclers of the very end of the war.

A similar pattern is to be found for the all-important financial documentation upon which so much of our knowledge of the war can be based. With the exception of a small number of later fourteenth-century accounts of the constables of Bordeaux (responsible for what might be termed war finance in the duchy) virtually nothing has been published.[7] The volume of material is very large, and it would be quite unrealistic to expect publication of the many particulars of account, with their multiple quittances, vouchers and warrants. But the enrolled accounts of

---

[1] K.A. Fowler, *The King's Lieutenant. Henry of Grosmont, First Duke of Lancaster* (London, 1969); H.J. Hewitt, *The Black Prince's Expedition of 1355–1357* (Manchester, 1958); R. Barber, *Edward, Prince of Wales and Aquitaine* (London, 1978).

[2] P. Tucoo-Chala, *Gaston Fébus et la vicomté de Béarn (1343–1391)* (Bordeaux, 1960).

[3] M. Vale, *English Gascony, 1399–1453* (Oxford, 1970); *The Angevin Legacy and the Hundred Years War, 1250–1340* (Oxford, 1990).

[4] See *Rôles Gascons*, ed. F. Michel and C. Bémont, 3 vols (Paris, 1885–1906).

[5] See *Gascon Rolls, 1307–1317*, ed. Y. Renouard and R. Fawtier (London, 1962).

[6] *Foedera, conventiones, litterare et cuiuscunque generis acta publica*, ed. T. Rymer, 4 vols (Record Commission, London 1816–30); *Catalogue des rolles gascons, normands, et françois conservés dans les archives de la Tour de Londres*, ed. T. Carte (London, 1742); J. Delpit, *Collection générale des documents français qui se trouvent en Angleterre* (Paris, 1847).

[7] T. Runyan, 'The Constabulary of Bordeaux: the Accounts of John Ludham (1372–73) and Robert de Wykford (1373–75)', *Medieval Studies*, 36 (1974), pp. 215–58; 37 (1975), pp. 42–84; J.R. Wright, 'The Accounts of John de Stratton and John Gedeney, Constables of Bordeaux, 1381–90', *Medieval Studies*, 42 (1980), pp. 238–307.

the constables and controllers of Bordeaux certainly deserve at least calendaring or extracting. This was what was done by Pierre Chaplais for the Renouard edition of the Gascon Rolls (1307–1317) and needs to be done again for later enrolments.[8] In present financial conditions that seems a pious hope. And what about the vast class of Ancient Petitions, not to mention the Ancient Correspondence, in the PRO? They are full of material for the war in Aquitaine, and reveal the conditions in which the war was fought as graphically as many a narrative account. Unless and until some joint project with the French is re-established, there is little hope that what Renouard described as 'la source principale de l'histoire des pays du sud-ouest de la France' will appear in print.[9] His words of 1962 still carry some weight: 'it is significant that . . . the history of the period of the Hundred Years War in Aquitaine – which was the main cause of the conflict – or the study of [its] institutions, because it was in the hands of the king of England, have as yet given rise only to superficial studies'.[10] The period of the Black Prince's rule in the 1360s, studied from the administrative point of view by Pierre Capra in his unpublished thesis, or of John of Gaunt's lieutenancy in the 1390s (which is almost totally unstudied) have especially suffered.[11] Some recent evidence from the University of Bordeaux, however, suggests that some work upon the English administration in the fifteenth century has been initiated. The influence of the *Annales*, with its excessive concentration upon economic, social and *mentalités* history at the expense of political, military and diplomatic aspects, may now be on the wane in France and we may well see a return to archivally-based research on the Hundred Years War by French historians. The resources of local (i.e. departmental) and municipal archives in France itself have not been fully tapped for the period, and there is a substantial amount of material concerning, for example, the role of the great noble families (Albret, Armagnac, Foix) in both 'public' and 'private' war at Pau and Montauban which has not been much worked upon. We lack a study of the house of Armagnac during the duration of the war: Charles Samaran's *La maison d'Armagnac au xve siècle* (1901), which did not use English unpublished sources, is all that we have – apart from a scattering of articles in regional periodicals for the fourteenth century.

That said, what *can* be found out about the war in Aquitaine? Two general points can be made: first, it was essentially a war of sieges and skirmishes; secondly, it was a war in which the greater conflict between England and France was often embroiled with private feuds and vendettas, some of which preceded the outbreak

8 See *The War of St Sardos (1323–25). Gascon Correspondence and Diplomatic Documents*, ed. P. Chaplais, Camden Society, 3rd ser., 87 (London, 1954).

9 *Gascon Rolls, 1307–1317*, p. 1.

10 'Il est significatif que . . . l'histoire de la période de la guerre de Cent Ans dans cette Aquitaine qui en etait le principal objet, ou l'étude des institutions de ce grand fief si particulier, puisqu'il était aux mains du roi d'Angleterre, n'aient encore donné matière qu'à des travaux estimables, certes, mais superficiels', *Roles Gascons, 1307–17*, p. I–II.

11 See P. Capra, 'Les bases sociales du pouvoir anglo-gascon au milieu du xive siècle', *Le Moyen Age*, 81 (1975), pp. 273–99, 447–73; 'L'histoire monétaire de l'Aquitaine anglo-gasconne au temps du Prince Noir (1354–72)', *Bulletin et Mémoires de la Société Archéologique de Bordeaux*, 64 (1968), pp. 93–151 and his account of the period of the Black Prince's rule in *Histoire de Bordeaux: III. Bordeaux sous les rois d'Angleterre*, ed. Y. Renouard (Bordeaux, 1965), pp. 369–404.

of the Anglo-French war. The great dispute between the houses of Foix and Armagnac, for example, dated back to the 1290s and did not end until the 1440s. Indeed, there were still signs of its dying embers at a later date. Public war in Aquitaine was also private war: the alignments of noble families could often follow pre-existing loyalties and contracts of *alliance* previously made with the greater families. When Foix inclined towards the Valois cause, so did many of the vassals and *alliés* of his house; those of his *alliés* and clients who were also liegemen of the king of England, as duke of Aquitaine, were placed in awkward dilemmas, sometimes, but not always, solved by clauses of exception in those *alliances*. But the feud with the neighbouring enemy – Armagnac – often emerged as the true determinant of the behaviour of the counts and *vicomtes* of Foix-Béarn, from Roger-Bernard III (1290–1302) through Gaston Fébus (1343–91) to Gaston IV in the fifteenth century. The course of the Hundred Years War could itself be changed by the ebb and flow of fortune among these warring nobles: in 1362, the great defeat of the Armagnacs and their Albret allies by Gaston Fébus of Foix at Launac led to the payment of enormous ransoms by Jean I of Armagnac and Arnaud-Amanieu of Albret.[12] Their subsequent appeal of 1368–9 to Charles V of France against the allegedly extortionate nature of the Black Prince's taxation policy in Aquitaine may have been partly fuelled by their already depleted resources after Launac. The appeal, of course, led to the renewal of the Hundred Years War in 1369.[13]

In a war which was intertwined with private feuds, the habits of *guerre privée* died hard. Raids, surprise attacks on seigneurial strongholds, burning of villages, the capture of ploughbeasts and other animals – these were the commonplace occurrences of a period stretching back into a much earlier age.[14] The picture was made more complex by the intervention of higher authorities. The local truces made by the English seneschals of Aquitaine in the fifteenth century look very like those concluded by their predecessors in the early fourteenth century. Military expeditions to the duchy – in the form of both English and French expeditionary forces – could often find themselves embroiled in the internal quarrels of the Gascon nobility. On the whole, the numbers in English expeditionary forces deployed in Aquitaine were relatively small: 3,000 to 6,000 men, of whom many were Gascons. The Black Prince might bring substantial companies in his entourage to the duchy in the 1350s and 60s, but this was exceptional. Gascon defence remained essentially self-defence. As we shall see a little later, the English administration continued to rely upon local sources for the majority of its fighting troops in its south-western French possessions, as it had done under Edward I during the Anglo-French war of 1294–1298 and the war of St Sardos under Edward II.[15] It

---

[12] See Tucoo-Chala, *Gaston Fébus*, pp. 85–92.

[13] For the significance of the appeal see E. Perroy, 'Edouard III et les appels gascons en 1368', *Annales du Midi*, 61 (1948–9), pp. 91–6; A. Loirette, 'Arnaud-Amanieu, sire d'Albret, ses rapports avec la monarchie française de 1364 à 1380', *Annales du Midi*, 43 (1931), pp. 5–39.

[14] See M. Vale, 'Seigneurial Fortification and Private War in Later Medieval Gascony', in *Gentry and Lesser Nobility in Late Medieval Europe*, ed. M.C.E. Jones (Gloucester/New York, 1986), pp. 133–48.

[15] See Vale, *Angevin Legacy*, esp. pp. 200–15, 230–44; and also Vale, 'The Gascon nobility and the

was hardly surprising that pre-existing loyalties and contracts should play their part in shaping the behaviour of these forces, raised almost exclusively from the petty nobility of the region.

As we have already seen, the war in Aquitaine was very largely a war of sieges and skirmishes. With the exception of the fight at Lussac in October 1370 (where Sir John Chandos met his death), the so-called *Male jornade* in 1450 and the more decisive engagement at Castillon in July 1453, it is hard to find true pitched battles. There was no Gascon Crécy, Poitiers, Agincourt, Verneuil or Formigny. Some fights, such as Castillon, took place outside a besieged place and engagements in the field between the besiegers and a relieving force seem to make up most of the encounters described in the sources. The innumerable border raids and plundering *chevauchées* of public and private war accounted for the rest of the field engagements of the period. By far the most significant form of military action was, however, the siege and counter-siege. This set a premium upon the fortified place. Castles were the *antennae* of 'English' Aquitaine. By the outbreak of the Hundred Years War, the duchy and its frontiers were already studded with forts, estimated at about 1,000 by Professor Gardelles (excluding the *vicomté* of Bearn).[16] They were the 'nervous system' of the administration, as J.P. Trabut-Cussac described the originally non-military, non-strategic *bastides* of an earlier period.[17] The great majority of them were in seigneurial hands, and the king-duke held only a small number of garrisoned fortresses in his own hands, and even then not always permanently: the castles of the Ombrière at Bordeaux, of Fronsac, Bourg, Blaye, Bayonne, Dax, St Sever and a few others on the frontiers which tended to slip in and out of Plantagenet or Lancastrian obedience. A few vital fortresses, some royal/ducal, some seigneurial, formed a network upon which the safe-keeping of the duchy depended. Sir William Faringdon, captain of Fronsac, put the point well in 1404 when he said (in a somewhat exaggerated, though perfectly normal, petition) that 'without sufficient wages for the said castle's garrison of 120 combatants . . . he cannot hold or keep the said castle against the French. This castle is the principal fortress of all Guyenne . . . for if all the other fortresses were lost, which God prevent, they could be recovered by means of the said castle of Fronsac . . .'.[18] At many points in the fourteenth and fifteenth centuries the duchy itself resembled an armed camp under siege. The point had been made by Richard Scrope in 1378 that 'Gascony and the other forts which our lord the king has over there are and ought to be as barbicans to the kingdom of England, and if the barbicans are well guarded, with the safe keeping of the sea, the kingdom will be in good peace, but otherwise we shall never have calm nor peace with our enemies'.[19] Scrope's words were to be echoed by Faringdon and by Sir John Tiptoft

French war, 1294–8', in *War and Government in the Middle Ages*, ed. J. Gillingham and J.C. Holt (Woodbridge/Totowa, 1984), pp. 134–46.

[16] J. Gardelles, *Les Châteaux du Moyen Age dans la France du Sud-Ouest: La Gascogne anglaise de 1216 à 1327* (Geneva, 1972), pp. 44–5.

[17] See J.-P. Trabut-Cussac, 'Bastides ou forteresses?', *Le Moyen Age*, 50 (1960), pp. 81–135.

[18] PRO, E.28/28, nos. 125, 126.

[19] *Rot. Parl.*, iii, p. 36b (22 Oct. 1378).

in fifteenth-century Parliaments.[20] Like a barbican, the duchy was perceived as an outwork thrown forward as an enclave into the territory of the enemy, with the sea as a moat between it and the kingdom of England. When the sea passage was blocked, however, the outpost could, as we shall see, be cut off, isolated and reduced to enemy obedience.

Geography had a part to play in determining the course of the war in Aquitaine. The possession of a few strongpoints on the frontiers gave command of communication and supply routes. Rivers, roads, their junctions and confluences, determined the location of the most important fortresses. Water supply was essential and the paucity of castles in the poorly endowed Landes to the south of Bordeaux reflected that fundamental fact. To the north, Bourg and Blaye served to control the course of the Gironde and its bifurcation into the Dordogne and Garonne; La Réole, Marmande, Tonneins and Clermont-Dessus commanded the Garonne above and below Agen. Fronsac, Libourne, Ste Foy-le-Grande, Bergerac, Limeuil, Domme and Beynac stood as manacles on the contested frontier area along the Dordogne. Inland fortresses such as Chalais and Puynormand in Périgod; Gensac, Rauzan, Sauveterre-de-Guyenne and Bénauge in the Entre-deux-Mers (all in seigneurial hands); and the cluster of fortified towns including Rions, St Macaire, Cadillac, and Langon in the immediate vicinity of Bordeaux were subject to siege and counter-siege throughout the war. It is perhaps surprising that the French, although coming extremely close to the city at a number of points during the war, were unable to take Bordeaux until 1451. But this was precisely what had happened during the war of St Sardos in 1324–5.[21] La Réole and other forts might fall to the French, but Bordeaux held out for the English. Despite its low-lying position it was an extremely defensible (and well-defended) city which even the most advanced siege-craft found a very hard nut to crack. Starvation and treachery, rather than bombardment and assault, were to prove the most valuable weapons in a besieger's armoury.

A second theatre of war in Aquitaine was constituted by the scatter of garrisons concentrated further south: at Dax, Gamarde, St Sever, Mont-de-Marsan, Roquefort-de-Marsan, Tartas, Pouillon and Guissen, somewhat isolated from the rest of the duchy by the sandy and infertile soils of the Landes. It is probably significant that the Landes, with the exception of those areas immediately bordering the *pays d'Albret* and the Bazadais, defended by the castles built by Pope Clement V and his relatives (Villandraut, Roquetaillade, Budos) saw little military action of any great consequence. No army of any size could sustain itself from local sources in such an infertile region.[22] Its very existence meant that an invading force had to divide itself into two separate armies, the one attempting to gain possession of the northern frontier castles on the Gironde, Dordogne and Garonne, while the other advanced through the relatively prosperous plains and river valleys of Chalosse to capture strongholds on the Adour and Midouze. This had happened

---

[20] See, for example, *Rot. Parl.*, iii, p. 579.
[21] See Vale, *Angevin Legacy*, pp. 237–39.
[22] R. Cuzacq, *Géographie historique des Landes* (Mont-de-Marsan, 1948), pp. 31–3, 43–6.

in 1294–98 and in 1324–5, as well as during the Hundred Years War itself. The final campaigns of the 1450s saw two French field armies attacking the duchy: one pressing down from the north towards Bordeaux (which explains why Castillon took place where it did); the other advancing westwards and southwestwards from Agen, Toulouse and the Languedoc to recover Bayonne and its hinterland.

It was not until 1442 that French strategy was successfully co-ordinated in these two areas – northern and southern – of warfare. It was then proved that an invading army, once it had gained control of strategically-sited castles on the Dordogne and Garonne, could effectively deprive Bordeaux of corn and other food supplies. In the event, the invasion failed, partly through the onset of disease in the French army. But in October 1453, the imposition of a French naval blockade in the Gironde, at the crucial time of the wine harvest, when Bourg and Blaye were already in their hands, completed the stranglehold on the city by preventing the arrival of aid from England.[23] Conversely, the stubborn resistance of an Anglo-Gascon garrison could immobilize and absorb the manpower of the enemy for many months. At La Réole in 1442 (as in 1324) and at Bénauge and Cadillac in 1453, the concentration of French forces at the decisive point – Bordeaux – was dispersed and delayed through their refusal to surrender. But the techniques of war in the fifteenth century were changing, and a more sophisticated and effective use of siege artillery tended to quicken the pace of siege-warfare.[24]

A castle – in Aquitaine as elsewhere – could serve at least two roles for an aggressor: it might serve to hold down a recently-regained area; and it might provide a secure centre from which raids could be made and the reduction of a region begun. The great advantage of getting hold of Rions, on the Garonne, within twenty miles of Bordeaux, was appreciated in letters patent of Charles VII issued on 14th June 1444, where it was stated that: 'from the said castle and town, many great hurts can be given to our said enemies . . . for it is said that there is no other fortress around the said town of Bordeaux under our obedience as near as . . . Rions'.[25] Again, in November 1451, the French considered the castle of Biron in Périgord, held by Anglo-Gascon forces until July 1450, to be 'a very fair and strong place, but it would have cost a very great deal to take and recover by siege; and if so, it would be much to the damage of the inhabitants of the . . . sénéchaussées . . . of Agenais and Quercy'.[26] Accordingly, Biron had been reduced by agreement with its English captain, although the tax-payers of the two sénéchaussées were constrained to contribute substantially to the costs of paying the English to go away. Another Anglo-Gascon garrison – at Clermont-Dessus – isolated amid

[23] See Vale, 'The Last Years of English Gascony, 1451–1453', *TRHS*, 5th ser., 19 (1969), pp. 133–6.
[24] See P. Contamine, *War in the Middle Ages*, tr. M.C.E. Jones (Oxford, 1984), pp. 256–70; M. Vale, 'New techniques and old ideals: the impact of artillery on war and chivalry at the end of the Hundred Years War', in *War, Literature and Politics in the Late Middle Ages*, ed. C.T. Allmand (Liverpool, 1976), pp. 57–72. For a more recent technical discussion see C.J. Rogers, 'The Military Revolutions of the Hundred Years War', *Journal of Military History*, 57 (1993), pp. 241–78.
[25] Pau, Archives Départementales des Pyrénées-Atlantiques (APA), E.643.
[26] APA, E.702, no. 8.

enemy territory, effectively impeded the commercial traffic of the Garonne valley as far as Toulouse.[27] Amanieu de Madaillan, captain of Clermont, as his predecessors had been, stated in March 1434 that 'I have been, and will always be, in the service of the king [Henry VI]'. But in March 1438 he evacuated the place after payment (bribe?) of 8,000 francs from Charles VII's receiver-general of *aides* in the *sénéchaussée* of Toulouse.[28] The systematic reduction of outposts such as these was imperative if the (admittedly) expensive benefits of peace to the local population were to be felt.

For the French the frontiers of Aquitaine appeared as marches, giving rise to problems very similar to those faced by the English in Wales and, above all, Scotland.[29] To deal with marcher societies was not an easy task, and the conditions of war in Aquitaine often resembled those found on the borders of England. Certain castles were acknowledged by the French, as by English and Anglo-Gascon captains, to be critical in the event of raids or invasions. Bergerac was said to be 'of great influence, situated . . . on the river Dordogne, key and principal entry to . . . the Bordelais' in December 1450.[30] William Faringdon's remarks of 1404 were fully endorsed by the French in June 1451, when an agreement for the surrender of Fronsac stated that 'it is the strongest castle of the marches of Guyenne, and has always been guarded by Englishmen born in England' (not entirely true, because it had a Dutch or German provost in 1409–12 and a partly Welsh garrison) 'because it is a royal *chambre* and the chief of Guyenne and Bordelais'.[31] Perched on its abrupt rocky outcrop, commanding the river valleys of the Dordogne, Dronne and Isle, the value of Fronsac can still be appreciated. Other castles in English hands possessed less spectacular advantages: at La Réole, the castle was said in 1446 to be 'in the low country and low marches of Guyenne' while the seigneurial castle of Blanquefort lay in flat meadow and marshland, but controlled the road from Bordeaux into the Médoc.[32] On both the English and French sides, the absolute necessity of maintaining garrisons 'on the frontier of war' was recognised, during both war and truces. That frontier often lay very close to the hub or nucleus of the Plantagenet and Lancastrian administrations – Bordeaux. In August 1423, for example, the castles of St Macaire, Rions, Sauveterre, Puynormand, Rauzan and Pujols were said to be 'on the frontier of

---

27 P. Wolff, *Commerce et marchands de Toulouse* (Paris, 1954), pp. 56, 62.
28 PRO, E.101/191/7, nos. 22, 24; Wolff, *Commerce et marchands*, p. 56; Paris, BN, ms fr. 26065/3654.
29 See J. Campbell, 'England, Scotland and the Hundred Years War in the Fourteenth Century', in *Europe in the Late Middle Ages*, ed. J.R. Hale, J.R.L. Highfield and B. Smalley (London, 1965), p. 214; R.R. Davies, *Lordship and Society in the March of Wales, 1280–1400* (Oxford, 1978), pp. 34–85.
30 *Ordonnances des rois de France de la troisième race*, ed. E.J. de Laurière et al. (Paris, 1723–1849), xiv, p. 111.
31 BN, MS Duchesne 108, fo. 27r (5th June 1451). The muster roll of its garrison on 4 Dec. 1412 names Henry van Emerik as provost and the list of archers includes names such as Johan Walshman, Gryffyn Daywath and Robert Denby (E. 101/185/6, no. 3).
32 AN, JJ 178, no. 19 (May 1446).

war, among the king's enemies and rebels'.[33] In July 1451 the fortified town and
port of Libourne (Leyburne) was described as being for a long time on the frontier
of war.[34] If an area was to be held down and occupied for any length of time, such
places had to be taken. Their walls could provide places of retreat for the local
inhabitants and for their beasts. It was difficult to sustain an army in the Bordelais,
as the French discovered to their cost between 1294 and 1453. The troops could not
live on wine, raw grapes and fruits without sufficient corn and bread supplies. To
launch expeditionary forces against the duchy without secure bases, close to the
theatre of war, in which to gather and store supplies and provisions was therefore a
risky undertaking. It was perhaps one reason why it took the French so long to
reduce the region to obedience.

The constant emphasis on watchful defence led to concern for the upkeep and
repair of fortifications by both the administration at Bordeaux and the towns of the
duchy. One of the most valuable aspects of the largely unpublished accounts of the
constables of Bordeaux, and of the documents subsidiary to those accounts
throughout this period, is the very detailed information they provide for the building, repair and maintenance of fortified places. It would probably be possible to
use both this evidence and architectural survivals to produce a substantial work on
the *King's Works in Aquitaine*. Responsibility for overseeing defensive fortifications had devolved upon the constable of Bordeaux – normally an English knight
or clerk – assisted by the controller who kept the counter-roll, or check, on
expenditure. John Bowet, the controller, gave a disturbing account of the state of
Fronsac castle in 1414: he told Henry IV that 'your castle of Fronsac has great
need of repair, and I do not yet know the cost of carpenters and masons until I have
shown them what shall be necessary; for the walls have fallen in part and are
falling down from day to day. All the gates . . . should be constructed anew, and I
have begun to make the first gate which will soon be finished, if God so pleases,
such as has never before been made for the castle . . .'.[35] We know from the
accounts that Bowet had been paid by the constable (Sir William Clifford) for
journeying to Fronsac with him to survey the place and inspect the repairs in
progress. From 1337 to 1453 the constables of Bordeaux – many of them clerks –
were required to inspect works of this kind and many, as Master Walter Colles in
the 1430s, were assiduous in performing this task.[36] Colles' successor, the Norfolk
knight and rival of Sir John Fastolf – Edmund Hull – spent the better part of the
months of November and December 1445 viewing fortifications at Bourg, Blaye,
Libourne and Fronsac.[37] In January 1446 his lieutenant, John Clement, was paid
for going with carpenters to Bourg to oversee the construction of certain walls
called the 'Bollewerk' (*boulevard*) for three days.[38] Guns were also provided for

[33] E.101/188/6, no. 6.
[34] *Ordonnances*, xiv, p. 161 (July 1451).
[35] BL, MS Cotton Caligula D III, f. 127; also PRO, E.101/192/8, f. 24r; 71/3, no. 871; 186/2, no.
85.
[36] E.101/191/7, no. 8; 191/13; 192/9, no. 28.
[37] E.364/84 (3 Nov. and 6 Dec. 1445).
[38] E.364/84 (3 Jan. 1446)

this species of early artillery fortification: some of the earliest evidence for the use of firearms in France in fact comes from the accounts of the constables of Bordeaux between 1337 and 1339.[39] Charges for the repair and stocking of forts are thus among the most regular items of expenditure in the constables' accounts throughout the Hundred Years War.

The towns of the duchy also played their part in the provision of defensive apparatus. The *jurats* of towns such as St Emilion or St Sever found that there was no better argument for permission to raise a new tax, or to be relieved of an old one, than the worthy cause of repair to the town walls.[40] Some communes were still unfortified as late as 1420, when the inhabitants of La Marque in Bigorre submitted themselves to the protection of Jean I, count of Foix for this very reason and because they were 'on the frontier of the English'.[41] On the other side of the political fence, the inhabitants of St Sever petitioned Henry VI in February 1433 that the town lay upon the frontier, near to the lordships of Foix, Armagnac and Albret.[42] Their predecessors had acted in precisely the same fashion in 1295, 1303, 1317 and no doubt at other points in the fourteenth century. A watch was necessary day and night, and the town maintained its own cannon and crossbowmen. They had also 'undertaken great repairs to the walls at their own expense, for because of the great excess of rain since a year ago, the foundations of a great part of the walls . . . have failed so that the said walls have fallen down'.[43] This was no laughing matter, given the importance of St Sever, and freedom from all tolls and taxes on their merchandise throughout the duchy was granted to them. But this type of dialogue between ruler and subject was nothing new. War had been a fact of life in Aquitaine for centuries: it was a reality to be lived with by all, lamented by some, but exploited by others.

Among those who gained from war – whether public or private – in Aquitaine, the nobility must be given pride of place. If a statistical count were taken of the numbers of nobles and their retinues who served the king-dukes of Aquitaine between 1294 and 1453 I have little doubt that the overwhelming majority would be Gascons. English expeditionary forces and castle garrisons would account for a relatively small, transient body of men. This was truly a warrior-nobility; it remained so until the seventeenth century. There appears to be a clear line of descent from the Bascot de Mauléon in the fourteenth century to Blaise de Montluc in the Wars of Religion. War, and the prospect of war, kept these men alive. Despite their relentless and often querulous petitions for payment of wages and redress of grievances, it was difficult for many of them to find any other gainful occupation. The poverty of the petty seigneurs of the Landes and Bazadais was legendary. As an exercise in the history of *mentalités*, a study of the Gascon nobility would emphasize the fact that for the man-at-arms of this period, the concept of peace

---

[39] See Vale, *Angevin Legacy*, p. 261, esp. nn. 191–4.
[40] *Archives Historiques de la Gironde* (Bordeaux, 1859–), 28, pp. 485–8; PRO, C.61/111, m. 3r.
[41] APA, E.429, no. 211 (21 June 1420).
[42] E.28/54, no. 7; C.61/125, m. 14.
[43] E.28/54, no. 7.

was unwelcome. They would have approved of Sir John Hawkwood's views on the subject as reported by Francesco Sacchetti.[44] At a lower social level, the Gascon crossbowmen and foot-serjeants commented on by Gilles le Bouvier, herald of Berry, in his *Livre de la description des pays* (c.1450) were the Ghurkas of the later Middle Ages.[45] They, like their Welsh contemporaries, served the English crown everywhere: France, Aquitaine, Wales, Scotland, the Low Countries, sometimes in garrisons. Aquitaine provided a reservoir of manpower (and horse-power) for both the Plantagenets and Lancastrians throughout the period.

Sources of manpower in the duchy fell into three main categories: firstly, the companies and retinues of the Gascon nobility, difficult to distinguish from the second type: hired captains and their followings; and thirdly, troops raised by the towns, either through short-term contracts with captains or from communal levies. In terms of quality and professionalism, the hired captains and the nobles clearly outdid the communal levies. The militia of Bordeaux, which had agreed in 1254 to serve the king-duke without pay for forty days within the diocese, was a force of dubious competence.[46] But it certainly served to recover castles from French hands between 1420 and 1423, supported by the city's tolerably effective artillery.[47] But well before the outbreak of war in 1337, the norm had become service for pay: this is exemplified by the payment of wages to troops (both cavalry and infantry) raised from both the nobility and the towns during the Anglo-French wars of 1294–5.[48] The forms of military contract for short-term service remained remarkably similar from the later thirteenth to the mid-fifteenth century. The addition of terms relating to gains of war appear to characterize some of the contracts (especially those of the Black Prince with Gascon nobles in the mid-fourteenth century) but the stipulation of service with men and horses at certain standardised rates of pay was already alive and well in the 1290s.[49] Compensation for horses lost while in service (the old feudal right of *restaur*), however, disappeared from the contracts by the middle of the fourteenth century. Over and above any 'feudal' obligations (which were in any case less clear and binding in Aquitaine than elsewhere) the Gascon nobility expected to be paid for its military activity on behalf of sovereign or immediate lords, whether Plantagenet, Lancastrian, Capetian or Valois. The feed man, or retainer, was by no means unknown in Aquitaine. Beneath the so-called 'non-feudal' *alliances* contracted by the greater families with lesser nobles, were bodies of retainers, *mesnies* or companies, some bound by contracts which seem very similar to the indentures of service in peace and war found in contemporary

---

[44] See the account cited in M.H. Keen, 'Chivalry, Nobility and the Man-at-Arms', in *War, Literature and Politics*, p. 32.

[45] See Gilles le Bouvier, *Le Livre de la description des pays*, ed. T. Hamy (Paris, 1908), pp. 45–52.

[46] *Archives Municipales de Bordeaux. Livre des Coutumes*, ed. H. Barckhausen (Bordeaux, 1890), p. 530.

[47] *AMB, Registres de la Jurade*, ii (Bordeaux, 1883), pp. 363, 401, 434.

[48] See Vale, *Angevin Legacy*, pp. 205–6, 239–40.

[49] See Capra, 'Les bases sociales du pouvoir anglo-gascon', pp. 274–82; Vale, 'The Gascon Nobility and Crises of Loyalty (1294–1337)', in *La 'France Anglaise' au Moyen Age* (Paris, 1988), pp. 213–14; 'The Gascon nobility and the Anglo-French War', pp. 135–46.

England.[50] We can glimpse these relationships rarely from the surviving evidence. But besides vassalic ties, there were clearly bonds of another kind. In July 1401, for instance, the Gascon esquire Petit de Pellegrue claimed that Guillaume-Amanieu de Madaillan, lord of Lesparre, had given him 'for the term of his life, one hundred francs of annual rent, and *bouche de court* (food in the household) for himself and three valets, and hay and oats for four horses by means of a letter sealed with own seal'.[51] Here was a life-retainer on the English pattern. How many more of them were there, hidden from us by the lack of documentation?

By whatever manner they were raised and sustained, there can be little doubt that the resources in armed men brought to the war by Gascon nobles were very substantial. It has been concluded (by Professor Pierre Capra) that during the Black Prince's operations in Aquitaine between 1354 and 1361 Gascon nobles, men-at-arms and serjeants accounted for 75% of the captains and 80% of the companies serving against the French at that time.[52] The remainder were English. All were contracted as both field troops and garrison forces. The pattern repeated that of the 1290s: indeed, the captains (and some of the rank-and-file) of these units were derived from precisely the same families – Caumont, Fossat, Pommiers, Montpezat, Caupenne, Estissac and so on. Numbers raised could be strikingly large: in 1297, a mere esquire (Auger de Mauléon) brought 11 mounted men-at-arms (*socii*) and 140 foot-serjeants to muster for Edward I in Aquitaine, while Garcie-Arnaud, Lord of Navailles had 15 men-at-arms and 111 serjeants in his company.[53] In 1337–8 Jean de Grailly, Captal de Buch, later a founder member of the Garter, had a company of 77 mounted men-at-arms and no less than 685 foot-serjeants, mostly in garrisons for Edward III, while Bernard d'Albret, lord of Rions and Vayres had 8 knights, 39 mounted and 37 unmounted men-at-arms, and 340 foot-serjeants at various castles between August and December 1338.[54] There is some evidence to suggest that the serjeants were armed with pikes or spears, as well as crossbows, so that the Gascon pikeman may soon make his appearance among the ranks of the known bodies of infantry who fought in the Hundred Years War. By the fifteenth century, Gascon nobles were providing the Lancastrian administration with rather larger companies of cavalry and fewer foot soldiers, although this might depend upon the nature of military operations and demands at a given time. In May 1417, for instance Gaston de Foix, Jean de Grailly's successor as Captal de Buch, had 110 men-at-arms 'of retinue', Gaillard de Durfort 60, and Bertrand de Montferrand 90, contracted to serve against Jean d'Armagnac, *vicomte* of Lomagne, who had recently taken Le Réole.[55] These men, like their

---

[50] See P.S. Lewis, 'Decayed and Non-Feudalism in Later Medieval France', *Essays in Later Medieval French History* (London, 1985), pp. 45–6, 61–2; Vale, 'The Anglo-French Wars, 1294–1340: allies and alliances', in *Guerre et Société en France, en Angleterre et en Bourgogne, xive-xve siècles*, ed. P. Contamine, C. Giry-Deloison and M.H. Keen (Lille, 1991), pp. 22, 24–5.
[51] PRO, C.61/108, m. 3 (12 July 1401); C.81/1356, no. 10.
[52] Capra, 'Les bases sociales du pouvoir anglo-gascon', pp. 293–99.
[53] Vale, *Angevin Legacy*, p. 202.
[54] Vale, *Angevin Legacy*, pp. 262–3.
[55] PRO, E.101/186/1, nos. 2, 3, 5.

ancestors, were military contractors, employing their kinsmen, vassals, and clients as sub-contractors. After 1337 they were more likely to be required to serve in the king-duke's 'public' war with France, for which they were paid by the Plantagenet and Lancastrian administrations, than in the suppression, on the king-duke's behalf, of private war and feuds within the duchy. In a sense, the Hundred Years War offered them greater scope for military activity, perhaps under stricter control than before, but it could also legitimitise the prosecution of essentially private quarrels subsumed in the greater conflict. The history of the Foix-Armagnac feud (still partly unwritten) during the Anglo-French war would suggest that royal lieutenancies could be used by their holders in the interests of their own houses. Yet another set of loyalties was therefore introduced into the complex pattern of allegiances within the duchy and on its borders. The dilemmas faced by the *alliés* of Foix, Albret and Armagnac were not entirely new, but no account of Gascon loyalties to England or France during the Hundred Years War can fail to take account of them. Pre-existing bonds, whether formalised by written contracts and pledges or not, could play a determining part in deciding the choices made by a nobility that lived from and by war.

I am very much aware that much has been omitted from this brief survey of some aspects of the war in Aquitaine. The question of economic and commercial connections between England and the duchy has not been broached and the wine trade has hardly been mentioned. To some extent this is intentional, as it seems to me that our knowledge of the trade and its ups-and-downs is comparatively great, stemming from the work of Professors Renouard, Bernard, Carus-Wilson and Miss James.[56] The economic and social impact of war upon the countryside was set out by Professor Boutruche many years ago – but only, in fact, for the Bordelais.[57] The areas in which the greatest lacunae seem to lie are in the field of military organisation and operations, especially the nature and course of the war in Aquitaine between about 1346 and 1399, and the behaviour of the Gason nobility in the period from about 1362 to the 1390s. Above all, a comprehensive history of the war in Aquitaine is unlikely to be written, in either England or France, until more of the primary material – particularly the Gascon Rolls and supporting documentation – is available, properly edited, in print. Until that time, unless the manuscript material attracts more scholars and researchers than it has done of late, the conflict in Aquitaine is likely to remain among the least well-known areas of our vastly improved knowledge of the war.

---

[56] Y. Renouard, *Etudes d'histoire médiévale* (Paris, 1968), i, pp. 225–336,579–86; ii, pp. 993–1008; J. Bernard, *Navires et gens de mer à Bordeaux, vers 1400-vers 1550*, 3 vols (Paris, 1968); E.M. Carus-Wilson, 'The Effects of the Acquisition and Loss of Gascony on the English Wine Trade', *BIHR*, 21 (1947), pp. 145–54; M.K. James, *Studies in the Medieval Wine Trade*, ed. E.M. Veale (Oxford, 1971).
[57] R. Boutruche, *La Crise d'une Société. Seigneurs et paysans du Bordelais pendant la Guerre de Cent Ans* (Paris, 1963).

5

The Domestic Response to the Hundred Years War

W. M. ORMROD

> This day is called the Feast of Crispian.
> He that outlives this day and comes safe home
> Will stand a-tiptoe when this day is named
> And rouse him at the name of Crispian.
> He that shall see this day and live t'old age
> Will yearly on the vigil feast his neighbours
> And say, 'Tomorrow is St Crispian.'
> Then will he strip his sleeve and show his scars
> And say, 'These wounds I had on Crispin's day.'
> Old men forget; yet all shall be forgot,
> But he'll remember, with advantages,
> What feats he did that day. Then shall our names,
> Familiar in his mouth as household words –
> Harry the King, Bedford and Exeter,
> Warwick and Talbot, Salisbury and Gloucester –
> Be in their flowing cups freshly remembered.
> This story shall the good man teach his son,
> And Crispin Crispian shall ne'er go by,
> From this day to the ending of the world,
> But we in it shall be remembered.
>
> (*Henry V*, Act 4, Scene 3)

THE MODERN CULT of Shakespeare has done more than anything else to perpetuate the popular belief that the Hundred Years War was the first great national enterprise in our island history. Coinciding as they did with the early flowering of English letters and the greatest glories of English Gothic, the French wars of Edward III and Henry V have traditionally been seen as an expression of that supreme confidence, inspired leadership and strong sense of communal purpose that characterised a lost and better age. That England was ultimately, and disastrously, defeated in those wars mattered less than that her warriors had acquitted themselves with honour. This chivalric-inspired romanticism still has many influential advocates: indeed, had the anonymous Elizabethan drama *Edward III* been admitted to the Shakespearean canon, it is likely that recreations of all the great set pieces of the Hundred Years War would still find a regular place on stage and screen.[1] Faced with this enduring and seductive tradition, it is no easy task to strip away several centuries of myth-making (Shakespeare's 'advantages') and to make an objective assessment of the domestic impact of the Anglo-French hostilities of the fourteenth and fifteenth centuries. For all these problems, however, it remains clear that the Hundred Years War brought about many profound changes in the political, social, economic and cultural life of England, changes which deserve both to be better understood and to be given a more prominent place alongside the purely military aspects of the war. Therein lies the purpose of this chapter.

To state that the population of late medieval England had no consciousness of participating in or living through a 'Hundred Years War' may seem an obvious point. But this is not to deny that the Anglo-French hostilities of 1337–1453 had begun to take on a certain historical coherence even before their conclusion.[2] Indeed, one of the main cultural consequences of the Hundred Years War was a new awareness of and interest in English history. For the crown itself, the long negotiations that preceded the opening of war in 1337 provided a major inducement to the ordering of official documents and the swift recovery of historical information: there is a very striking contrast between Edward I's desperate pleas for monastic librarians to search their chronicles for evidence in support of his claims in Scotland and the detailed (if not always completely accurate) accounts of Anglo-French relations since the Treaty of Paris 1259 drawn up by the agents of Edward I, II and III.[3] There were also appeals to the more distant past: both Edward III and Henry V, for example, seem to have entertained the notion that they were entitled to the duchy of Normandy not simply as a dependency of the French crown but also through their ancient patrilineal right extending back to William the Conqueror. That this notion finds echoes in both semi-official and unofficial literature of the 1340s and 1410s is an interesting indication of the widespread popularity attached to the practice of justifying current action by an appeal to the past.[4] Consequently, it is not surprising to find that the tradition of historical writing was itself stimulated by the Anglo-French struggle: the early phases of the Hundred Years War witnessed new refinements in the chronicling of warfare, as more detailed accounts of battles, often provided from eye witnesses and other reliable sources, were formed together into consecutive and sustained accounts of English military enterprise.

Until the beginning of the fifteenth century, however, English warfare in France tended to be seen as a natural fulfilment of the more general policy of

---

[1]   R. Proudfoot, 'The Reign of King Edward the Third (1596) and Shakespeare', Proceedings of the British Academy, 71 (1985), pp. 159–85.

[2]   K. Fowler, The Age of Plantagenet and Valois (London, 1967), pp. 13–15.

[3]   Edward I and the Throne of Scotland, ed. E.L.G. Stones and G.G. Simpson (Oxford, 1978), 2, pp. 137–48; G.P. Cuttino, English Diplomatic Administration 1259–1339, second edition (Oxford, 1971), pp. 112–26; E.B. Fryde, Studies in Medieval Trade and Finance (London, 1983), chapter V, p. 251.

[4]   W.M. Ormrod, 'England, Normandy and the Beginnings of the Hundred Years War' and A. Curry, 'Lancastrian Normandy: The Jewel in the Crown?', England and Normandy in the Middle Ages, ed. D. Bates and A. Curry (London, 1994).

expansionism to which the English crown had committed itself since the time of Edward I and which found almost as much expression in the Scottish as in continental campaigns. It was the extraordinary revival of enthusiasm for the French wars in the 1410s and the particular insistence of Henry V and his brothers on effecting the dual monarchy envisaged by the Treaty of Troyes that really began to give a particular significance to the extinction of the Capetian dynasty in 1328 and the declaration of Edward III as king of France in 1340 and therefore to identify 1337 as the effective beginning of a consistent diplomatic and military history. Furthermore, it was only natural that in the immediate aftermath of the final English defeat in 1453, many writers, whether historians or polemicists, should have begun to use the great theme of the Anglo-French struggle for didactic purposes either, in the case of the humanists, to question the utility of war or more influentially, in the case of William Caxton's continuation of the *Brut* chronicle and Lord Berners' translation of Froissart, to preserve and honour the memories of the greatest heroes of English chivalry.[5] That this literary tradition itself drew not only on the established chronicles of the fourteenth and fifteenth centuries but on oral traditions and folk memories is a powerful reminder of the extraordinary psychological and cultural response that the Hundred Years War had provoked in the population of England.[6]

That developing sense of a collective experience is perhaps all the more remarkable given that so few English people witnessed the realities of war in the fourteenth and fifteenth centuries. In sharp contrast with certain parts of France, the kingdom of England knew nothing of what is now called 'total war': the phenomenon of enemy armies occupying the land, living off its fruits and grinding away at the economic and psychological wellbeing of its dependents was unknown. On the other hand, the country certainly knew the threat, and sometimes the reality, of invasion. Scottish raiders during the reign of Edward II had brought widespread devastation and hardship to the north of England and provided a salutary reminder of the lasting damage that could be inflicted even by temporary incursions. From the 1330s, the south of England had to face similar threats from across the Channel. The attack on Southampton in 1338, which put a stop to trade in the port for over a year, is the best documented and best known case, but small-scale raids, and rumours of schemes for full-scale invasions, created periodic scares along the south and east coasts for the rest of the fourteenth century. Indeed, it can be argued that the failure of the crown and nobility to organise coastal defence and ward off the French threat was one of the principal grievances of the Kentish rebels who rose in support of the Peasants' Revolt in 1381.[7]

Moreover, although the vast majority of the inhabitants of England living away from the Channel and the northern march knew nothing of enemy raids, they were

[5] A. Gransden, *Historical Writing in England* (London, 1974–82), 2, pp. 454–79.

[6] For the varied sources used in the composition of *Henry V*, see *Narrative and Dramatic Sources of Shakespeare*, ed. G. Bullough (London, 1957–75), 4, pp. 347–75.

[7] E. Searle and R. Burghart, 'The Defense of England and the Peasants' Revolt', *Viator*, 3 (1972), pp. 365–88.

certainly not immune from other side-effects of war. It was particularly fortunate for the crown that the wealthiest and most productive parts of the country, those which provided so many of the material resources necessary to sustain the war effort, lay a good distance from the coast in midland England. Here, the biggest threat of disruption came not from foreign raiders but from fellow-Englishmen in the shape of the unscrupulous royal agents who collected money and supplies for the king's armies and the demobilised troops who often continued the habits of violence and pillage picked up on active service in enemy territory. Although such experiences in no way compared with the horrific deprivations suffered by non-combatants in France, it would therefore be a great mistake to assume that the Hundred Years War did not impinge, both practically and psychologically, on the lives of the English population.

A similar point can be made about the record of English military service during the period 1337–1453. Much effort has been given over to assessing the size both of the military contingents and of the support services that were raised for campaigns in France, and it now seems unlikely, even on the most generous estimate, that more than ten per cent of the adult male population of England was directly engaged in war at any one time during the Hundred Years War.[8] A good deal less attention, however, has been given to the more challenging question of whether those left at home perceived themselves as being indirectly engaged in the same struggle. During the early stages of the Hundred Years War the crown continued to use older methods of compulsion in order to secure infantry and light cavalry for its armies, and since the communities were sometimes required to provide the arms and wages of these soldiers, it is not unreasonable to suggest that the non-combatant population developed some sense of corporate interest in the activities of those men they sent to war. Increasingly, however, the emphasis on highly trained and well equipped mounted archers meant that the lower ranks of royal armies were recruited not from the peasantry but from the lesser gentry, and many urban and rural communities may have perceived the French wars as the preserve – perhaps even the playground – of the elite. But precisely because the military classes also provided the political and governing elite within England, it is quite possible that peasant communities were encouraged to identify as closely with the martial pretensions of local landed society as with the small numbers of their own kind who continued to venture overseas. The idea that the French wars were intended to protect and promote the interests not only of the king and the aristocracy but of the 'nation' as a whole may have been largely a piece of political propaganda designed to placate an often ambivalent non-combatant population, but it remains true that the period of the Hundred Years War witnessed the rapid development of a much closer contact between the state and the people. Even if the majority could express that identity only through an often obscene contempt for the lecherous and treacherous French, it does not follow that the sense of involvement

[8]   M.M. Postan, *Essays on Medieval Agriculture and General Problems of the Medieval Economy* (Cambridge, 1973), pp. 63–5.

in what was sometimes projected as a form of national crusade was any less real than that invoked by other, later wars in England's history.[9]

To move from the mentality of war to its material costs is to enter an entirely different sphere of historical study where hard facts and statistical analysis become the order of the day. It is interesting to observe, however, that the conclusions based upon these objective data have varied widely. Few would now deny that the fourteenth century witnessed an enormous increase in the financial demands of the English state: K.B. McFarlane calculated that the crown raised approximately £8.25 million from the profits of direct and indirect taxation during the conventional chronological limits of the Hundred Years War, and the present author's researches on the same material have indicated that the true total stood at over £9.5 million.[10] But what do these figures actually mean in economic terms? Was the investment in war offset by the profits that England derived from it, as McFarlane believed, or did the Hundred Years War represent a major drain on natural resources that contributed significantly to the economic stagnation of the fifteenth century, as suggested by M.M. Postan?[11] To answer these questions properly requires not only more space but also more research, and the present contribution seeks only to address one aspect of the subject, albeit perhaps the most fundamental one, namely the direct burden of royal taxation in England during the fourteenth and first half of the fifteenth centuries.

It is important to realise that the initial stages of the Hundred Years War witnessed few fiscal novelties; ever since the late twelfth century, and more particularly from the time of Edward I, the English crown had been developing remarkably sophisticated methods of mobilising the country's wealth to support its various military and diplomatic policies. Consequently, it was very much on the precedents set during his grandfather's reign that Edward III at first relied to fund his wars in France. Apart from the conscription of soldiers and the compulsory levies of foodstuffs that caused so much controversy in the shires, the principal elements within this financial system were three-fold: the raising of huge cash loans from foreign (chiefly Italian) merchant bankers; the imposition of heavy surcharges on the existing customs duties on wool in order to provide security for those loans; and the negotiation of a series of direct taxes from the clergy (who were assessed on their incomes) and the laity (who contributed according to the

---

[9] J. Barnie, *War in Medieval Society. Social Values and the Hundred Years War 1337–99* (London, 1974), pp. 32–55; V.J. Scattergood, *Politics and Poetry in the Fifteenth Century* (London, 1971), pp. 35–107; N. Housley, 'France, England and the "National Crusade", 1302–1386', *France and the British Isles in the Middle Ages and Renaissance. Essays in Memory of Ruth Morgan*, ed. G. Jorndorf and D.N. Dumville (Woodbridge, 1991), pp. 183–98.

[10] K.B. McFarlane, *England in the Fifteenth Century* (London, 1981), pp. 142–3; materials for the revised figures are stored in the European State Finance Database Project (hereafter ESFDB) held by the Economic and Social Research Council Data Archive. For what follows see W.M. Ormrod, 'Medieval England', *The Rise of the Fiscal State in Europe, 1200– 1800*, ed. R.J. Bonney (Oxford, 1995).

[11] McFarlane, *Fifteenth Century*, pp. 139–49; Postan, *Essays*, pp. 49–80.

value of their movable property). It is not easy to calculate either the size or the general economic impact of these various levies, but it is now generally agreed that the burdens imposed on the country by Edward III in 1337–41 surpassed even those of Edward I in 1294–8 and, coinciding as they did with a series of natural and man-made economic crises, created considerable hardship and widespread disaffection among the population of England. Up to the 1340s, indeed, scholarly chroniclers and popular versifiers alike were virtually unanimous in their belief that the French campaigns, like the Scottish wars before them, had an inhibiting and sometimes devastating impact on the domestic economy.[12]

After the 1340s, however, both the scale and the nature of the crown's exactions altered significantly, as the methods of Edward I gave way to a new financial system that would endure for the rest of the Hundred Years War. Large-scale and often uncontrolled lending by Italians was now replaced by more modest and usually manageable borrowing from English nobles, prelates and merchants. From 1342 the extra subsidies on wool exports became permanent impositions and vastly increased the amounts of money made from the indirect taxation of overseas trade. Consequently, the earlier dependence on direct taxation gave way to a system in which the customs and subsidies on overseas trade regularly provided the bulk of the crown's tax revenues (fig. 5.1). And just as conscription gave way to voluntary service, so too were the arbitrary levies of arms and victuals abandoned in favour of a more efficient, if more expensive, system of contract purchasing on the open market.

Lest it be thought that the period 1350–1450 marked some kind of golden age of English taxation in which the demands of the state were reconciled with the interests of its subjects, it is as well to remember that the system of taxation remained blatantly inadequate and inequitable. Governments continued to overspend, sometimes disastrously so: both Richard II in the 1380s and Henry VI in the 1440s were driven to the verge of financial (and therefore political) bankruptcy by their failure to match increased expenditure with appreciable increases in revenue. From the perspective of the taxpayer, the system of direct taxation in particular was palpably unfair. For nearly a century after 1334, the crown continued to charge fixed quotas from village and town communities as their contributions to lay subsidies, largely ignoring the massive changes both in population and in the geographical and social distribution of wealth that followed the Black Death and the recurrent plagues of the later fourteenth century. Parliament's attempts to establish a fairer system of contributions in the 1370s proved fundamentally misguided, ending in the disastrous poll tax of 1380 and the débâcle of the Peasants' Revolt. For both the state and the taxpayer, the Hundred Years War was a challenging and often cheerless burden.

For all this, however, there are some important signs that the new financial

---

12 W.M. Ormrod, 'The Crown and the English Economy, 1290–1348', *Before the Black Death. Studies in the 'Crisis' of the Early Fourteenth Century*, ed. B.M.S. Campbell (Manchester, 1991), pp. 149–83, provides a full bibliography; a dissident voice is raised by A.R. Bridbury, 'Before the Black Death', *EcHR*, second series, 30 (1977), pp. 393–410.

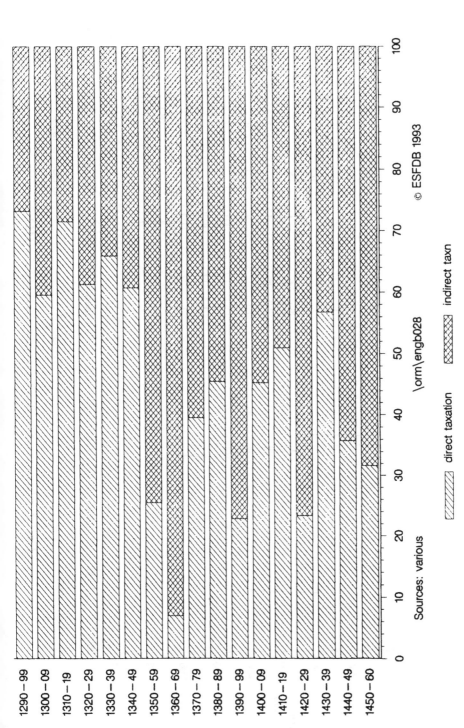

Fig. 5.1 The relative value of direct and indirect taxation in England, 1290–1460.

1290−99
1300−09
1310−19
1320−29
1330−39
1340−49
1350−59
1360−69
1370−79
1380−89
1390−99
1400−09
1410−19
1420−29
1430−39
1440−49
1450−60

0   10   20   30   40   50   60   70   80   90   100

Sources: various   © ESFDB 1993

\orm\engb028

direct taxation   indirect taxn

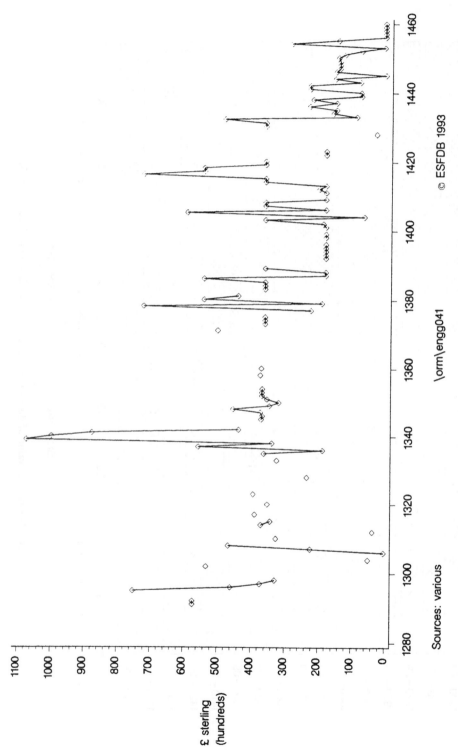

Fig. 5.2 Net receipts from direct taxation of the laity, 1290–1460.

Sources: various

\orm\engg041

© ESFDB 1993

£ sterling (hundreds)

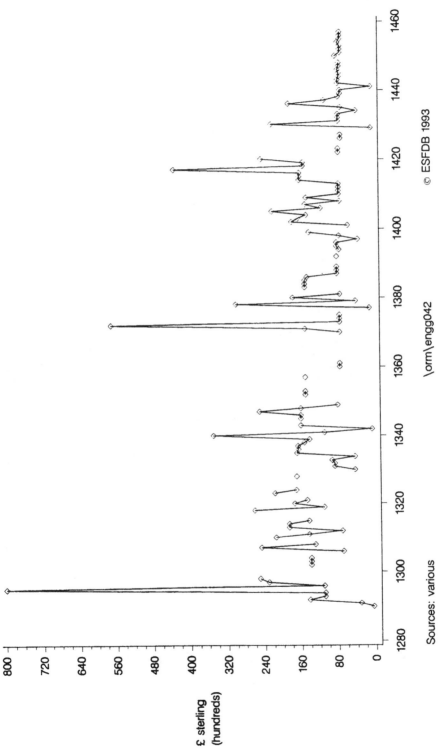

Fig. 5.3 Net receipts from direct taxation of the clergy, 1290–1460.

£ sterling (hundreds)

Sources: various

\orm\engg042

© ESFDB 1993

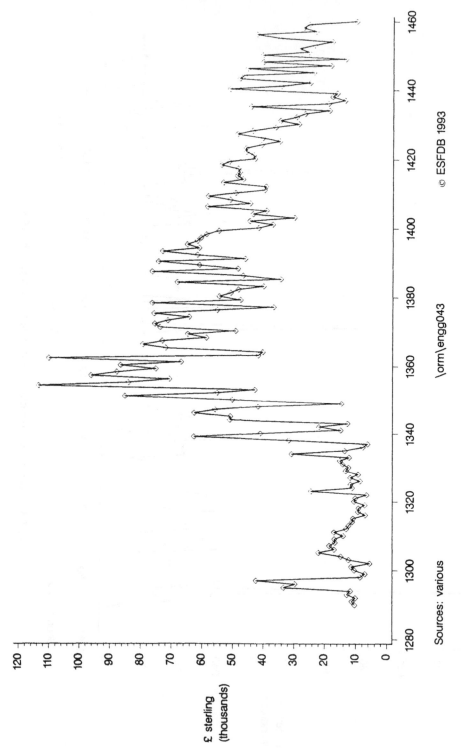

£ sterling
(thousands)

Sources: various   \orm\engg043   © ESFDB 1993

Fig. 5.4   Total revenue from indirect taxation of overseas trade, 1290–1460.

dispensation that operated after the 1340s had a very different impact on the domestic economy from the system that it replaced. To begin with, there is the striking evidence demonstrated by figures 5.2–5.4 of the overall decline in the value of both direct *and* indirect taxation over the course of the fourteenth and first half of the fifteenth centuries. Although economic factors had a part to play in this, the downturn in revenue that is so particularly apparent under Henry VI arose largely from political considerations. Direct taxes paid by the clergy and laity could not be collected without the formal consent of convocation and parliament, and despite some interesting efforts by Richard II, Henry IV and Henry V to extend the list of occasions on which such subsidies might be sought, both the clergy and, to a greater extent, the commons were only generally prepared to accept that taxation was an *obligation* in cases of real military necessity.[13] In the later stages of the war, when France was supposed to be paying for itself, convocations and parliaments therefore became increasingly adept at spreading the payment of direct levies over longer periods and in the meantime effectively immunising themselves from further impositions. Their success in blocking or compromising most of the initiatives for a reform of direct taxation also meant that considerable sections of the economy and society remained unexploited. Indeed, for every impoverished community struggling under its antiquated tax quota there was a town, a noble family or an unbeneficed priest enjoying substantial under-assessment or even total immunity from royal exactions. At least so far as direct taxation is concerned, then, the decline in yields between the fourteenth and fifteenth centuries represented not the cumulative effects of sustained fiscal pressure on the economy but the political conventions that had created an increasingly wide gulf between the potential and the real tax bases.

The explanation for the very dramatic decline in revenue from indirect taxation after its extraordinary peak in the middle of the fourteenth century is rather more complicated. The crown collected the customs duties as of right, and the only parliamentary taxes on overseas trade, the wool subsidy and tunnage and poundage, were conceded in a virtually unbroken series irrespective of whether or not the country was at war. From the 1340s to the death of Henry V, revenue from the taxation of overseas trade was therefore conditioned largely by the state of the export trade in wool, which contributed by far the largest proportion of the customs and subsidies. The French wars themselves have often been blamed for the decline in wool exports that set in during the later fourteenth century. But there were many other factors influencing the state of trade, not all of them within the control of the English crown; and in many ways it was the success of the wool merchants in resisting such vicissitudes that was the most remarkable feature of the English economy at the turn of the fifteenth century.[14] It is therefore important to realise that the marked decline in royal income from indirect taxation under Henry VI arose not simply from a slump in trade but also from the decision taken by the

[13] G.L. Harriss, 'Theory and Practice in Royal Taxation. Some Observations', *EHR*, 97 (1982), pp. 811–19.
[14] T.H. Lloyd, *The English Wool Trade in the Middle Ages* (Cambridge, 1977), pp. 225–56.

parliament of 1422 to reduce the wool subsidy paid by native merchants by a massive 23 per cent in line with its general policy of throwing the fiscal burden onto the king's new dominions in northern France.[15] Still more striking in this respect is the political pressure that parliament was able to bring to bear on any royal proposals for extending the duties on other commodities passing the ports, most obviously on the increasing numbers of English cloths that were now being exported to the continent. Once again, then, the decline in revenue from taxation denotes not an equivalent decline in the real tax base but an inability on the part of the state to adapt to new economic conditions. The figures are rough and ready, but revealing: in the 1350s, the crown's income from the customs and subsidies represented approximately 18.5 per cent of the total value of exports and imports; but in the 1390s the proportion had already fallen to 15 per cent; and by the 1440s it stood at under 12 per cent.[16]

It therefore appears that, despite the undoubted economic problems that England faced in the fifteenth century, the fall in taxation during the later stages of the war represented a reduction in the willingness, rather than the sheer ability, of the political community to pay. At particular times – in the 1340s, the 1370s, and the 1410s – the population of England had probably been pushed to the very limits of endurance in order to subsidise royal campaigns in France. But in the final analysis it cannot be said that the country was bled white by the fiscal pressures of the Hundred Years War. The greatly reduced financial commitment which is such a feature of Henry VI's regime was an expression not of destitution but, quite simply, of the loss of political will.

To understand why this great crisis of public confidence came about, it is necessary not only to analyse the slow breakdown of English military control in central and northern France after the 1430s but also to assess the criteria by which the political society of England had judged the crown's diplomatic and military policies since the time of Edward III. For all the expressions of national fervour and communal endeavour, the war was popular principally because it offered the participants the opportunity for profit, advancement and honour. The material benefits to be derived from active service in France were well understood, though inevitably somewhat exaggerated: neither Thomas Walsingham's comments on the matrons of England who decked themselves in the finery plundered during the

---

[15] The denizen rate fell from 43s. 4d. to 33s. 4d. per sack. Contrary to the author's statement, the figures given by G.L. Harriss, *Cardinal Beaufort. A Study of Lancastrian Ascendancy and Decline* (Oxford, 1988), p. 123, represent the *total* charge in customs and subsidies.

[16] These calculations are based on the following data. Michaelmas 1352–Michaelmas 1362: value of overseas trade, T.H. Lloyd, Overseas Trade and the English Money Supply in the Fourteenth Century', *Edwardian Monetary Affairs (1279–1344)*, ed. N.J. Mayhew, British Archaeological Reports, 36 (1977), pp. 113–15; tax revenue, W.M. Ormrod, *The Reign of Edward III. Crown and Political Society in England 1327–1377* (London, 1990), p. 207. Michaelmas 1391–Michaelmas 1399: value of overseas trade, T.H. Lloyd, *England and the German Hanse, 1157–1611* (Cambridge, 1991), pp. 104, 106; tax revenue, ESFDB \orm\engd006. Michaelmas 1442–Michaelmas 1452: value of overseas trade, J.L. Bolton, *The Medieval English Economy 1150–1500* (London, 1980), p. 307; tax revenue, ESFDB \orm\engm009.

great campaign of 1346–7 nor John Leland's claims in the early sixteenth century that many of the great baronial residences of England had been built *ex spoliis bello Gallico* should perhaps be taken too literally.[17] On the other hand, the investment of the profits of war in conspicuous consumption undoubtedly created important tangible symbols of England's military fortunes which could have a powerful impact on more general public perceptions of the war. Although attention tends now to be concentrated on the outstanding royal and aristocratic castles of Windsor, Warwick, Bolton, Bodiam, Sudeley, and so on, it is important to recognise that there once existed many other more modest but still potent expressions of the particular advantages to be had from the French war. The brass commissioned for the tomb of Sir Hugh Hastings at Elsing (Norfolk) and the heraldic devices incorporated into the east window of Gloucester Abbey by Sir Thomas Bradestone not only provided memorials to these seasoned campaigners but also linked them directly with some of the most distinguished royal and noble commanders in Edward III's early campaigns.[18] The countless other tomb effigies, brasses, inscriptions, armorial bearings and private chapels that were erected in English churches to commemorate the members of the military elite in the course of the war provided a constant reminder of the long struggle to which the realm had committed itself.

It was the desire to keep faith with these heroes and to uphold the honour of the individual, the family and the crown that also seems to have provided the necessary political resolve at those times when the nature of the fighting in France was a good deal less glamorous and the conditions generally unfavourable to the English cause. It has been suggested by M.R. Powicke and M.H. Keen that the long intermission in the war brought about by Richard II's truce with Charles VI broke the tradition of military service that had bound together landed society in the fourteenth century and that the occupation of northern France in the fifteenth century was the work of a comparatively narrow group of quasi-professional soldiers who became increasingly isolated from the domestic political community. This evidence could certainly be used to explain the striking decline in the financial commitment that the English parliament made towards the war effort under Henry VI. On the other hand, it should be stressed that there were few occasions, even in the darkest days of the war, when the political community as a whole was prepared to countenance the idea that the crown might simply cut its losses and withdraw from France.[19] In a proclamation of May 1389, Richard II tried to appeal

---

[17] H.J. Hewitt, *The Organization of War under Edward III* (Manchester, 1966), p. 110; K.B. McFarlane, *The Nobility of Later Medieval England* (Oxford, 1973), pp. 22–3, 92–3.

[18] *Age of Chivalry. Art in Plantagenet England 1200–1400*, ed. J. Alexander and P. Binski (London, 1987), pp. 497–8; N. Saul, *Knights and Esquires. The Gloucestershire Gentry in the Fourteenth Century* (Oxford, 1981), p. 77.

[19] M. Powicke, 'Lancastrian Captains', *Essays in Medieval History Presented to B. Wilkinson*, ed. T.A. Sandquist and M.R. Powicke (Toronto, 1969), pp. 371–82; M. Keen, 'The End of the Hundred Years War. Lancastrian France and Lancastrian England', *England and her Neighbours 1066–1453. Essays in Honour of P. Chaplais*, ed. M. Jones and M. Vale (London, 1989), pp. 297–311; M.H. Keen, 'English Military Experience and the Court of Chivalry. The Case of Grey v. Hastings',

to the practical instincts of his subjects by stressing what would now be called the peace dividend and promising the remission of taxation at the conclusion of a final treaty. Yet when the terms of that treaty were presented to parliament in 1394, the knights of the shire found them quite unacceptable, arguing that the feudal homage demanded from Richard II as duke of Aquitaine would mean that 'every single Englishman having the king of England as his lord would pass under the heel of the French king and be kept for the future under the yoke of slavery'.[20] Here, then, lay the basic problem confronting every English king between 1337 and 1453: what A.R. Myers called the 'tragic dilemma' between a ruinous war and a shameful peace.[21] It was on the same notions that Richard of York was to play in his Shrewsbury manifesto of 1452 when he spoke of the 'worship, honour and manhood asserted of all nations to the people of England, whilst the kingdom's sovereign lord stood possessed of his lordship in France', contrasting this with the 'derogation, lesion of honour and villainy reported generally unto the English nation for the loss of the same'.[22] What really changed under Henry VI was that the English parliament would no longer countenance the real financial investment required to make such proud and still popular sentiments a reality.

It is evident, then, that the general course of the Hundred Years War was increasingly determined by domestic public opinion, a collective viewpoint expressed not simply by a handful of peers and prelates in the king's council but generated in the localities and articulated in the proceedings of the county courts and the commons in parliament. The marked shift in the military priorities of the English crown away from the preservation of distant Aquitaine and towards the maintenance of the English positions in the more familiar and fertile territory of northern France, already evident long before Henry V's conquest of Normandy, is an interesting example of the way in which the original war aims of the crown had to be adapted to accommodate the interests and enthusiasms of the elite. The long parliamentary debates on the economic importance and military necessity of maintaining the English garrison at Calais also demonstrate the degree to which strategy was becoming a matter of public concern and, to some extent, of public control. Consequently, the ability of the king to mobilise support for his wars depended increasingly on the extent to which he and his lieutenants fulfilled public expectations; or, to put it another way, the extent to which he was able to manipulate public opinion in his own favour. It is to the domestic propaganda of the Plantagenet regime that we must therefore turn our attention in the remainder of this chapter.

Guerre et société en France, en Angleterre et en Bourgogne xive–xve siècle, ed. P. Contamine, C. Giry-Deloison and M.H. Keen (Lille, n.d.), pp. 123–42. See also M. Stansfield, 'John Holland, Duke of Exeter and Earl of Huntingdon (d. 1447) and the Costs of the Hundred Years War', *Profit, Piety and the Professions in Later Medieval England*, ed. M. Hicks (Gloucester, 1990), pp. 103–18.
[20] A. Tuck, 'Richard II and the Hundred Years War', *Politics and Crisis in Fourteenth-Century England*, ed. W. Childs and J. Taylor (Gloucester, 1990), pp. 126, 127.
[21] A.R. Myers, *England in the Later Middle Ages*, eighth edition (Harmondsworth, 1971), pp. 15–36.
[22] Keen, 'End of the Hundred Years War', p. 298.

The formal public information system that operated in fourteenth- and fifteenth-century England was based around two principal agencies: the sheriffs, who were responsible for making proclamations before the county courts and in markets and other public places; and the church, which was periodically requested to perform prayers, masses, processions and sermons in support of the king's wars. So much has been written on these channels of communication that it is perhaps as well to take a critical, even cynical, approach to their effectiveness. In particular, the idea that the clergy acted as a kind of advertising agency for the late medieval state clearly exaggerates the evidence and distorts the nature of the institution. In the well documented diocese of Lincoln, there were only 34 occasions between 1337 and 1453 when royal requests for prayers in connection with the war are known to have been implemented.[23] Moreover, it is now impossible to tell how many of the clergy actually obeyed episcopal instructions and enthusiastically imparted the news of projected campaigns or recent victories to their parishioners. Since a good deal of the protest and anti-war literature of the later Middle Ages flowed from clerical quills, it is tempting to suggest that there was at least a proportion of the clergy who were opposed on ideological or practical grounds to acting as the mere mouthpieces of a warlike monarchy: there is certainly no reason to think that the sentiments expressed by Thomas Brinton, John Wyclif and John Gower in the later fourteenth century were notably unusual for their time.[24] But even if proclamations and sermons in favour of the war did indeed reach a significant proportion of the population and persuade them of the righteousness of the king's cause, it is not necessary to assume that these were the only means by which the crown sought to influence the attitudes of its subjects. There were other less structured, more subtle but still potent means of propaganda which were put to particularly effective use by the image-conscious Plantagenets during the course of the Hundred Years War.

It is interesting to note that the written word had little part to play in the public relations exercises undertaken by the English monarchy prior to 1450: the production and circulation of official chronicles of the French wars was not part of their political scheme. Even those historical and biographical works that were produced within the court circle and express what might be called the official line were often intended for very specific, private consumption: the anonymous *Gesta Henrici Quinti*, for example, which made such a spirited defence of Henry V's policies in France, was written in the language of scholarship and survives in only two manuscripts.[25] This is not to say, of course, that royal propaganda was not repeated, consciously or unconsciously, in a great deal of contemporary literature. But in tracing the 'official' origins of fourteenth- and fifteenth-century writings on kingship and war, it is as well to remember that public attitudes were influenced a great

[23] A.K. McHardy, 'Liturgy and Propaganda in the Diocese of Lincoln during the Hundred Years War', *Studies in Church History*, 18 (1982), pp. 215–27.

[24] J.R. Maddicott, 'Poems of Social Protest in Early Fourteenth-Century England', *England in the Fourteenth Century. Proceedings of the 1985 Harlaxton Symposium*, ed. W.M. Ormrod (Woodbridge, 1986), pp. 130–44; Barnie, *War in Medieval Society*, pp. 117–38.

[25] Gransden, *Historical Writing*, 2, p. 204.

deal more easily by visual than by written media. The regency government of Henry VI demonstrated a particularly keen awareness of this fact in producing illustrated royal genealogies for dissemination among the king's new French subjects. The peculiar potency of imagery, whether expressed in illuminated manuscripts, courtly ritual or architectural symbolism, had indeed been appreciated by the English monarchy long before the start of the Hundred Years War, but it had been given much greater prominence since the mid-thirteenth century as a result of the religious, cultural and political pretensions of Henry III and Edward I. The images of the pious prince and the chivalric hero which these kings sought to project became the basic models for the public representation of the English crown throughout the Hundred Years War.

For Edward III, the image of kingship was inextricably bound up in that extraordinary combination of cultural refinement and physical brutality that we call chivalry. Edward's success in harnessing the natural belligerence of the aristocracy and turning it on his foreign enemies has long been discussed, but it is only comparatively recently that historians have begun to appreciate his equally remarkable record in transforming the royal court into the centre of chivalric, and therefore also of political, culture within England. Tournaments, for instance, which had long been regarded as potentially subversive gatherings of discontented nobles, were now made a deliberate and regular feature of court life and carefully stage-managed in order to ensure maximum publicity for the king and his aristocratic lieutenants. Picking up on a precedent set by his grandfather, Edward III also set out deliberately to project himself as the new King Arthur; the fact that a number of unofficial literary works elaborated on this idea is an important demonstration of the widespread popularity of the king's new public image. It is particularly significant that Edward chose his own birthplace of Windsor, rather than any of the sites more obviously associated with the Arthurian legends, as the headquarters of his new Order of the Garter, created deliberately to commemorate the victories of Crécy and Calais and to epitomise the aristocratic *esprit de corps* that had made those triumphs possible. The enormous building programme that turned Windsor from a modest Norman castle into a major Plantagenet palace – the Versailles of its age – was itself a statement of Edward's military and political achievements, while the dedication of both the Order of the Garter and its chapel at Windsor to St George did more than anything else to turn a previously international symbol of Christian knighthood into the patron saint of England. The culture of chivalry as espoused by Edward III had therefore not only captured the mood of exultant confidence existing in the age of Crécy and Poitiers but also focused particular attention on the king and his court as a symbol of the nation's unity.[26]

This new emphasis on the monarch as both mirror and protector of the integrity of the realm took on a further dimension in the fifteenth century as a result of a new interest in the king's ability to provide 'good governance' by preserving and

---

[26] J. Vale, *Edward III and Chivalry. Chivalrous Society and its Context 1270–1350* (Woodbridge, 1982); R.A. Brown, H.M. Colvin and A.J. Taylor, *History of the King's Works. The Middle Ages* (London, 1963), 1, p. 163.

enhancing the political, legal and economic interests of his subjects.[27] One of the most effective ways in which a ruler could demonstrate his good intentions towards the people was by emphasising his personal piety and suggesting that his inner worth provided a guarantee of wise government. Henry V appears to haver placed almost as much emphasis on his role as the scourge of heretics and the founder of saintly religious communities as on the triumph of Agincourt in public representations of his kingship, and both the quasi-official and unofficial accounts of his deeds consistently stressed his personal devotion to the heavenly hierarchy.[28] It therefore seems no accident that the fifteenth century witnessed a striking new emphasis on the physical representation of kingship in a specifically religious context. During the second half of the fourteenth century the crown itself had patronised the new artistic concern with portraiture: the tomb of Edward III and the extant panel paintings of Richard II (the Westminster portrait and the Wilton Diptych) are usually accepted as the earliest genuine, if stylised, likenesses of English kings. By the fifteenth century this courtly preoccupation was finding imitations in some of the principal churches of England, where it became fashionable to decorate the choir screens with statues representing parallel series of Old Testament kings (the ancestors of Christ) and recent English rulers (his successors on earth). At Salisbury, the existing thirteenth-century gallery of kings was extended shortly before 1399 to accommodate representations of Henry III's successors, while both Canterbury Cathedral and York Minster appear to have commissioned the still extant (though now altered) schemes of royal statues for their screens during the early decades of the fifteenth century. Indeed, it has been suggested that the York screen was intended specifically to commemorate the conquest of Normandy by Henry V, whose own later image there may well be a rather crude attempt at portraiture.[29] The increasing interest in such artistic representations of English kings was later to find secular expression in the sets of royal portraits that adorned the great houses of Tudor and Stuart aristocrats. Under Henry V and Henry VI, however, the symbolic merging of Old Testament and Plantagenet kingship in prominent ecclesiastical settings provided a particularly powerful statement of the divine nature of monarchy and, by extension, of the inextricable bond that now existed between the fortunes of the crown and the good of the people.

Perhaps the most loaded of all the visual images produced by the English monarchy during the Hundred Years War, however, was the heraldry resulting from Edward III's claim to the throne of France. From 1340 the Plantagenets quartered their arms to incorporate the French fleur de lis, which remained part of the royal device until George III finally dropped the pretensions of his ancestors in 1801–02.

---

[27] G.L. Harriss, 'Introduction', *Henry V. The Practice of Kingship*, ed. G.L. Harriss (Oxford, 1985), pp. 1–29.

[28] J. Catto, 'Religious Change under Henry V', *Henry V*, ed. Harriss, pp. 97–115.

[29] J.H. Harvey, 'Architectural History from 1291 to 1558', *A History of York Minster*, ed. G.E. Aylmer and R. Cant (Oxford, 1977), pp. 181–6; Harriss, 'Introduction', p. 28, n. 69. For the Canterbury and other screens see L. Stone, *Sculpture in Britain. The Middle Ages* (London, 1955), pp. 118, 174–6, 181, 204, and references.

The heraldic, dynastic and political union of the leopard and the lily was an attractive theme picked up more than once in fourteenth- and fifteenth-century literature. It found expression not only in the ubiquitous use of the royal arms on public buildings but also, more occasionally, in the depictions of English kings wearing the coronation robes of France, which appeared long before Henry VI made his great-great-grandfather's dream come true at Paris in 1431, and, perhaps most interestingly of all, in the multiple and imperial crowns associated with the regimes of Edward III, Henry V and Henry VI.[30]

In a sense, however, the dual monarchy represented in these visual images typifies the dichotomy which this chapter has attempted to identify in the English response towards the Hundred Years War. When Edward III assumed the title of king of France in 1340, he did so primarily to ensure an alliance with the county of Flanders; more grandiose notions of fulfilling a dynastic destiny were at most a secondary consideration. Nor, quite clearly, was the English political community impressed by this novel development, for parliament promptly extracted from the king a statutory guarantee that 'the realm of England and the people of the same, of whatever estate or condition they be, shall not in any time to come be put in subjection to us, nor our heirs or successors as kings of France'.[31] When Edward III's fortunes changed in the 1340s, there is every indication that at least a proportion of his subjects became convinced empire-builders: the political literature of the mid-fourteenth century is thick with allusions to the Arthurian conquest of Gaul, and there may have been some degree of disillusionment in England as a result of Edward's declared willingness to renounce his dynastic claim to France in 1360.[32] Yet when the prospect of a dual monarchy finally seemed set to become reality after the Treaty of Troyes of 1420, the English once more proved reluctant to accept the consequences: not only did parliament again insist on the strict separation of the two realms, it also argued that the king's French dominions should now bear the cost of the continental war and that England should be relieved of the long-standing burden of war taxation.

In this respect, the very considerable propaganda mounted by the minority government of Henry VI has to be taken as a sign of the weakness, rather than the strength, of his regime. After Henry's return from his French coronation, he entered the city of London in February 1432 to a carefully organised public display intended to glorify his achievement of the two greatest monarchies in western

---

[30] For coronation robes and crowns see, for example, D. Styles and C.T. Allmand, 'The Coronations of Henry VI', *History Today*, 32 (May 1982), pp. 28–33; E. Danbury, 'English and French Artistic Propaganda during the Period of the Hundred Years War. Some Evidence from Royal Charters', *Power, Culture and Religion in France c. 1350–c. 1550*, ed. C. Allmand (Woodbridge, 1989), pp. 75–97. For hints of imperial imagery see J.W. McKenna, 'How God Became an Englishman', *Tudor Rule and Revolution. Essays for G.R. Elton from his American Friends*, ed. D.J. Guth and J.W. McKenna (Cambridge, 1982), p. 35 and n. 33; Harriss, *Cardinal Beaufort*, pp. 324–5 and n. 51.
[31] *English Historical Documents 1327–1485*, ed. A.R. Myers (London, 1969), p. 70.
[32] See the references cited in W.M. Ormrod, 'The Personal Religion of Edward III', *Speculum*, 64 (1989), p. 849; W.M. Ormrod, 'The Double Monarchy of Edward III', *Medieval History*, 1 (1991), 76–7.

Europe. In Cheapside stood 'a royal castle of green jaspar, and therein two green trees standing upright, showing the right titles of the king of England and of France, conveying from St Edward and St Louis by kings unto the time of King Harry the Sixth, every king standing with his coat of armour, some leopards and some fleur de lis; and on the other side was made the [Tree of] Jesse of Our Lord ascending upward from David to Jesus'.[33] Unfortunately for Henry, such posturing meant little when set against the recent triumphs of Joan of Arc and the ceremony at Reims that had effectively turned Charles VII into the rightful king of France. To say that the ensuing war was doomed simply because the English political community lost interest in it would be too simplistic, but it is difficult to escape the fact that the reality of Henry VI's rule in France proved a good deal less acceptable than the fantasy in which his predecessors and their subjects had indulged. Thus, the claim to the throne of France turned full circle and became, as it had originally been in 1340, a rod with which to beat the king. In this sense at least, the Hundred Years War did indeed create an impossible challenge for the English crown.

---

[33] J.W. McKenna, 'Henry VI of England and the Dual Monarchy. Aspects of Royal Political Propaganda, 1422–1432', *Journal of the Warburg and Courtauld Institutes*, 28 (1965), pp. 160–1 (spelling modernised).

6

War and Fourteenth-Century France*

MICHAEL JONES

THE EFFECTS of the Hundred Years War on France in the fourteenth century can be discerned in almost every sphere besides the strictly military: political and institutional, economic and social, religious and intellectual. Attention can only be directed here to a few aspects of an enormous subject. It was one which already fascinated contemporary writers, for example, Froissart or Jean de Venette in their contrasting appreciations of the martial events which fill their chronicles. In more recent times the war has engaged the energies of several generations of outstanding historians and resulted in a formidable literature. Among recent additions one need only mention Jonathan Sumption's splendid narrative account, 250,000 words of text for the war's first decade, or there is Philippe Contamine's yet more massive study of the composition of French royal armies, which may be conservatively estimated at some half a million words.[1] Even when in the late twentieth century it is often the indirect consequences of warfare that come under scrutiny because of a primary concern with broader institutional, economic and social matters rather than with military affairs *tout court*, the *histoire événementielle* of the war continues to grow almost exponentially as investigation of previously untapped archival sources reveals, for instance, the movements of soldiers, the response of rulers and administrators to perceived danger and the impact of war on combatant and non-combatant alike. In particular, local or regional contexts have been illuminated by a series of major monographs.

Here a pattern set with exemplary clarity by Robert Boutruche's study of the Bordelais, first published in 1947, has been followed with further notable success for other provinces like the Ile-de-France, Normandy, Auvergne and Anjou,[2] or by

---

* This chapter is offered as a brief and partial synthesis, deliberately based on a limited number of modern, chiefly detailed French studies; its only claim to originality is in presenting some results of this work to a more general English readership and in providing a guide to other important recent literature.

[1] J. Sumption, *The Hundred Years War, i. Trial by Battle* (London, 1990); P. Contamine, *Guerre, état et société à la fin du moyen âge. Etudes sur les armées des rois de France, 1337–1494* (Paris, 1972).

[2] R. Boutruche, *La crise d'une société. Seigneurs et paysans du Bordelais pendant la Guerre de Cent Ans* (Strasbourg, 1947; revised edition, Paris, 1963); G. Fourquin, *Les campagnes de la région parisienne à la fin du moyen âge* (Paris, 1964); G. Bois, *La crise du féodalisme* (Paris, 1976) [*The Crisis of Feudalism. Economy and society in Eastern Normandy, c.1300–1550*, trans. Jean Birrell

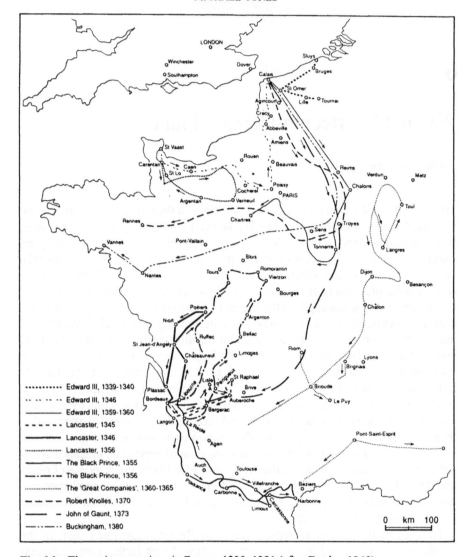

Fig. 6.1   The main campaigns in France, 1339–1381 (after Fowler, 1969).

(Cambridge, 1984)]; P. Charbonnier, *Une autre France. La seigneurie rurale en Basse Auvergne du XIVe au XVIe siècle*, 2 vols (Clermont-Ferrand, 1980); M. Le Mené, *Les campagnes angevines à la fin du moyen âge (vers 1350–vers 1530)* (Nantes, 1982). *L'Histoire médiévale en France, Bilan et perspectives*, ed. Michel Balard (Paris, 1991), is a valuable guide to work since c.1970 on all the themes touched upon in this paper but I have not yet seen his companion volume *Bibliographie de l'histoire médiévale en France (1965–1990)* (Paris, 1992).

taking a particular town as the main focus and putting local military events in a broader context. Among outstanding studies in which the effects of war on urban society are clearly seen are those of Toulouse, Tours, Périgueux, Poitiers, Reims and St-Flour, to mention but a selection.[3] The result is that both the diversity of experience and more general patterns within France at large during this 'temps d'épreuves' can be fully appreciated. Whilst there are clearly still problems in disengaging the exact contribution of warfare, as opposed to that of the two other major scourges of the period, disease and famine, in the overall pattern of demographic decline and social and economic dislocation that characterizes the fourteenth century, war's importance in that triad, sometimes questioned on the grounds that medieval armies were usually modest, devastation localized and hostilities intermittent, is assuredly undeniable. Here I simply want to evoke something of the atmosphere war created in this period, its particular characteristics and some responses to it. The wider political and institutional effects – the fragmentation of Capetian France with emerging principalities and appanages challenging the crown, and the creation of the administrative and taxation system that later served the monarchy during the Ancien Regime – must largely be neglected.[4]

We may start with some maps and then by quoting one of the most poignant contemporary descriptions of how warfare impinged on ordinary people as a commentary upon these. Fig. 6.1 shows the principal English campaigns in France fought between 1339–81, the brief apogée of the classic *chevauchée*. Many remarks could be made, including two obvious ones. First, the route taken by most English invasions of France, by entering or exiting via Calais and its Pale, inevitably meant that north-eastern France – Artois, Picardy, Champagne, the Ile-de-France – suffered directly on numerous occasions. We might expect to find evidence from these regions for some of the worst destructive and long-lasting effects of late medieval warfare. The other area of France which *prima facie* may have suffered to a comparable degree is in the south-west. Here during the lieutenancies of Henry of Lancaster and Edward, Prince of Wales, regions under French control facing Guyenne were the scene of much serious fighting, whilst the recovery of French military fortunes after 1369 was marked by swift inroads into the greater Aquitaine established by the treaty of Brétigny-Calais (1360). This ensured that Guyenne and neighbouring regions in the often neglected Midi, remained a major theatre of warfare in the late fourteenth century just as

---

[3] P. Wolff, *Commerce et marchands de Toulouse (vers 1350 – vers 1450)* (Paris, 1954); B. Chevalier, *Tours, ville royale (1356–1520)* (Paris & Louvain, 1975); A. Higounet-Nadal, *Périgueux aux XIVe et XVe siècles. Etude de démographie historique* (Bordeaux, 1978); R. Favreau, *La ville de Poitiers à la fin du moyen âge. Une capitale régionale*, 2 vols (Poitiers, 1978); P. Desportes, *Reims et les Rémois aux XIIIe et XIVe siècles* (Paris, 1979); A. Rigaudière, *Saint-Flour, ville d'Auvergne au Bas Moyen Age. Etude d'histoire administrative et financière*, 2 vols (Paris, 1982); J-P. Leguay, *Un réseau urbain au moyen âge: les villes du duché de Bretagne aux XIVe et XVe siècles* (Paris, 1981) also pays considerable attention to the impact of war.

[4] C. Allmand, *The Hundred Years War. England and France at War c.1300–c.1450* (Cambridge, 1988) is the best brief introduction; J. Henneman, *Royal Taxation in Fourteenth Century France*, 2 vols (Princeton & Philadelphia, 1971–6), exhaustively deals with this central theme.

Sumption's ambitious narrative underlines the scale of fighting in the south during the first decade of the war.[5]

Secondly, however, we should remember that regions which seem to have been spared full-scale invasion (apparent blanks on the map like Brittany and its Marches, especially those south of the Loire towards Poitou, parts of central France, Languedoc and the south-east) were by no means free from warfare. Some of this was generated by local causes but then prosecuted under the cover of the general Anglo-French war. The feuding of great lords, most obviously the long-term though intermittent rivalry of the houses of Foix and Armagnac and the often conflicting interests of other great Gascon noble families like the Albret, Comminges, Durfort and L'Isle Jourdain added to the mayhem.[6] Examples of shorter violent interludes, since in many parts of France the nobility still exercised the right to make private war, may be widely found. That in the county of Burgundy between the duke and the lords of Chalon-Arlay in the early years of the war is a good example, and that between the vicomte de Polignac and the sire de St-Ilpize in the Auvergne in the early 1360s is another; while the family of Mirepoix was deeply divided around 1360.[7] In the case of the duchy of Brittany there was for over twenty years from 1341 a civil war for possession of the ducal throne, a war of siege and counter-siege, attrition and guerilla actions, though one not entirely devoid of more significant encounters: Morlaix (1342), La Roche Derrien (1347), Mauron (1352) and Auray (1364), in the event a high ratio of battles to other forms of warfare for the period [fig. 6.2]. Even after the victory of Jean de Montfort and his English allies at Auray, the duchy was far from peaceful. It witnessed further extensive military activity between 1372–81 and again intermittently to the mid 1390s, whilst from 1342–97 an English garrison held Brest in a hostile fashion despite an Anglo-Breton alliance.[8]

Brittany was one of the first regions in which bands of free-booting adventurers, *routiers*, absent from France since the defeat of John Lackland by Philip Augustus early in the thirteenth century, began to proliferate again. Individual captains seized strongholds from which to exploit and terrorize the surrounding countryside by levying *rançons* and *patis*, demands for money and provisions, often raised on a

---

[5] H.J. Hewitt, *The Black Prince's Expedition 1355–57* (Manchester, 1958), K.A. Fowler, *The King's Lieutenant. Henry of Grosmont, First duke of Lancaster 1310–1361* (London, 1969) and A. Goodman, *John of Gaunt* (London, 1992) provide accessible accounts of most important fourteenth-century campaigns in the Midi.

[6] Malcolm Vale, *The Angevin Legacy and the Hundred Years War, 1250–1340* (Oxford: Blackwell, 1990) provides much detail on the Gascon nobility; R.W. Kaeuper, *War, Justice and Public Order. England and France in the Later Middle Ages* (Oxford, 1988), esp. pp. 225–60 for private war.

[7] Dom U. Plancher, *Histoire générale et particulière de Bourgogne*, 4 vols (Dijon, 1739–81), ii. *Preuves*, no. cclxi for letters of Philip VI announcing terms of peace between Duke Eudes IV and Jean de Chalon, sire d'Arlay, 13 June 1337, and cf. R. Cazelles, *La société politique et la crise de la royauté sous Philippe de Valois* (Paris, 1958), pp. 116 & 121n; Dom Cl. Devic and Dom J. Vaissete, *Histoire générale de Languedoc* [cited as *HL*], ed. A. Molinier et al., 16 vols (Toulouse, 1872–1904), x, *Preuves*, 1083–4, 1096–9, 1180–1 (Mirepoix), 1300–1 (Polignac).

[8] Michael Jones, *Ducal Brittany, 1364–1399* (Oxford, 1970); idem, *The Creation of Brittany* (London, 1988).

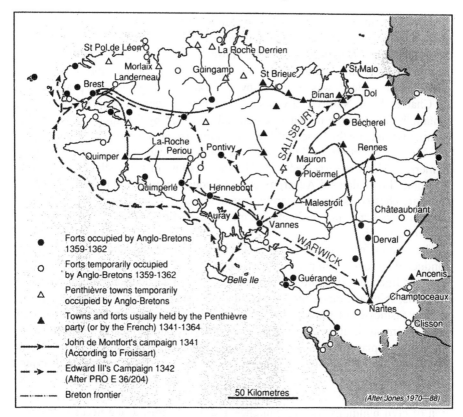

Fig. 6.2 The Breton civil war 1361–64 (after Galliou and Jones, 1991).

regular basis at set times of the year; such captains frequently paid only the loosest lip-service to their nominal sovereign, the king of England or France.[9] Such behaviour, even in a country which knew noble lawlessness, was deeply atavistic, a reversion to far-off days before the Capetians had established their dominance and ensured that, at least in northern France, the majority of the population normally lived in peace. By the 1350s other provinces like Poitou (plate IX), the Limousin and Normandy witnessed a similar development. Mounting their own unofficial *chevauchées* like the raid of Robert Knolles on Auxerre and the Auvergne or the ravaging of Normandy and the Ile-de-France by James Pipe in 1358–9, and culminating between 1360–8 in confusing movements as far afield as Alsace, Provence and Languedoc by the Great Companies, hardened professional soldiers and adventurers wreaked havoc on many other regions.

It was now that English, Gascon, Breton and other captains with yet more exotic

[9] S. Luce, *Histoire de Bertrand du Guesclin et son èpoque. La jeunesse de Bertrand, 1320–1364* (Paris, 1876) is a classic account; K.A. Fowler, 'Les finances et la discipline dans les armées anglaises en France au XIVe siècle', *Les Cahiers Vernonnais* 4 (1964), pp. 55–85, for a good modern discussion of 'ransoming'.

origins (German, Spanish, Italian, even Hungarian) established a stranglehold over many remote and inaccessible communities in central and southern France up to the Pyrenees and Alps: one such garrison used Lourdes as a base for several years, Tarbes likewise. Anse on the Rhône served as a repair for the band of Seguin de Badefol, whose death was attributed by Froissart to eating poisoned pears offered by Charles II of Navarre, anxious to terminate a contract with this notorious captain.[10] This was the period so colourfully recalled by the light of a November evening fireside by the Bascot of Mauléon, reminiscing to Froissart, 'At the sign of the Moon' at Orthez in 1388, and the one regretted by the famous *routier* Aymerigot Marchès (executed in 1391) after his loss of the castle of Aloise near St-Flour: 'Les villains d'Auvergne et de Limousin nous poureoient et amenoient en nostre chastel les bles et la farine, le pain tout cuit, l'avoine pour les chevaulx et la littiere, les bons vins, les buefs, les moutons, les brebis, tous gras et la poulaille et la vollaille'.[11]

The chronic fear and insecurity created by major invasions and localized warfare conducted by roving companies or permanent garrisons naturally prompted efforts by the indigenous population to protect itself. Town accounts are full of payments to scouts, spies and messengers sent to discover the proximity of enemy troops not only in fastnesses of the Massif Central but even in regions normally far distant from the main theatres of war like Provence. The authorities at Carpentras, for example, displayed an understandable paranoia over the whereabouts of the Companies and the no-less undisciplined Spanish troops who gathered around Henry of Trastamara during his exile in the Midi and menaced public order wherever they went.[12] The fortification of towns and castles and the hasty adaptation of civil buildings such as churches and monasteries to the needs of defence was another obvious response.

Figs 6.3 and 6.4 provide some indication of the intensity of efforts in this regard. In 1367, with the Companies still at large, Charles V instructed the *baillis* of Champagne, Burgundy, Auvergne, Bourbonnais and Nivernais to visit all the fortresses in their jurisdiction in the company of two knights in order to take appropriate measures for their defence or to destroy them if the former could not be easily effected. A return survives from the *bailli* of Melun which provides details on the density of fortified places bordering the forest of Fontainebleau, south-east of Paris. Within an area some 30 km by 40 km there were six major

---

[10] Jean Froissart, *Chroniques*, ed. S. Luce et al., 15 vols (Paris, 1869 – continuing), vi. pp. xxxv n. 3, 74–6, 269–71 and *HL*, x, 1340–7 (Badefol); P. Tucoo-Chala, *Gaston Fébus et la vicomté de Béarn, 1343–1391* (Bordeaux, 1960), pp. 106, 305–6, 312 (Lourdes); M. Hébert, 'L'armée provençale en 1374', *Annales du Midi* 91 (1979), pp. 5–27 at p. 19 for Hungarians.

[11] Jean Froissart, *Voyage en Béarn*, ed. A.H. Diverres (Manchester, 1953), pp. 87ff. (Mauléon); R. Delachenal, *Histoire de Charles V*, 5 vols (Paris, 1909–31), ii. 29 n. 2 (Marchès) citing Jean Froissart, *Oeuvres*, ed. Kervyn de Lettenhove, 28 vols (Brussels, 1867–77), xiv. 164.

[12] R. André-Michel, ' "Anglais", Bretons et routiers à Carpentras sous Jean le Bon et Charles V', *Mélanges d'histoire offerts à M. Charles Bémont par ses amis et ses élèves* (Paris, 1913), pp. 341–52; *HL*, x. 1224, 1233–4 (Trastamara); K.A. Fowler, 'News from the Front: letters and despatches of the fourteenth century', *Guerre et société en France, en Angleterre et en Bourgogne xive–xve siècle*, ed. P. Contamine, C. Giry-Deloison & M. Keen (Lille, 1991), pp. 63–92.

Fig. 6.3 Fortifications in the area south of Fontainebleau Forest in 1367 (after Contamine, 1972).

castles, four fortified manors, five towers, 12 forts and 28 fortified churches; a ratio of one strongpoint for each 20 or 25 km^2, though two forts and two churches were subsequently deemed untenable and were demolished.[13] Some of these defences naturally date from earlier periods, but many had been created as a direct response to the hostilities of recent decades.

Fig. 6.4 shows a similar dense configuration of fortified places on one of the most sensitive 'frontiers of war' in the fourteenth century: Saintonge.[14] Here the 'Hundred Years War' can be said to have begun in 1294, if not in 1259 when the treaty of Paris delivered the province into English hands, since its possession was hotly disputed both during Edward I's war with Philip IV and during the War of St-Sardos (1323–5). After Charles of Valois's invasion, the English regained Saintes in 1331 and the region saw some of the first military operations after the official outbreak of war in 1337. From that point onwards Saintonge normally remained divided into rival zones of allegiance. Even before the arrival of Lancaster in 1345, the province had witnessed many minor skirmishes with the capture or recovery of towns and castles from enemy hands: the daily coinage of warfare in France throughout this period. It was in Saintonge in the early 1350s that the leader of the Great Companies at the battle of Brignais (1362), the formidable Arnaud de Cervole, archpriest of Vélines in the diocese of Périgueux, who had recently forfeited his clerical status because of earlier acts of brigandage, gained his spurs and was rewarded by John II with a formal grant of the castellany of Châteauneuf-sur-Charente for services against the Anglo-Gascons. The iron hold which he exercised over his own men is demonstrated by his execution of 31 of them for 'homicides, rapines et viols' committed whilst they were holding Cognac in 1354–5.[15]

Later, by the treaty of Brétigny-Calais, Saintonge was officially handed over entirely to Edward III, much to the chagrin of many of its inhabitants. French campaigns to repossess it recommenced promptly in 1369, and 1372 saw them making major gains north of the Charente with the return to their allegiance of La Rochelle (plate X), Rochefort, Surgères and other strongholds. Cognac was re-gained in 1375 shortly before the truce of Bruges was agreed. When hostilities broke out again in 1377 the Charente continued to demarcate the frontier with English garrisons holding Taillebourg ('le plus bel chastel de Poictou . . . la clef de Poictou'), Bourg-Charente, La Faon and Verteuil. Though Bouteville fell briefly to the French in 1379, it soon returned to English hands and it required several campaigns by Louis, duke of Bourbon, and Louis de Sancerre, marshal of France, from 1384 to recover Taillebourg, St-Séverin and Verteuil, to demolish the castle at Jarnac and defences at Bourg-Charente considered too difficult to defend, and to

---

[13] Contamine, *Guerre*, p. 10.

[14] Vale, *Angevin Legacy* and R. Favreau, *La commanderie du Breuil-du-Pas et la guerre de Cent Ans dans la Saintonge méridionale* (Jonzac, 1986) for all that follows on Saintonge.

[15] Favreau, p. 41, Contamine, *Guerre*, p. 173, H. Denifle, *La désolation des églises, monastères et hôpitaux en France pendant la Guerre de Cent Ans*, 2 vols (Paris, 1897–9), i. 188–211 and A. Cherest, *L'Archiprêtre: episodes de la Guerre de Cent Ans au XIVe siècle* (Paris, 1879) for Cervole.

Plate I The battlefield of Crécy, looking south-eastwards from the observation tower thought to be on the site of the windmill from which Edward III viewed the field.

Plate II The battlefield of Crécy, looking north-eastwards from Edward's supposed viewing point towards the village of Wadicourt.

Plate III Bois de Crécy-Grange, near to which was placed the English baggage park behind the English lines.

Plate IV The battlefield of Poitiers.

Plate V Sir John Cressy's retinue in the muster roll of 26 March 1441 (PRO, E101/53/33. Crown copyright).

Plate VI The castle of Beynac (Dordogne) on its promontory.

Plate VII The keep of the castle of Beynac (Dordogne).

Plate VIII The town defences of Libourne (Gironde).

Plate IX The castle of Moncontour (Vienne), finally retaken by the French in 1372

Plate X The port defences of La Rochelle, after 1372.

Plate XI The fortified church of Esnandes (Charente-Maritime).

Plate XII The town defences of Avignon, c.1355–70.

Plate XIII Portsmouth: seaward defences constructed in the sixteenth and seventeenth centuries.

Plate XIV Southampton: Back of the Walls excavations showing remains of late thirteenth-century dovecote and fourteenth-century half-round tower.

Plate XV Southampton: the arcaded machicolation on the western defences of the town.

Plate XVI
Winchester: the West Gate.

Plate XVII Carisbrooke: the main gatehouse.

Plate XVIII The inner gatehouse of Cooling castle.

Plate XIX The outer gatehouse of Cooling castle.

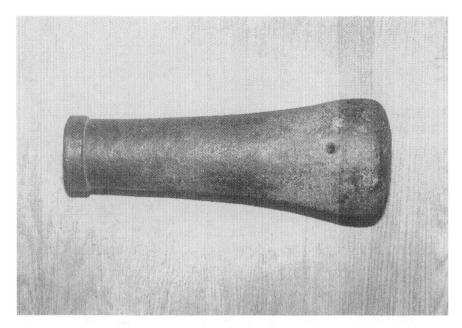

Plate XX Fourteenth-century gun, National Museum, Stockholm.

te XXI Fourteenth-century bronze gun, National Museum, Stockholm.

Plate XXII   Bronze gun, Turin.

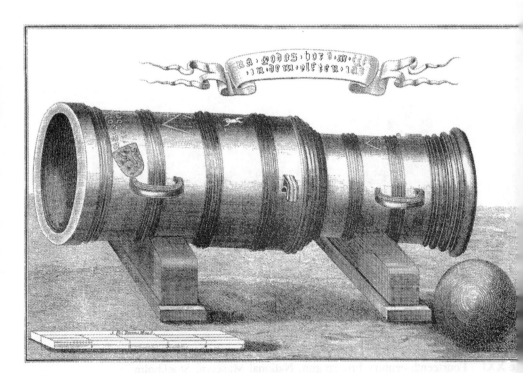

Plate XXIII   Eighteenth-century drawing of late medieval bronze gun preserved at Brunswick.

Plate XXIV Fifteenth-century English longbowmen from the *Warwick Pageant* (British Library, MS Cotton Julius EIV, f.20b).

Plate XXV More longbowmen from the *Warwick Pageant* with cavalry and banners (British Library, MS Cotton Julius EIV, f4).

Plate XXVI A battle piece of Scots against English, from the Chronicles of Froissart (Bibliothèque Nationale, Paris).

Plate XXVII A late medieval military waggon train (Bibliothèque Royale, Brussels, MS 9242, f.184).

Plate XXVIII Simon Stanley shooting the tests for the Mary Rose 'approximation' bow of 140 lb draw-weight, using a heavy war arrow with a long steel bodkin head.

Plate XXIX Simon Stanley shooting a Mary Rose 'approximation' bow at point blank.

Plate XXX Dodford (Northants). Sir John Cressy (d.1445).

Plate XXXI Meriden (Warwickshire). John Wyard (c.1405).

Plate XXXII North Cadbury (Somerset). Probably William Lord Botreaux and Lady Botreaux (d.1433). Detail of tomb-chest showing the couple kneeling beside the Virgin and Child.

Plate XXXIII North Leigh (Oxon). William Wilcotes (d.1411).
Detail showing the name 'Jesus of Nazareth' above the forehead.

Plate XXXIV Lowick (Northants). Ralph Greene (effigy made 1412–20). Detail showing the name 'Jesus of Nazareth' above the forehead.

Plate XXXV Willoughby-on-the-Wolds (Notts). Sir Hugh Willoughby (d.1448). Detail of tomb-chest showing the Holy Trinity.

Plate XXXVI Willoughby-on-the-Wolds (Notts). Sir Hugh Willoughby (d.1448). Detail of tomb-chest showing the Virgin and Child.

Plate XXXVII
Wingfield (Suffolk).
Sir John Wingfield
(d.1361).

Plate XXXVIII
Ingham (Norfolk). Sir
Roger and Lady de
Bois (later fourteenth
century). Detail of
tomb-chest showing
two angels presenting
souls of the deceased
to Christ or the Holy
Trinity.

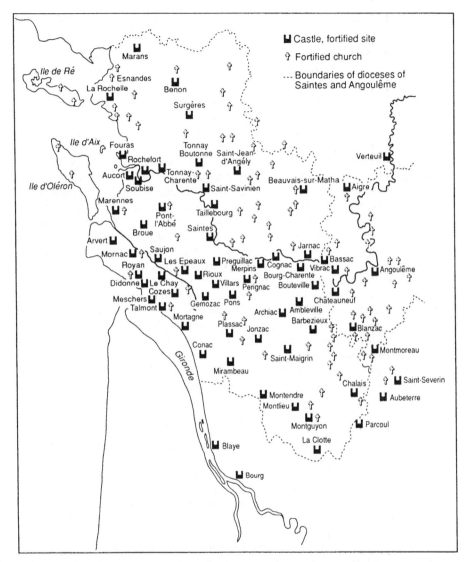

Fig. 6.4 Fortifications in Saintonge during the Hundred Years War (after Favreau, 1986).

relieve Rioux, though the otherwise isolated garrison at Bouteville still remained unconquered when the regime of general truces inaugurated in 1388 came into force and only fell finally to the French in 1392. Is it any wonder then that this map of Saintonge during the Hundred Years War shows more than 70 castles and fortified towns and almost 90 fortified churches, some like that of Esnandes in the *plat pays* north of La Rochelle not simply adapted from earlier work but designed *ab initio* for the physical defence it could offer as much as for any spiritual consolation it might provide (plate XI). Or that Favreau comments bleakly and with only mild hyperbole that in Saintonge by the 1380s 'tout est reduit au désert'.[16]

The fear and suffering created by all this military activity is perhaps best caught in a letter to posterity written on the inside cover of a manuscript belonging to his house by the prior of Brailet (Yonne) in 1359. This was a year after the Jacquerie compounded the effects of foreign invasion by stirring up class hatred and civil war which had allowed Anglo-Navarrese and other lawless soldiery to ravage the Ile-de-France at will. First published in 1857,[17] it still retains its power to shock:

In A.D. 1358 the English came to Chantecoq and took the castle on the eve of All Saints [31 Oct.]. At the same time they burned almost all the town and afterwards reduced the whole countryside to their control, ordering the towns, both great and small, to ransom all their possessions, viz., bodies, goods, and movables, or else they would burn the houses. This they did in many places. Confounded and completely terrorized in this fashion, very many of the people submitted to the English, paying them money by way of ransom and agreeing to provide them with cash, flour, oats, and many other necessary supplies [remember Aymerigot Marchès and the *rançons*!], if they would stop for a while the aforementioned persecution, because they had already killed many men in different places. Some they shut up in very dark dungeons, threatening them daily with death, and continually punishing them with whippings, wounds, hunger and want beyond belief. But others had nothing with which to pay ransom or they were unwilling to submit to the power of the English. To escape from their hands these made themselves huts in the woods and there ate their bread with fear, sorrow, and great anguish. But the English learned of this and they resolutely sought out these hiding places, searching numerous woods and putting many men to death there. Some they killed, others they captured, still others escaped. Among the latter I, Hugh de Montgeron, prior of Brailet in the parish of Domats in the deanery of Courtenay, diocese of Sens, contrived a hiding place in the Bois des Queues beyond the swamp of the lord of Villebon and there remained with many of my neighbours seeing and hearing every day about the vicious and wicked deeds of our enemies, namely, houses burned and many dead left lying in brutal fashion through the villages and hamlets. Seeing and hearing such things, I decided on the Sunday after St Luke's day [20 Oct.] to go to the city and remain there. But it happened that very night that these wicked English found their way to my hut so quietly that, in spite of the watchfulness of our sentinels, they almost captured me while I was asleep. But by God's grace and through the help of the Blessed Virgin Mary I was awakened by the noise they made and escaped naked, taking nothing with me because of my haste except a habit with a hood. Crossing into the middle of the swamp I stayed there shivering and shaking with the cold, which was very great at the time, while my hut was completely despoiled. Afterwards I went to Sens to the house of John Paysans, a priest and one of my relations, who received me kindly, showing me such charity from the goods that God had bestowed upon

---

[16] Favreau, p. 50.

[17] *Bibliothèque de l'école des chartes* xviii (1857), pp. 357–60, published here with minor amendments after *The Chronicle of Jean de Venette*, ed. and trans. R.A. Newhall and J.A. Birdsall (New York, 1953), pp. 253–4.

him that it is impossible for me adequately to describe it. And still [the English] never stopped coming to our aforementioned priory, sending me letters threatening destruction and intimating that they would set it on fire unless I came to them under safe conduct which they would send me. On this account I went and obtained from them a respite from the feast of St Peter's throne [22 Feb. 1359] until the feast of St John the Baptist [24 June 1359]. But little good this did because the man who was captain at the time was taken prisoner by the French and so all my trouble went for nothing. So I lived in the midst of troubles from the feast of All Saints until the feast of the Baptist. Again they took me prisoner but, not recognizing me, they left their booty behind because there was so little of it, for which God be praised. During this time they stripped the house of all movable goods, drank up four *queues* of wine, they carried off a *modius* of oats according to the measure in use at Courtenay, they took all my clothes, and at Easter [21 April 1359] and again on the Sunday after the feast of St Peter and St Paul [30 June 1359] they ate up the pigeons. And so by God's grace, I have escaped in the name of the Lord out of their hands up until now. But unless I wish to lose thirty arpents of the best grain, it is necessary to make again a settlement with these fellows lest worse happen and the last state of affairs be worse than the first.

I am writing this out behind our barn on Wednesday, the festival of St Martin 1359 [4 July 1359, though it was in fact a Thursday], because I do not dare write elsewhere. Do you who live in cities and castles ever see trouble equal to my trouble? Farewell.

Hugh

We need not dwell at length on the lot of the prior of Brailet and his kind: evidence of damage to ecclesiastical properties as a result of war in fourteenth-century France is overwhelming. Père Denifle's famous compendium, published between 1897–9 first traced the extent of the devastation; recent work simply refines and augments his findings.[18] Such information provides a valuable index to the regions where destruction was at its most severe as in the dioceses of Amiens, Tournai and St-Omer in the north-east, Cahors, Tulle, Rodez and Castres in the Midi, which Michèle Bordeaux estimated to have suffered even more than the group of central-western dioceses (Tours, Poitiers, Angers, Saintes, Limoges) and north-eastern ones (Reims, Laon, Cambrai, Noyon, Sens, Chalons, Troyes) from which evidence has already been cited for the devastation of war.[19] Whilst it is especially by exploiting accounts and other financial records of ecclesiastical corporations (which have survived more frequently than those from lay estates, though where these do they tell much the same story) that Boutruche and his successors have charted in such bold detail the fluctuating economic fortunes of landlords in the late fourteenth century.

This evidence has established for the countryside a pattern of decline in income and productivity, sometimes catastrophic in its incidence, more often cumulative, alternating with phases of reconstruction marking the periods when warfare ceased

---

[18] Denifle, *La désolation, passim*; cf. Favreau, *La commanderie*.

[19] Michèle Bordeaux, *Aspects économiques de la vie de l'église aux XIVe et XVe siècles* (Paris, 1969).

(truces were officially in force for two years out of three during the fourteenth-century phase of the war).[20] Thus, in northern France between c.1365 and c.1410, despite all that has been said so far about the impact of war, there was one such period of general remission. Fourquin heads a chapter in his *Campagnes de la région parisienne* 'tentative agrarian restoration, c.1365–1410'; Bois likewise speaks of 'the first reconstruction, c.1364–1410' in his account of neighbouring rural Eastern Normandy. Le Mené, dealing with Anjou, a region less directly afflicted by war than those two provinces (though not entirely immune from it as fig. 6.5 shows),[21] similarly discerns economic recovery, though its effects are deemed to be more patchy. Here there was no single great wave of destruction and desertion followed by a general movement of recolonization, but rather piecemeal efforts leading by the end of the century to 'l'impression . . . d'un pays en pleine convalescence'.[22] Rental values in the Angevin countryside, for example, had perhaps fallen by 30–40% from the mid-century. Orchards and vineyards (as in Saintonge or the Bordelais) particularly suffered physical destruction and took a long time to re-establish, but arable land had rarely been entirely abandoned. Of that which had been between 1363–75, the period when Anjou was most obviously affected by warfare, all but 10% was back in cultivation by 1400. As Bois demonstrated for Normandy, in Anjou too it seems it was easier to re-establish peasant holdings in late fourteenth-century conditions rather than larger seigneurial estates. These latter required considerable capital investment in mills, barns and other installations, so often the object of deliberate destruction, as well as administrative expertise and determination to restore them to their full revenue-earning potential.[23] With nuances, to take into account differing phases in the cycle of warfare and natural disaster which afflicted all of France during the period, the picture in the Angevin and Norman countryside seems to be repeated throughout much of the kingdom.

How did experience of war in towns compare? Perhaps even more than in the countryside the impact of war on towns is difficult to measure because of differences in size, variety of municipal institutions and forms of administration, economic and commercial interests, social complexion and many other factors distinguishing one urban community from another. Great cities already well-provided with sound defences when the war began like Bordeaux, even though in an exposed strategic position, were clearly less at risk than small *bourgades*. Unless there was some unfortunate accident such as treason or revolt, they were less likely to be besieged or suffer damage during a *chevauchée*, though

---

[20] K.A. Fowler, 'Truces', *The Hundred Years War*, ed. K.A. Fowler (London, 1971), p. 184; R. Boutruche, 'The devastation of rural areas during the Hundred Years War and the agricultural recovery of France', *The Recovery of France in the Fifteenth Century*, ed. P.S. Lewis (London, 1972), pp. 23–59, an article originally published in 1947, first sketched the broad outlines of the story.
[21] *Atlas historique français (Monumenta Historiae Galliarum): Anjou*, ed. Robert Favreau (Paris, 1973), Pl. VIII no. 4.
[22] Le Mené, p. 221.
[23] Le Mené, pp. 211ff.

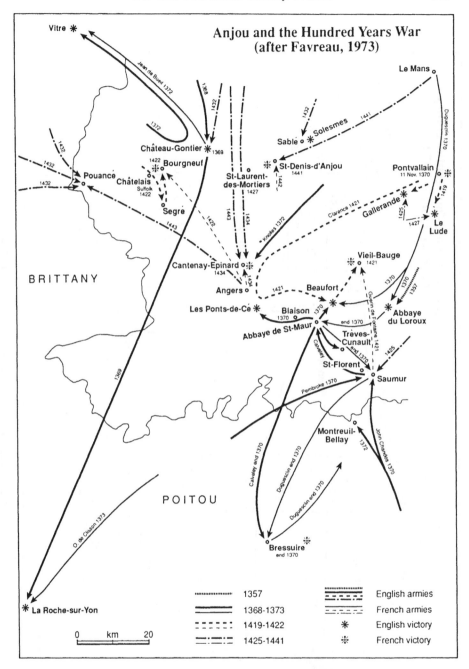

Fig. 6.5 Anjou and the Hundred Years War (after Favreau, 1973).

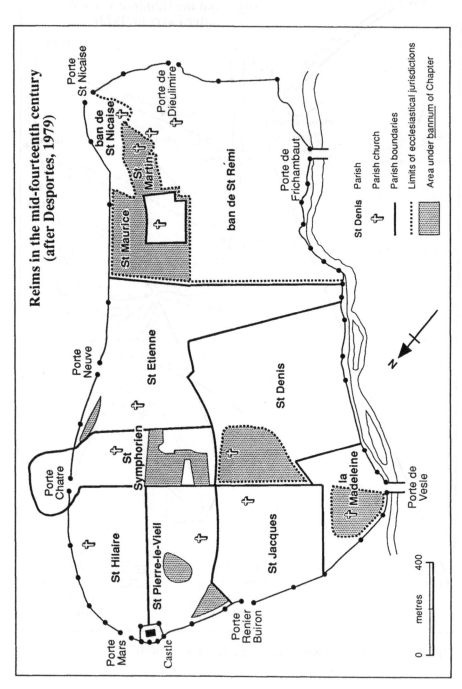

Fig. 6.6 Reims in the mid-fourteenth century (after Desportes, 1979).

Reims in the mid-fourteenth century
(after Desportes, 1979)

Porte St Nicaise

ban de
St Nicaise

Porte de
Dieulimire

St
Martin

Porte de
Frichambaut

St Maurice

ban de St Rémi

St Denis   Parish

✝ Parish church

——— Parish boundaries

········· Limits of ecclesiastical jurisdictions

▨ Area under bannum of Chapter

Porte
Neuve

St Etienne

St
Symphorien

Porte
Chatre

St Denis

la
Madeleine

Porte de
Vesle

St Hilaire

St Pierre-le-Vieil

St Jacques

Porte
Renier
Buiron

Porte
Mars

Castle

N

0   metres   400

unprotected suburbs were at risk like those of Narbonne and Carcassonne destroyed during the Black Prince's great raid of 1355. A full-scale siege of even a modest walled town was not undertaken lightly and required considerable logistical expertise: it would be an interesting exercise to establish the proportion of successful sieges during this phase of the war before combustible artillery helped to speed the process. But even the Companies, lacking the specialist technical services that regular authorities soon developed in response to the war, could inflict much damage directly on urban property besides laying waste the *plat pays*.

Failing to take Amiens in 1358, for example, Navarrese troops set fire to the suburbs and, according to Froissart, more than 3000 houses were burnt in a conflagration the signs of which could still be seen fifty years later.[24] But systematic destruction of whole towns or even of *quartiers* was relatively rare as was massacring or expulsion of entire populations; even though it conformed with contemporary laws of war, the sacking of Limoges in 1370 by the Black Prince is exceptional.[25] In this respect at least the Anglo-French war in the fourteenth century appears less vicious in retrospect than the Albigensian Crusades when wholesale slaughter of civilian populations occurred. Nor, with the exception of the hapless inhabitants of Calais who found themselves in no-man's land between the English and French armies after their expulsion by Edward III, are there any fourteenth-century incidents comparable to Louis XI's attempt to expunge Arras from the map in 1479 by ejecting its citizens, razing the town and renaming the site, Franchise.[26] Nevertheless, some towns because they lay in the path of a *chevauchée* (like Caen in 1346) or because of their strategic or symbolic national or regional importance (Paris, Reims, Nantes and Rennes) naturally attracted the attention of enemy armies and were attacked or besieged on several occasions. A rich documentation allows us to take Reims (with a population in 1300 of about 20,000) as an extreme case of the way war affected urban life in this period.[27]

Like many French towns at the beginning of the war, its defences were in an unprepared state [fig. 6.6]: a new enceinte begun under Philip Augustus and pushed forward under Philip the Fair remained incomplete, often nothing more than earth banks and wooden palisading. As rumours of war began to spread in 1336 the échevins advised Philip VI of the need to inspect the defences which the *bailli* of Vermandois was ordered to repair in July 1337. But the town was still chiefly in the jurisdiction of the archbishop and division between ecclesiastical and lay authorities delayed action for several years though able-bodied men between the ages of 15 and 60 were formed into 'dizaines' (four of which formed a

[24] Delachenal, ii. 17–21.
[25] Cf. M.H. Keen, *The Laws of War* (London & Toronto, 1965), passim. R. Barber, *Edward, Prince of Wales and Aquitaine* (London, 1978), pp. 225–6, critically surveys the evidence and concludes that Froissart exaggerates the casualties.
[26] H. Sée, *Louis XI et les villes* (Paris, 1891), pp. 134–7; H. Stein, 'Les habitants d'Evreux et le repeuplement d'Arras en 1479', *Bibliothèque de l'école des chartes* lxxxiv (1923), pp. 284–97; idem, 'La participation du pays de Languedoc au repeuplement d'Arras sous Louis XI', *ibid.*, xcii (1931), pp. 62–9.
[27] Desportes, *Reims*, esp. pp. 526ff. for the following account.

'connétablie' about 100 strong) as an urban militia, the town walls and gates were temporarily reinforced, a system of watches was organized, especially at night, export of foodstuffs was prohibited, strangers in particular were carefully checked and the town was dispensed from sending recruits to the general *arrière-ban* so that it could better defend itself. Edward III's campaign in the Cambrésis (1340) added urgency to the citizens' efforts to complete their defences but it was the battle of Crécy that finally roused them to a frenzy of activity, with the clergy reluctantly accepting the necessity of contributing to the expenses of the fortifications.

As in many French towns which had not developed their own administrations during the thirteenth-century communal movement, Reims was a city where 'the ramparts gave birth to municipal institutions'.[28] Neighbouring Troyes and Chalons and more distant Tours, Angers, Nantes, Blois and Orléans were other important centres which evolved in the same way during the first decades of the war which saw the raising and completion of many major enceintes.[29] That of Avignon not only survives largely intact today but its construction between 1355–70 is well documented (plate XII).[30] At Reims, under Gaucher de Lor, appointed captain by Philip VI, a small committee was formed to supervise raising the necessary taxes and their expenditure. As Desportes comments, 'On peut voir en ce corps la première institution commune de la ville', since it united for the first time representatives of the archbishop, the chapter and the abbey of St-Rémi as well as citizens.[31] More generally, a familiar pattern can be discerned; as Favreau has written, 'Un peu partout la guerre impose la défense, la défense exige le budget, la gestion du budget entraîne le développement des libertés muncipales.'[32]

Although the Black Death interrupted work on the defences at Reims, building continued at a more leisurely pace in the early 1350s before the battle of Poitiers had a galvanising effect similar to that of Crécy. Traditional artillery weapons were bought from Paris, St-Quentin and Rouen, an expert *artilleur* was hired from Verdun, metal and wooden grills were placed in the bed of the river Vesle to prevent horses crossing and agreements for mutual military aid were made with Chalons and the county of Rethel.[33] Despite further disputes between the townspeople and their archbishop over whether his castle of Porte-Mars should be

---

[28] Cf. P. Contamine, 'Les fortifications urbaines en France à la fin du moyen âge: aspects financiers et économiques', *Revue historique*, cclx (1978), pp. 23–47 [reprinted in his collected essays *La France au XIVe et XVe siècles. Hommes, mentalités, guerre et paix* (London, 1981), no. V] at pp. 30–3.

[29] Cf. B. Chevalier, 'Pouvoir royal et pouvoir urbain à Tours pendant la guerre de Cent Ans', *Annales de Bretagne* 81 (1974), pp. 365–92.

[30] R. Michel, 'La construction des remparts d'Avignon au XIVe siècle', *Congrès archéologique de France, lxxvi session, Avignon 1909* (Paris, 1910), pp. 341–60; A-M. Hayez, 'Travaux à l'enceinte d'Avignon sous les pontificats d'Urbain V et Grégoire XI', *Actes du 101e Congrès national des Sociétés savantes* (Paris, 1978), pp. 193–223.

[31] Desportes, p. 542.

[32] Favreau, *Poitiers*, i. 188.

[33] Desportes, p. 556 after P. Varin, *Archives administratives de la ville de Reims*, 10 vols (Paris, 1839–53), iii. 120–6.

incorporated into the enceinte (as it finally was in 1364), the summer of 1358 saw the effective enclosure of the town. But it was at a considerable material and human, as well as financial, cost (in the event an investment calculated at no less than 100,000 livres): houses, churches, hospitals and monasteries lying outside the enceinte were ruthlessly demolished and in the surrounding countryside woods were felled, villages cleared and *maisons-fortes* destroyed, their inhabitants being offered shelter within the city in an effort to create a *cordon sanitaire* around the city. It was not a moment too soon: on 4 December 1359 Edward III finally arrived before the newly-constructed defences to besiege the city. Nor was this the only occasion the defences of Reims were put to the test since the city later lay in the path of the successive *chevauchées* of Knolles (1370), Gaunt (1373) and Thomas of Woodstock (1380).[34]

The impact of war on Reims and its citizens was thus dramatic: alarms and excursions since 1337, institutional developments, especially in response to urban defence, the declining control of the archbishop, major alterations to the physical environment in and immediately around the town, social change too as the city provided a haven for refugees (in some years up to 50% of the population in some parishes were newcomers) whilst the role of the formerly dominant patriciate waned in worsening economic conditions. The Black Death, of course, contributed its share to the misery of these years: a quarter or third of the population was lost and it had similar consequences to those observed elsewhere – legal proceedings disrupted, rising wage rates, difficulties in filling tenancies, and so on. But because of a deteriorating military position, conditions became even worse in the Rémois between 1356–64. For part of this period the city was virtually cut off by routier bands and foreign invasion from its close trading partners, Laon, Soissons, Paris, Troyes, let alone its more distant markets. Scarcity drove up the price of basic cereals which doubled or tripled in cost; whilst the Anglo-French peace agreed in 1360 simply added to the inhabitants' tax burden. Reims owed 20,000 écus towards the first tranche of John II's ransom (600,000 écus) and was forced to raise loans to meet its obligations, including the maintenance of hostages in England, from Italians in Paris. These were still outstanding in 1365.

The extent to which Reims could take advantage of the rural economic recovery noted elsewhere from the 1360s was limited. Factors other than warfare need to be considered in explaining this. The town's textile industry, on which its economic fortune had been built, was by now in sad decline, in part because of the contraction of wider European markets and reduced demand but also because its products were no longer fashionable as replacement by products from the Low Countries, Germany and England in former Rémois markets shows. Yet we can see that the fiscal pressures generated by war (one of the factors to which Bois gives most attention in assessing changing social relations in rural Normandy in this period) also imposed an enormous burden on an impoverished urban population. Tax

---

[34] Modern accounts have only marginally modified the classic narratives of these expeditions by Delachenal, iv. 301–42 (Knolles), 480–503 (Gaunt); v. 364–85 (Buckingham).

demands absorbed an increasing proportion of reduced urban wealth: the need to respond to royal requests for money, costs of maintaining the defences and equipping troops, problems caused by a continual flow of rural refugees into the city because of rural insecurity, all drained local resources. Despite its prestige as the city where the king was crowned, coronations were a mixed blessing since they cost the city dear (at least 7712 1. 18s 5d in 1364). Other fortuitous circumstances could similarly wreck careful budgeting. In 1382, for instance, the brother of Guy, marshal of Burgundy, Jean de Pontailler, *en route* for Flanders, was taken prisoner by some Rémois, and the city had to spend 35,000 francs it could ill-afford in legal costs and reparations to regain the good will of the duke of Burgundy.[35] To put this comparatively huge sum into perspective it may be noted that between 1364–80 about 60,000 francs had been raised from the citizens by means of *fouages* but often only after much protest. It was thus not until the late 1380s that Reims really began to show signs of a genuine revival of fortunes. In the event it was both a short and very partial period of remission: the second decade of the fifteenth century brought renewed crisis.

I had hoped to discuss some technical and specialised developments in warfare itself – the spread of gunpowder artillery and amphibious warfare along some of France's great river systems – as further illustrations of the changing impact of war in the fourteenth century.[36] But space precludes that and I must conclude. A succession of leading scholars, including last century Siméon Luce and Père Denifle, and in the early part of our own, Roland Delachenal, have all quoted the remarks of Petrarch returning to France after the treaty of Brétigny as testimony to the destructive effects of war in this period: 'I had difficulty in convincing myself that this was the country I had seen in former times . . . I scarcely recognized anything that I had once seen in this kingdom once so rich and now reduced to ashes, beyond city walls and fortresses there remained, it may be said, not a house which was left standing'.[37] Hyperbole, of course, nevertheless these are images which we do well to remind ourselves constituted the daily reality of war for many ordinary people in fourteenth-century France: images, moreover, that have been enhanced rather than diminished by the steady accumulation of detail culled from non-literary sources on which most serious scholars since the mid-nineteenth century have increasingly chosen to base their research on the effects of war on fourteenth-century France.

---

[35] Desportes, pp. 589–90.
[36] For example, A. Merlin-Chazelas, *Documents relatifs au Clos des Galées de Rouen et aux armées de mer du roi de France de 1293 à 1418*, 2 vols (Paris, 1977–8) provides much material on ship and troop movements on the Seine from the late 1350s; for the amphibious siege of Rolleboise in 1363–4 see also Luce, *Du Guesclin*, pp. 417ff. and Delachenal, ii. 356–9.
[37] Cf. Delachenal, ii. 21.

7

The Fourteenth-Century French Raids on Hampshire and the Isle of Wight

MICHAEL HUGHES

> They set out with their fleet, which carried at least a thousand fighting-men of various kinds, and sailed for England, coming into Southampton harbour one Sunday morning when the people were at mass. The Normans and Genoese entered the town and pillaged and looted it completely. They killed many people and raped a number of women and girls, which was a deplorable thing. They loaded their ships and vessels with the great plunder they found in the town, which was rich and well-stocked, and then went back on board. When the tide was high again, they raised anchor and sailed with a good wind towards Normandy, putting in at Dieppe, where they shared out their booty.[1]

FROISSART's colourful description of the attack on Southampton in 1338 is a reminder of the French raids on the English coast in the fourteenth century. Although the raids have been the subject of a number of Hundred Years War studies, albeit brief ones, only Colin Platt's excellent book on medieval Southampton describes, in detail, the effects of the fourteenth-century French raids on any English town. But even he had not benefited at the time of his research from the excellent work on the cartularies of the two religious houses St Denys' Priory and God's House Hospital, that owned properties in medieval Southampton, the publication of the Southampton Terrier of 1454, and the results of the more recent archaeological excavations that have taken place between the late 70s and 1990.[2] However, there has never been a comprehensive survey or commentary on the French raids on other parts of Hampshire and the Isle of Wight and their subsequent effects on the local population. Consequently, the contents of this chapter attempt to provide a more comprehensive study drawing on earlier published works

---

[1] Froissart, *Chronicles*, ed. and trans. G. Brereton (Harmondsworth, 1968), pp. 60–1.

[2] C. Platt, *Medieval Southampton: the Port and Trading Community, A.D. 1000–1600* (London, 1973); *The Cartulary of the Priory of St Denys near Southampton*, ed. E.O. Blake (Southampton, 1981), vol. 1; *The Cartulary of God's House, Southampton*, ed. J.M. Kaye (Southampton, 1976), vol. 1; *The Southampton Terrier of 1454*, ed. L.A. Burgess (London, 1976); *Archaeology in Hampshire*, ed. M.F. Hughes (Winchester, 1976–). These annual reports published each year by Hampshire County Council contain summary reports of excavations etc. undertaken in the county for the previous twelve-month period.

Fig. 7.1 Hampshire and the Isle of Wight in the fourteenth century.

as well as more recently published (and unpublished except for brief interim reports) archaeological, architectural and documentary evidence.

The Channel became strategically very important as rivalry between France and England grew in the late thirteenth century, and as a long term policy the French were intent on having access to the ports on both sides. There was already a royal naval base at Rouen, which employed Genoese shipwrights, and in order to enhance their channel fleets the French constructed a new base at La Rochelle.[3] In addition, the French sought the assistance of the galley fleets from Genoa and Castile as they could not themselves provide sufficient numbers of ships for their royal fleet. Consequently the combined enemy fleet was able to harry English ships in local coastal waters, all part of the intermittent but long-drawn-out conflict at sea between the English and the French that dates back to the first half of the thirteenth century.

Important coastal targets at this time would have included Portsmouth and Southampton and the sheltered waters of the Solent. Portsmouth's importance in the thirteenth century was as a naval port with shipbuilding and repair facilities and as a centre where ships were mustered by the king for war. Throughout the thirteenth and fourteenth centuries ships were collected at Portsmouth mainly for raids on France. In contrast there were occasions when the conflict with France was put to one side. In 1270, for example, thirteen ships were mustered in preparation for Prince Edward and the earl of Lancaster, amongst other nobles, who sailed to join Louis IX of France for the relief of Jerusalem.[4]

Apart from its naval significance, it would also appear from the excavations at Oyster Street, in Old Portsmouth (fig. 7.4), that a period of consolidation and expansion was taking place during the fourteenth and fifteenth centuries in the commercial dockside facilities, which were located to the south of the naval port.[5]

Southampton also prospered as a port throughout the thirteenth and fourteenth centuries from the wine trade with Bordeaux and English-held Gascony, and trade with Venice and Genoa. For a century and a half Venetian and Genoese galleys were frequent visitors to the town which, although mainly a trading port, was also a victualling port for royal ships.[6] Southampton, like its near neighbour Portsmouth, was also of direct military value to the Crown and to France.

The fourteenth-century raids (fig. 7.2)

Although the French raid of 1338 has caught the imagination of most historians of the Hundred Years War, Southampton, and probably Portsmouth, had been subjected to raids, not by French ships, but by Englishmen from the Cinque Ports in

[3] C.T. Allmand, *The Hundred Years War: England and France at War c.1300–c.1450* (Cambridge, 1988), pp. 82–3.
[4] *Victoria County History: Hampshire and the Isle of Wight*, ed. W. Page, vol. 5 (London, 1912), p. 362.
[5] R. Fox and K.J. Barton, 'Excavations at Oyster Street, Portsmouth, Hampshire, 1968–71', *Post-Medieval Archaeology*, 20 (1986), pp. 31–255.
[6] *VCH: Hampshire*, 5, p. 362.

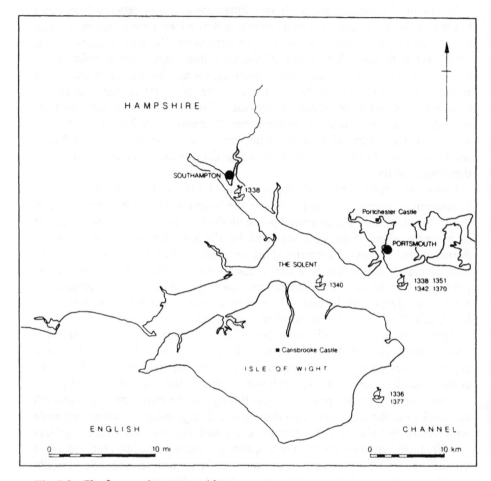

Fig. 7.2   The fourteenth-century raids.

the 1320s who had taken advantage of the problems that beset Edward II and the civil disorders that occurred during this time. In September 1321 a fleet of thirty ships from Winchelsea burnt seventeen vessels at Southampton and left damage estimated six years later at over £8,000.[7]

By 1336 hostilities between England and France were on the increase and Philip VI, the French king, planned to invade England. In August a force of French vessels made for the Isle of Wight where a number of English royal ships and merchantmen were anchored. The English ships were boarded and some were scuttled whilst others were taken over to Normandy as booty. The English royal fleet, unfortunately dispersed at the time, was called to intercept the enemy ships but the French had already returned to their bases.[8]

As a result of this disaster southern England was gripped with the fear of invasion. Since August commissioners of array had been selecting men in coastal towns and villages to assist in the defence of the coast. Beacons were established on local hilltops to warn of an impending French invasion. Ships were requisitioned by the king ready to defend the southern and eastern coasts, and there was a mass recruitment of men in these areas. The French king then abandoned his plan to invade England, and in October 1336 the English fleets were disbanded and the recruitment of men cancelled. This change of French policy, it appears, was due to the lack of reinforcements. Instead Philip VI decided to concentrate on naval raids on south-east England.[9]

Consequently in March 1338 a French fleet under Nicholas Bechuchet, Admiral of France struck an effective blow against the English. He landed at Portsmouth with a large force, plundered and burnt the town, leaving only the parish church of St Thomas (now the cathedral of Portsmouth) and the hospital, Domus Dei (God's House), still standing. Portsmouth, like Southampton, was ill-prepared, and the French met little resistance, because the English fleet previously mustered at Portsmouth before the attack had been sent in two directions away from the Solent area and the Hampshire coastline was completely undefended.[10]

During the later months of 1338, attacks were made by French galleys under Bechuchet on the Channel Islands as well as on English merchant ships in the Channel. Then in October the French fleet, this time with the addition of Genoese and Catalan galleys, attacked Southampton with a large force, plundering and burning the town.[11] Inevitably, narratives of the raid vary and there is even some doubt as to the date, but the story as Froissart chronicles it is one of the most dramatic, as we have already seen.

The next attack on the Solent coastline was made in 1340 by the men of a French fleet under the command of Bechuchet's successor, Robert Houdetot. The French had encountered an English convoy in the Channel and had captured some

[7] Platt, *Medieval Southampton*, p. 107.
[8] *CCR, 1337–39*, pp. 43–5.
[9] J. Sumption, *The Hundred Years War: Trial by Battle* (London, 1990), pp. 167–8.
[10] Sumption, *The Hundred Years War*, p. 226.
[11] Platt, *Medieval Southampton*, pp. 109–10; Sumption, *The Hundred Years War*, pp. 248–9.

merchant ships. They then sailed in to the Solent and landed on the Isle of Wight. Although the French inflicted a great deal of damage, they were eventually driven back to their ships by the island militia. Houdetot then proceeded to raid the Isle of Portland in Dorset, and Teignmouth in Devon.[12]

Portsmouth was the subject of another raid in 1342 when the French came ashore and burnt the town. After the attack the enemy fleet lay off the Hampshire coast for several days, alarming the local inhabitants.[13] In 1351 a Flemish ship was attacked at Portsmouth by armed boats belonging to a French vessel from Bayonne, leaving eight sailors killed in the skirmish.[14]

The first phase of the Hundred Years War ended in 1360 as it had begun, with more enemy threats to the English coast. The years 1359–60 saw widespread fear in England of a French invasion, although actual raids did not take place until March 1360 when Winchelsea was attacked.[15] There was a respite after the Treaty of Brétigny in 1360, but when hostilities broke out again in 1369 they were accompanied by an escalation of French naval involvement. The 1370s witnessed coastal attacks of greater intensity and frequency than before, which left widespread damage along the south and east coasts. Once again Portsmouth was one of the first targets. Thirty French ships landed forces in July 1370 and burnt the town.[16] In 1377 the Isle of Wight was invaded, Carisbrooke Castle besieged and a number of places damaged, the French leaving only after a substantial ransom had been paid.[17] In 1385 and 1386 there were further threats of invasion and although nothing happened, the knowledge caused panic once again amongst the local populace. French attacks ceased in 1389 for the remainder of the fourteenth century period of the Hundred Years War.

The effects of the raids

Edward III's reaction to the raids on both Portsmouth and Southampton in 1338 was immediate – especially when he learnt of the cowardice on the part of the coastal militia and the arrayers of men in the county who appeared to have fled when the French ships were sighted.[18] The raid had also been followed by looting in Southampton of royal stocks of wool and wine on a considerable scale by local people as well as men from Berkshire and Wiltshire. Edward punished the guilty by imprisonment in the Tower of London or elsewhere.[19]

The damage to Southampton was considerable, as is vividly demonstrated in the

---

[12] Sumption, *The Hundred Years War*, p. 347.

[13] *CCR, 1340–43*, pp. 562, 575, 579.

[14] *CPR, 1350–54*, p. 166.

[15] *VCH: Hampshire*, 5, p. 365.

[16] *VCH: Hampshire*, 5, p. 365.

[17] J.R. Alban, 'English Coastal Defence: some Fourteenth-Century Modifications within the System', in *Patronage, The Crown and The Provinces in Later Medieval England*, ed. R.A. Griffiths (Gloucester, 1981), p. 58.

[18] *CPR, 1338–40*, pp. 180–1.

[19] Platt, *Medieval Southampton*, p. 110.

cartularies of the hospital of God's House (founded in the 1190s) and the Augustinian Priory of St Denys (founded in 1127), which together provide the chief sources for the topography of the town in the thirteenth and fourteenth centuries. They also record a number of devastated properties purporting to be the result of the French raid.[20] The results of archaeological investigations that have taken place inside the medieval town since the late 1950s have also revealed the extent of the damage. These investigations, mainly as a result of re-development programmes, both large and small, have provided evidence of destruction by burning and the demolition of buildings (fig. 7.3). It should, however, be pointed out that a number of the excavations are not as yet fully published and observations made in this paper are based on summary reports published each year.[21]

Surveys of the God's House properties in the town indicate that the total number in 1338 was 130. Of these, 47 were destroyed during the raid, and a further nine probably destroyed, the majority of which were located in the west of the town in the parishes of St Michael and St John. If this is a sample of the level of destruction to other properties in this part of the town then it would suggest that a loss of between 40% and 50% of all buildings occurred as a result of the French raid. Some properties were also lost in Above Bar Street, outside the medieval town. However, it would appear that the French raid was selective, with adjacent properties apparently treated differently.[22]

Apart from forays north of Bargate and east of God's House Gate, the documentary evidence suggests that the French concentrated on the area between their landing place at the bottom of Bugle Street and the properties which surrounded the castle on the south and east. Timber-framed houses and a number of stone houses and vaults are also recorded as being badly damaged. The Weigh House in French Street (the remains of which still survive, see fig. 7.3), for example, was rebuilt in the late fourteenth century to replace a building damaged in the 1338 raid.[23]

Within a year of the raid, St Denis Priory, the religious house situated to the north of the medieval town that owned urban property, pleaded poverty and distress because a greater part of its land holdings in Southampton and elsewhere in adjacent areas had been laid waste. It also claimed that many of its buildings had been burnt and their charters and other monastic records badly damaged by the French, restricting the ability of the priory to sustain its level of activity.[24] However, whether the reason for the priory's poverty was actually due to the depredations caused by the French raid or to the damaging effects of the fourteenth-century plagues, is uncertain; the priory claimed the former.

---

[20] *God's House*, ed. Kaye; *St Denys*, ed. Blake.
[21] *Archaeology in Hampshire*, ed. Hughes.
[22] *God's House*, pp. lv–lvi.
[23] C. Platt and R. Coleman-Smith, *Excavations in Medieval Southampton 1953–1969* (Leicester, 1975), p. 78.
[24] *St Denys*, p. xl.

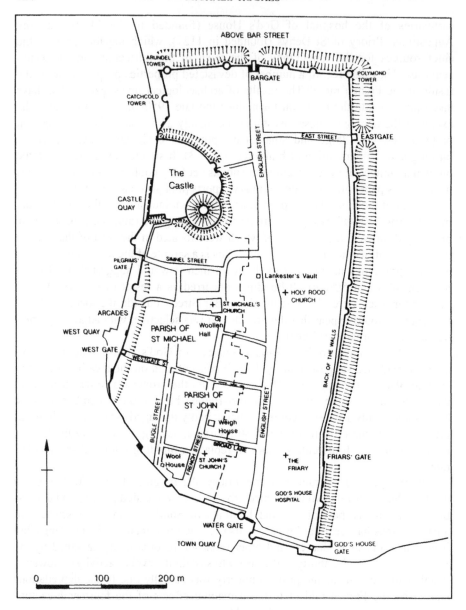

Fig. 7.3   Southampton, showing sites and streets referred to in text.

The archaeological evidence from inside the medieval town also reveals a picture of destruction, in some cases by burning, followed by a period of abandonment. A series of large pits had been dug, for example, in the open ground behind a house on English Street (modern High Street) to dispose of unusable building debris possibly left as a result of the raid. The pits were filled to the top with rubble and burnt slate.[25] Recent investigations at Lankester Vault, near the remains of Holy Rood church (fig. 7.3), revealed that a metalled street level of flint cobbles overlay a layer of limestone cobbles that lay directly on top of a layer of building material, burnt *in situ*. Unfortunately the pottery from this burnt level ranged from 1250 to 1350, which prevents dating this destruction layer more accurately.[26]

At various sites on both sides of the High Street, excavations or watching briefs in recent years have shown the existence of widespread layers, approx. 10cm thick, of burnt material, including roofing slates.[27] Once again no positive dating evidence has been found for this ubiquitous burnt layer, but its widespread distribution away from the town walls would suggest that it may be connected with a single, dramatic conflagration, possibly the result of the French raid.

One of the problems in Southampton has been the lack of closely datable material for these 'destruction' layers and there has been a natural inclination to attempt to fit the archaeological evidence with the more 'glamorous' documentary and literary evidence concerning the French raid and its after-effects on the town. However, it is possible that it was the construction of a new stone wall, with its towers and gates, on the western and southern sides of the town in the mid- to late fourteenth century that caused the demolition of properties on the waterfronts. The act of demolition could also have created 'destruction' layers in the archaeological stratigraphy of the excavations in that part of the medieval town.

In French Street a number of properties of wealthy owners (evident from the range of exotic pottery and the presence of internal fireplaces), may have been abandoned prior to the 1338 raid and subsequently destroyed during the attack on the town. A destruction level of burnt and unburnt artefacts was recorded during the excavations, on top of which was a layer of unburnt household rubbish. This suggests that the fire-damaged properties lay abandoned for some years during which time the area was used for refuse disposal. The properties were then redeveloped in the late fourteenth or early fifteenth centuries.[28]

The evidence from archaeological investigations, in French Street, backed up by that from documentary sources, has also demonstrated that the process of rebuilding may have taken some time. Some empty plots were used as gardens by the occupiers of neighbouring properties. In contrast, other documentary sources suggest that some properties in St Michael's parish were rebuilt quickly.[29]

It would also appear from documentary sources that in the mid- to late 1300s,

---

25 *Excavations in Medieval Southampton*, p. 37.
26 *Archaeology in Hampshire* (1990), p. 35.
27 *Pers. comm.*, A. Russel.
28 *Archaeology in Hampshire* (1990), pp. 35–6.
29 *God's House*, p. lv.

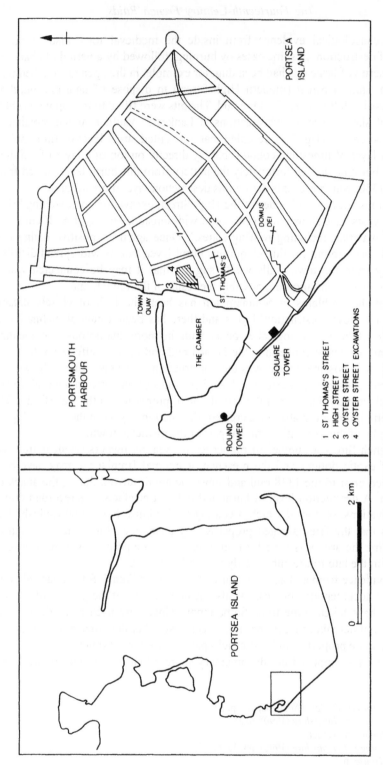

Fig. 7.4 Oyster Street site and line of sixteenth-century fortifications.

Southampton went into a recession. Foreign merchants, upon whose trade and contacts with Europe Southampton had become increasingly dependent, had been frightened off by the war. Florentine wool merchants transferred their business to Bristol after the 1338 raid and no wool exports were recorded for over a year. Other trade also came to a standstill. Portsmouth suffered a similar fate – no customable goods passed through the port during the year following the 1338 raid.[30]

Although the raid created problems in trade, they may have been due more to a general lack of confidence brought on by the prolonged conflicts with France and its allies and compounded by the effects of the fourteenth-century plagues and allied diseases such as typhoid. In 1351, for example, there is a reference in the Patent Rolls to the impoverished and oppressed state of the town brought on as much by the pestilence as by the destruction caused by the French raids.[31] It was economically, socially and politically an unstable time for the people of the town.

In the last decade of the fourteenth century prosperity gradually returned but it was due more to the business acumen of local merchants and traders than to the renewed activities of foreign businessmen.[32] This is reflected in some of the archaeological evidence from High Street properties. The evidence of exotic artefacts from France and the Mediterranean showed that some parts of the town had retained some semblance of prosperity and a few influential Southampton merchants still had the ability to entertain visitors from Italy and elsewhere.

Although as vulnerable as Southampton to French attack, Portsmouth showed no comparable long term interruption to its development. Activity on the commercial waterfront increased. The excavations at Oyster Street, Old Portsmouth, were the first large-scale investigations within the medieval walled town (fig. 7.4). The site fronted onto The Camber, a landlocked deep-water basin, inside Portsmouth Harbour. According to excavated evidence the site consisted of a complex of stone and timber buildings and other features such as pits, stone-lined wells and a timber water cistern used for the storage of fresh water, all probably dating to the late thirteenth or early fourteenth century. In the fourteenth and fifteenth centuries the existing buildings were removed and the remaining structures improved. The cistern was enlarged, two fresh wells were dug and a garden area was laid out in the centre of the site. As the status and prosperity of the site increased, an attempt was made to reclaim part of the shoreline with stone walling, and a quay and docking area were constructed, 20 metres south-west of the main complex.[33] This evidence suggests that by the late thirteenth century and throughout the fourteenth and fifteenth centuries, Portsmouth was a flourishing commercial port providing berths, storage and victualling facilities, and any temporary disruption to trade, as suggested by the documentary evidence, was balanced by the need to supply the king's and other ships.

It was not only Southampton and Portsmouth that suffered from the war with

---

[30] Platt, *Medieval Southampton*, p. 111.
[31] Platt, *Medieval Southampton*, p. 119.
[32] Platt, *Medieval Southampton*, p. 111.
[33] Fox and Barton, 'Oyster Street, Portsmouth', pp. 31–255.

France and the threats of invasion. In Winchester the cloth industry went bankrupt; foreign merchants avoided other Hampshire ports, and the need to support the king's armies in France drained the economy of local Hampshire towns, including Lymington, Fareham and Emsworth as well as other coastal settlements such as Hamble, Hook (Warsash) and Hurst.[34] The Cistercian abbey at Netley, on the shores of Southampton Water, petitioned the Crown in 1338, alleging that it had become impoverished because of its coastal location and because of the 'frequent coming and going of marines'.[35]

A similar picture is portrayed in the records of Southwick Priory, which claimed that a number of its nearby manors had suffered from the passage of English armies, and that its coastal properties, including those in Portsmouth and Southampton, had been burnt during French raids. It also complained of the severe strain put upon its resources during the reign of Edward III who continually demanded hospitality for himself and his entourage whenever they were making for ports of embarkation on the Hampshire coast.[36]

A glimpse of personal tragedies caused by the fourteenth-century conflicts with France is occasionally found in records. At Crofton, on the coast near Fareham, a death was reported in 1351 of a man who had been killed at sea 'by enemies from Normandy', whilst two years previously another had been captured at sea – 'in time of war by enemies of the King and taken outside the realm of England and had not returned'.[37]

Town and castle defences

Although there had been a general, but often slow improvement in castle and town defences throughout the twelfth century, the wars with France in the thirteenth, fourteenth and fifteenth centuries saw a massive increase both in royal and local expenditure and in manpower to construct new defences as well as to improve and repair older fortifications, especially in the coastal counties of England where enemy invasion was feared. The early thirteenth century saw the establishment by the Crown of murage, a new tax which permitted towns to levy tolls on goods coming into their markets for sale. The proceeds were to go towards the building of new town walls. In 1369, it was ordered that all castles, abbeys, priories, cities, towns and boroughs should be surveyed and put into order, and that walls, ditches and gates should be repaired.[38]

---

[34] *CPR, 1345–48*, p. 167.

[35] *VCH: Hampshire*, 2, p. 148.

[36] *The Cartularies of Southwick Priory*, Part 1, ed. K.A. Hanna (Winchester, 1988), pp. xvii and xxiv.

[37] D.G. Watts, 'The villages on the manors of Titchfield Abbey', *Proceedings of the Hampshire Field Club and Archaeological Society*, 21, Pt 1 (1958), p. 34.

[38] H. Turner, *Town Defences in England and Wales* (London, 1971), pp. 31–2.

Portsmouth. The earliest reference to any form of fortification at Portsmouth occurs in the early thirteenth century when an order is directed to the sheriff of Southampton to enclose the docks at Portsmouth with a strong wall for the preservation of the king's ships,[39] although there is no physical evidence today of such a fortification. However, in 1342 a levy of murage was made on Portsmouth for eight years for fortifications against the French following the attack of 1338,[40] which may imply that there was an earlier fortification and that the grant was given for its repair.

Not much progress can have been made with the defences of Portsmouth for in 1386 a commission was appointed to take measures to wall the town. As a result of the commission's findings a simple bank and ditch was probably constructed around the town. The defences of the fourteenth and fifteenth century are now difficult to determine, however, as the town was re-fortified in the sixteenth century. The earlier defences may only have consisted of an earthwork along the side of the harbour, which by the end of the fifteenth century included the Round Tower (c.1415) and the Square Tower (c.1494) (fig. 7.4). Leland, the Tudor antiquary, however, describes the defences in the sixteenth century as still only an earthen and timber wall, built around the town, with a ditch on the outside and gates of timber.[41] By the late sixteenth and seventeenth centuries, further bastions and a stone curtain wall had been built (plate XIII).

Southampton. As a result of the 1338 raid Edward III gave orders for work to begin on new defences at Southampton, especially as another French attack was expected daily. The town was garrisoned and Edward required 'a stone wall to be built forthwith towards the water', so that the town should be 'surrounded with a stone wall' (fig. 7.3).[42]

The earliest references to Southampton's defences date from the early thirteenth century. In 1203 there is an allowance made to enclose the town,[43] whilst in 1217 a deed refers to the 'portam orientalem' which implies the existence of an East Gate (fig. 7.3). 'The bridge of Eststrete' and 'the ditch of Hampton' are recorded prior to 1217 in the St Denys Cartulary which suggests the presence of earthwork fortifications.[44] Excavations undertaken in the north-eastern corner of the medieval town in 1986 (the site known as York Buildings being close to the Polymond Tower, see fig. 7.3), have shown that these earthen defences may have originally been built over existing properties of late Saxon or early medieval date. The remains consisted of a bank of re-deposited brickearth at least two metres high, from which pottery of c.1200 was recovered.[45] The Bargate, the town's north gate (fig. 7.3), has been

[39] *VCH: Hampshire*, 5, p. 361.

[40] *CPR, 1340–43*, pp. 562–3.

[41] S. Quail, 'Stone towers: the fortifications of Portsmouth', in *The Spirit of Portsmouth* (Chichester, 1989), pp. 53–5.

[42] *CPR, 1338–40*, p. 237; *CCR, 1339–41*, p. 101.

[43] *Pipe Roll 5 John* (Pipe Roll Society, N.S. xvi 1938), p. 145.

[44] *St Denys*, pp. 59, 111, 122–42.

[45] *Archaeology in Hampshire* (1987), p. 28

dated on architectural grounds to the late twelfth century,[46] whilst the East Gate, later demolished, appears in a mid-sixteenth century picture as a stone gate structure with two flanking towers.[47] Contrary to previous suggestions that these gates were later inserted into the earthen defences,[48] it is possible that they were constructed towards the end of the twelfth century as free-standing symbols of urban pride rather than for defensive reasons, and that the earthen defences were added in the early thirteenth century, after England had lost Normandy, and consequently control of the Channel, to the French Crown. There is also a reference of c.1233 to a gate of the Friars Minor, on the eastern side of the town (fig. 7.3).[49]

The other two sides facing the open water were not defended at this time, for on the shorelines of the western and southern sides there was a group of private quays, accessed by a network of lanes from twelfth- and thirteenth-century merchants' houses and warehouses which lay in this part of the medieval town and whose mercantile activities were of paramount importance to the town's prosperity.

It has been argued on documentary and structural grounds that the northern and eastern stone walls were constructed in the late thirteenth century.[50] Certainly, during the last half of the thirteenth century a series of murage grants are recorded for Southampton, and excavations in the 1970s on the north-east corner of the town have suggested that a fairly crude stone wall was built against the outside, and into the top of, the earthen rampart during this period.[51]

It would appear that these poor quality wall foundations consisted of only three courses of masonry. This suggests that the process of constructing town walls in stone may have been a slow process. On top of these three courses only a thin wall (0.76m) was constructed. When a comparison is made between the width of this wall with other medieval town defences in England, where the wall thickness varied between 1.9 and 2.1m, it can be seen just how poor a construction was the medieval wall at Southampton.[52] In the fourteenth century it appears that the rampart was heightened, probably to strengthen the poorly constructed wall, whilst a trench was dug into the rampart immediately behind the wall in the fifteenth century and filled with masonry in order to strengthen once again the badly constructed, and by now weakened, defences.[53]

It does appear that the defensive towers and intervening curtain walls around the northern and eastern sides of the town were not built in one operation. Some of the stone towers, of probable late thirteenth-century date, may have been constructed over a filled-in inner town ditch, and before the curtain wall was built in between.

[46] P.A. Faulkner, 'The surviving medieval buildings', in *Excavations in Medieval Southampton*, p. 56.
[47] Turner, *Town Defences*, p. 167.
[48] J.S. Wacher, 'The excavations, 1956–1958', in *Excavations in Medieval Southampton*, p. 142.
[49] *St Denys*, p. 129.
[50] B.H. St J. O'Neil, 'Southampton town wall', in *Aspects of Archaeology in Britain and beyond: Essays presented to O.G.S. Crawford*, ed. W.F. Grimes (London, 1951), pp. 243–57.
[51] Wacher, 'Excavations', in *Excavations in Medieval Southampton*, pp. 146–8.
[52] J.R. Kenyon, *Medieval Fortifications* (Leicester, 1990), p. 187.
[53] Wacher, 'Excavations', in *Excavations in Medieval Southampton*, pp. 147–9.

In contrast, investigations on the line of the south-east wall (Back of the Walls, fig. 7.3), near God's House, indicated that a late thirteenth-century dovecote, probably owned by the medieval hospital, was demolished and its footings used for the construction of a half-round tower, sometime in the second quarter of the fourteenth century (plate XIV). The excavations also revealed that the former earthen rampart abutting the eastern wall was used as a working platform, possibly for the construction of the stone curtain wall sometime in the mid- to late fourteenth century,[54] to which an inquisition of 1353 may refer '. . . the parapet on the eastern wall was made with poplar boards and earthen walls . . . and has been destroyed by wind and rain to the danger of the town'.[55]

In the late thirteenth and first half of the fourteenth century, there is nothing more positive to imply any defence of the southern or western waterfronts than the gating of the streets.[56] Even if the castle had been in a state of readiness, it could have given no more than a nominal defence as virtually no substantial walls or gates existed along the quays on the south and west of the town. This lack of defence was due mainly to the overriding demands of the wealthy merchants who occupied much of the area immediately behind the wharves, who, together with the king, wanted unrestricted access to their warehouses. The construction of a defensive wall would certainly have impeded these mercantile activities. However, documentary sources mention that as part of a programme initiated by Edward II, the merchants and townspeople may have constructed a wooden barbican somewhere on the docksides – discretion being the better part of valour – and in 1336 there was a move to replace the wooden construction with a stone version,[57] although it cannot have been very substantial in preventing an attack, let alone an enemy landing force, as was proved two years later.

The eventual walling of the western and southern sides of the town took place in the mid- to late fourteenth century, as suggested by the orders given in 1360, 1369 and 1376 for the urgent repair or building of the walls. Because of rising costs, the walls were still not completed in 1386 and the King was petitioned by the townspeople to find the necessary finance to complete the project. This petition coincided with a fresh threat of invasion and new efforts were made to complete the wall circuit and to improve the castle's fortifications.[58] The new walls destroyed the older pattern of lanes and quays and concentrated trade at the public quays, Town Quay and West Quay (fig. 7.3), a new pattern that enhanced the commercial and social importance of the High Street and its properties, as demonstrated by the rich artefacts recovered from excavations.

Recent excavations carried out in advance of restoration work on the western town walls, revealed the limestone foundations of a half-round tower at Simnel

---

[54] *Archaeology in Hampshire* (1990), pp. 43–4.

[55] *CIM, 1348–77*, p. 38.

[56] *Excavations in Medieval Southampton*, p. 37.

[57] Turner, *Defences*, p. 172.

[58] A.D. Saunders, 'The Defences of Southampton in the Later Middle Ages', in *The Southampton Terrier*, p. 21.

Street (fig. 7.3), blocking or defending the gateway there. This tower then appears to have been levelled when the 'arcades' were inserted in the late fourteenth century (fig. 7.3). The curtain wall between Westgate (built at the same time as God's House Gate in the first half of the fourteenth century), and Simnel Street was finally completed around the same time. All the openings except for the postern were blocked, and gunports inserted into suitable doorways and windows. The house immediately north of Blue Anchor Lane projected beyond the general line of the wall, and this was demolished and rebuilt almost one metre to the east. The foundations of three half-round towers along this section of the defences were also discovered during the excavations. Finally the curtain wall itself was strengthened by adding to the west face a line of machicolated arcading, which supported a battlement in front of the houses (plate XV). The southernmost of the towers was demolished early in the seventeenth century, and it may have been at this time that the remainder of the arcades were destroyed along that part of the town defences. The other towers survived until 1775, when they were demolished to widen the road.[59]

Both from documentary sources and archaeological evidence it would appear that very little work was carried out on the refurbishment of the castle (fig. 7.3), from the last quarter of the thirteenth century to the last quarter of the fourteenth, although evidence from a programme of excavations undertaken in the early 1980s, suggests a flurry of building activity in the late thirteenth century. Consequently, there may have been a considerable amount of dereliction of the castle buildings and defences during those hundred years, possibly because after the raid of 1338 all expenditure was targetted at the town walls. The emphasis on urban defence at this time throughout western Europe was shifting away from a single heavily fortified stronghold to that of a strong-walled town. In the early fourteenth century there were orders to fortify and guard the castle, but there is little evidence of new work being undertaken before 1378. The succeeding ten years however, saw the castle almost completely rebuilt with work, according to archive material, concentrating on a new keep, probably similar in style to other castle towers in this period. However, there is little archaeological evidence for this work on a new keep because it appears that most of the late fourteenth century-work was undertaken on other areas of the castle. The castle rebuilding programme was, however, undertaken to more stricter standards than those used in the construction of the town walls, probably because it was financed by the royal purse and under the supervision of the king's mason, Henry Yevele.[60]

Possible evidence of French casualties from the 1338 raid came from the excavations in the outer bailey of the castle where a group of skeletons, all but one of which, were found buried unceremoniously in a disused lime kiln pit, which had gone out of use by the end of the thirteenth century.[61]

Accustomed to the benefits of a stable economy and unused to disorder and

[59] *Archaeology in Hampshire* (1989), p. 25.
[60] *Excavations at Southampton Castle*, ed. J. Oxley (Southampton, 1986), pp. 109–117.
[61] *Ibid.*, pp. 60–3.

invasion scares, the town found it hard, as Edward III would discover, to take seriously the task and burden of repairing existing fortifications or building new ones. In contrast to the high standards of workmanship on the castle defences in Southampton, it is clear from archaeological investigations that the workmanship on the town walls was shoddy and inadequate during the fourteenth century.

During the reign of Richard II when French invasion once more threatened the English coasts on a number of occasions, several castle and town defences had gunports either added to them or inserted into new or older town or castle walls and towers. Documentary evidence for the use of artillery in Southampton in the fourteenth century is scarce but there is the rather humorous reference to the 'appointment of Thomas Tredington, chaplain to serve the king in his new tower of Southampton, both to celebrate divine services and to keep the armour, artillery, victuals and guns for its garrison and defence. He is retained for this service expressly because he is an expert in guns and the management of artillery'.[62] Gunports were apparently inserted into the ground floor openings of the castle hall in the late fourteenth century, at the same time as other defences of the town that were redesigned for artillery. The introduction of artillery, however, rendered the new keep and the castle somewhat redundant by the fifteenth century, when there are numerous references to artillery in Southampton. The introduction and use of artillery in Southampton, however, is discussed in more detail elsewhere.[63]

The fourteenth- and fifteenth-century defences at Southampton have their closest parallels with those around Canterbury and have similar characteristics to other town defences constructed during the period of the Hundred Years War in southern and eastern England such as at Exeter, Poole, Norwich and Great Yarmouth. In other towns such as Winchester and Chichester, earlier walls, often of Roman date, were refurbished or rebuilt. The fortifications of English towns, however, were never as complete or as sophisticated as their equivalents in France at such towns as Falaise, Caen, Rouen and Mont-St-Michel, in Normandy, where the impressive remains of the fourteenth- and fifteenth-century fortifications still survive.

Winchester. Activity on the walls at Winchester closely reflected the course of the Hundred Years War, and in particular the French raids on the Hampshire coast or the threat of them. Murage was still collected on a regular basis during the fourteenth century but can have covered no more than routine maintenance. In 1338 special efforts were made to collect money and carry out repairs to the walls in case the raids were repeated.[64] The work continued sporadically at first, but between 1374 and 1378 virtually the full length of the wall surrounding the episcopal

---

[62] *CPR, 1385–89*, p. 162.

[63] See John Kenyon's chapter in this volume in addition to his 'Early artillery fortifications in England and Wales: a preliminary survey and reappraisal', *Archaeological Journal*, 138 (1981) and *Medieval Fortifications*; D.F. Renn, 'The Southampton Arcade', *Medieval Archaeology*, 8 (1964); D.F. Renn, 'The earliest gunports in Britain', *Archaeological Journal*, 125 (1968); Saunders, 'Defences of Southampton', pp. 22–31; A.D. Saunders, *Fortress Britain* (Liphook, 1989).

[64] *CPR, 1338–40*, pp. 180, 212, 281.

palace of Wolvesey was rebuilt at the bishop's expense, the 1377 raid in the Solent area probably providing an added incentive. The raids caused widespread alarm in Winchester and the inhabitants walled up the Durngate and pulled down the bridge outside it. Considerable work then took place on the city walls until the end of the fourteenth century due to fears of further French attacks.[65]

Excavations on the site of the Assize Courts indicated that Gar Street (now Trafalgar Street) had been remetalled five times and houses refloored frequently down to the mid- to late thirteenth century. In the fourteenth century the street was once again resurfaced but the houses went out of use and the area was heavily dug into by pits, evidence perhaps of the effects of the fourteenth-century plagues or the instability created by the French raids.[66]

Excavations near the East Gate of the city and in sections of the North Walls indicated that by the twelfth century the Roman wall had been reduced to its footings. In the thirteenth century the wall was reconstructed on the line of the front of the Roman defences, and was repaired in the fourteenth century. From archaeological investigations near Wolvesley Palace, it would appear that in the late fourteenth century part of the city wall was partly rebuilt or repaired. It is also thought that the battlements were added to the top of the wall at this time.[67] Excavations in Tower Street showed that the city wall had been repaired on a number of occasions and a tower added in the late thirteenth or fourteenth century.[68]

The refronting of the West Gate with its provision for cannon probably took place in the late fourteenth century (plate XVI), and in 1390 a sum was set aside for the repair of walls, gates and towers of the castle.[69] The work was carried out under the supervision of Henry Yevele and William Wynford, who were also responsible for the rebuilding of the nave of Winchester Cathedral and the construction of Winchester College.[70]

Portchester Castle. Throughout much of the fourteenth century Portchester Castle was kept in a state of defensive readiness against the threat of French attack. In the first half of the fourteenth century, Richard earl of Arundel was keeper of the maritime district in Hampshire, part of the coastal home-defences system and was ordered to keep 10 men-at-arms and 40 archers in the castle for its safekeeping. Both the castle's main gates were reconstructed in the 1320s and the Watergate was further extended in 1336/37 by an external construction on the east side as a further defence against enemy galleys. The castle's ditches were re-dug in 1325 and

[65] D. Keene, *Survey of Medieval Winchester*, Winchester Studies 2.i, Pt I (Oxford, 1985), pp. 42–8.
[66] *Object and Economy in Medieval Winchester: Artefacts from Medieval Winchester*, ed. M. Biddle, Winchester Studies 7 ii, Pt ii ed. M. Biddle (Oxford, 1990), p. 1154.
[67] B. Cunliffe, 'The Winchester City Wall', *Proceedings of the Hampshire Field Club and Archaeological Society*, 22, pt II (1962), pp. 51–81.
[68] *Object and Economy in Medieval Winchester*, p. 1201.
[69] *CPR, 1377–81*, p. 111.
[70] R. Allen Brown, H.M. Colvin and A.J. Taylor, 'The Middle Ages', in *The History of the King's Works*, 2nd edn, ed. H.M. Colvin (London, 1963), p. 863.

1326. The medieval south postern gate was blocked up in the mid-fourteenth century, no doubt to provide greater security, and amongst other defensive measures undertaken to protect the castle, may have been the construction of an outer earthwork, consisting of a bank and ditch, which commanded the landward approach. Although the pottery evidence from small-scale excavations of the earthwork suggests a fourteenth-century date for its construction, it may indicate the refurbishment of an earlier outer defence. Further renovation work was started in 1369 when hostilities with France were renewed, and no doubt quickly completed as a direct result of the raid on Portsmouth in 1370. Walls and towers were heightened, a section of the wall on the south-east corner brought down by the sea was rebuilt, both gates were repaired and the castle ditches once again cleared out.[71]

As well as being a base for assembling royal armies, weapons and equipment, Portchester played its part in defence. Delays kept Edward III at Portchester through June 1346 as his army of 15,000 men assembled, until he finally sailed for the campaigns in Normandy that was to lead to victory at Crécy and the taking of Calais.

Between the French raids and the assembling of armies, however, the castle continued to function as a residence. As a result of the invasion scare of 1360, supplies were sent to the castle in readiness for a siege, and in 1361 the inhabitants of Portchester, the settlement outside the castle, were granted remission for taxes for having assisted in the defence of the castle and settlement at the time of the raids.[72]

Sir Robert Assheton, who became keeper of the castle in 1376, was responsible for the construction of Assheton's Tower which had gunports built into the private apartments – the earliest example in England of a purpose-built structure with provision for artillery. Firearms are recorded for the first time at Portchester in 1379 and were becoming an essential part of the equipment of any major castle at the time.[73]

Isle of Wight. Between 1294 and 1298 documentary evidence points to considerable activity on the defence of the Isle of Wight because of its strategic importance, including expenditure for a new drawbridge at the main gate of Carisbrooke Castle. In 1335/36 further repairs were undertaken to the castle prison, and work was begun on the construction of the new drum towers of the gate together with repairs to the portcullis and drawbridge. In 1352 the king's chamber was adapted for the storage of provisions by blocking up the windows, and the battlements were renovated.[74]

The French attacked the Island in 1377 and 'utterly burnt and destroyed the town

---

[71] B. Cunliffe, *Excavations at Portchester Castle, III, Medieval: the Outer Bailey and its Defences* (London, 1978), pp. 120–173, 300–6.
[72] *CCR, 1360–4*, pp. 14, 31, 39, 193.
[73] Kenyon, 'Early artillery fortifications in England', p. 209.
[74] *History of the King's Works*, pp. 591–5.

of Carisbrooke and unsuccessfully besieged the castle' which necessitated further repairs.[75] In 1380, under the watchful eye of Henry Yevele, the King's Mason, further fortifications were undertaken, the main work being the heightening of the main gatehouse.[76] The alterations to Edward III's gatehouse, previously assigned to the fifteenth century, have now been dated to the last two decades of the fourteenth century, suggesting that the machiolation above the gateway and the gunports in the top levels of the gatehouse towers can also be assigned to the late fourteenth century, when two cannon were brought to the castle (plate XVII).[77]

The earliest examples of gunports in England also come from the Isle of Wight and were built to defend Quarr Abbey (fig. 7.1) against French attack. The abbot was responsible for the defence of the Island and around 1365 was given a licence to crenellate. In the surviving precinct wall there are a number of simple, circular gunports possibly of this date.[78]

General coastal defence in the thirteenth and fourteenth centuries

> It was also decreed that in the coastal areas and islands, such as Cornwall, Guernsey, Wight, Hampshire and Sheppey, no men-at-arms or defence personnel should be moved away, regardless of any levy called by the King, but should guard their coasts and borders and should train their children in the use of arms and archery, in return for twopence each a day drawn from the duties on the wool within their districts.[79]

Whatever the purpose of the French raids, serious damage was done, and alarm, especially in the coastal counties, was widespread. The likelihood of an attempt by the French to invade must have been foreseen for some time, indeed, ever since the early thirteenth century when Philip Augustus took Normandy, with its Channel coast and ports from the English. Although some steps may have been taken to protect English Channel ports from French ships, they proved useless against the fourteenth-century raids. The French could land without the need for port facilities and English ships could be burnt in harbour without landing, so no part of the south coast could be regarded as immune from attack.

The traditional way of signalling news of a threatened landing in England was by a system of hill-top beacons. The control of these beacons in the coastal counties was with the 'keepers of the maritime land', the 'maritime land' being a coastal strip that extended six leagues from the shore.[80] In 1337/38 some of the south coast keepers were instructed by the king to have the beacons in their areas prepared without delay, whilst sheriffs throughout England were ordered to have

[75] *CCR, 1385–89*, p. 356.
[76] *CPR, 1377–81*, p. 486.
[77] *History of the King's Works*, p. 594.
[78] Saunders, *Fortress Britain*, p. 18; D.F. Renn, 'The *enceinte* wall of Quarr Abbey', *Fort*, 8 (1980), pp. 5–6.
[79] *Froissart*, ed. Brereton, p. 58.
[80] Alban, 'English Coastal Defence', pp. 59–60; H.J. Hewitt, *The Organization of War under Edward III, 1338–62* (Manchester, 1966), p. 7.

beacons ready on hilltops far from the sea as well as on the coasts because massed French galleys sailing through the Channel created an invasion scare. Edward III gave orders that beacons were to be prepared on hilltops near Southampton in anticipation of French attacks.[81]

Churches situated within six leagues of the sea were instructed to ring only one bell for normal services but to ring all bells if the French were sighted.[82] It is possible, in this context, that a number of church towers on or near the coast were crenellated and used as look-outs during the fourteenth century, as for example at St Andrew's, Hamble, All Saints, Fawley, and Christchurch Priory in Hampshire. Freshwater, and St Helens are examples of churches on the Isle of Wight with late medieval battlemented towers (fig. 7.1). Also on the Island, St Catherine's Tower, built on the coast in the fourteenth century, may have had a dual role both as a lighthouse and as a look-out for French ships (fig. 7.1).

As well as attempts to defend the major ports, other important measures were those taken for general defence. Much of the existing system, including the use of beacons, however, had its roots in earlier centuries. Those counties bordering the English Channel were called upon to fulfil their military obligations to defend their localities in the thirteenth century. For example, in 1296 the bishop of Winchester was put to great expense in order to guard the coast at or near his manor of Fareham in southern Hampshire.[83]

Edward I understood the strategic importance of the Isle of Wight and skilful manipulation bought the island under Crown control in 1293. During his reign elaborate preparations were also made to protect the island against French attack. According to Worsley, the nineteenth-century Island historian, a list was made of the men-at-arms and archers for whom each landholder was liable – 54 men-at-arms and 141 archers in all. The Island militia was divided into two, one to serve the east of the Island and the other the west. Each was then divided into districts under the command of a leading landowner. Watches were organised and beacons prepared on the headlands around the coast with horsemen ready to sound the alarm around the Island on sighting the enemy.[84] Carisbrooke Castle was strengthened and Yarmouth, East Cowes, Ryde and Quarr Abbey were fortified,[85] although there is no physical evidence surviving of any other fourteenth-century fortifications on the Island except at Carisbrooke and Quarr.

During the period of insecurity in the fourteenth century, men living in the maritime land were exempt from service in France and ordered to stay in their shires for the defence of the realm. Men living in counties away from the coast were also liable to be ordered to serve in the maritime land, as occurred in 1338,

---

[81] *CCR, 1337–39*, p. 179; Hewitt, *Organization of War*, p. 5.
[82] Hewitt, *Organization of War*, p. 5.
[83] M.F. Hughes, *The Small Towns of Hampshire* (Winchester, 1976), p. 63.
[84] *VCH: Hampshire*, 5, p. 312.
[85] *CCR, 1333–37*, pp. 469–70.

for example, when men from Oxfordshire were sent to Hampshire whenever they were required.[86]

A number of problems, however, arose in ensuring that the maritime lands were kept manned. One problem was the evasion of military service, which tended to cause an exodus of men from the Isle of Wight and the environs of Portsmouth and Southampton, as well as from other coastal regions where French attacks had occurred or were predicted. This is well illustrated in the Close Rolls which record that Bartholomew de l'Isle, who had left the Isle of Wight, received a rebuke '. . . it is not becoming for belted knights to eloign (remove) themselves from places where deeds of war may take place but rather to go to those places and stay there . . .'. There were a number of repeated orders to those who lived on the coast to remain there, and for those who had moved away to safety there were instructions to return to their homes. The sheriff of Hampshire was instructed, for example, that men in Southampton were to build houses 'and dwell therein for the safe-keeping of the town'.[87]

Another problem concerned the owners of estates scattered throughout southern England who were often forced to provide service for the defence of maritime lands in a number of coastal counties. For example, the abbot of Hyde Abbey in Winchester had to provide service, not only in Hampshire, but also in the maritime lands of Sussex and Dorset, where he also held properties. The medieval hospital in Southampton was not only having to provide men for the protection of the town, but also in Dorset, where it owned estates.[88]

Other religious houses and prelates were also ordered to assist in coastal defence. In 1342 the Abbot and the Prior of St Swithun's, Winchester, were given a commission to be 'keepers of Southampton against incursions by the French who, as the King had learned, are planning an attack on it with galleys and ships of war'.[89] The Bishop of Winchester complained to the king in July 1338 that he had to assemble men-at-arms as well as members of his household and his tenants on his manor of Fareham to repel an invasion by the French who had recently attacked Portsmouth and other coastal towns,[90] whilst Quarr Abbey, had to provide men-at-arms and archers for the defence of the Isle of Wight.[91] On the Isle of Wight the population protested that they were 'supporting great labour and heavy expense in the defence' and managed to gain some respite from payment. Carisbrooke Castle was used as a food store and orders were issued that no grain was to be taken from the island.[92]

Predictions of French invasion on the Hampshire or Isle of Wight coasts in 1346, 1352 and 1360 were followed by strict orders against evacuation, and in 1355 and

[86] CCR, 1349–54, p. 545; CCR, 1339–41, p. 19.
[87] CCR, 1339–41, pp. 444, 101.
[88] CCR, 1337–39, p. 109.
[89] CPR, 1340–43, p. 476.
[90] CCR, 1337–39, pp. 124–5.
[91] CPR, 1338–40, p. 6.
[92] CCR, 1339–41, pp. 285, 352.

1356, when England intended to invade France, extensive measures were once again taken for the defence of the realm. In August 1356 militia men in all the coastal counties between Norfolk and Hampshire were to be arrayed, armed and provided with horses to resist invasion, and beacons were to be prepared. In 1360 the arrayers of the inland counties were ordered to array their men and to be ready to assist Hampshire in the protection of its coastline once they had received an order from the king or from the Hampshire arrayers.[93]

Castles such as those at Portchester, Southampton, Christchurch, Carisbrooke and Corfe, in Dorset must also have played key roles in coastal defence. The garrisons of coastal towns and castles could be reinforced by units raised by the commissions of array in the rural areas of the counties. For example, Warin de l'Isle's garrison at Portsmouth was strengthened by men from Bedfordshire, Buckinghamshire and Northamptonshire in 1369.[94]

Attack or invasion by the French and their allies during the fourteenth-century phase of the Hundred Years War was ever present, often stretching resources, both manpower and financial, to the limit. During the period in question the coastal defensive system in England underwent continual experimentation and modification, reflecting the wishes of the Crown to improve efficiency and to secure the defence of the realm. The system that evolved was to last into the fifteenth century, and it was not until the military requirements of the Henrican period that Hampshire and the Isle of Wight, as well as the rest of southern and eastern coastal counties, saw a major change in defence strategy.

---

[93] Hewitt, *Organization of War*, p. 16; *CCR, 1354–60*, pp. 337–9; *CCR, 1360–64*, pp. 97–8.
[94] Alban, 'English Coastal Defence', p. 72.

8

Coastal Artillery Fortification in England in the Late Fourteenth and Early Fifteenth Centuries

JOHN R. KENYON

THE BUILDING of fortresses along the southern coast of England which was initiated by King Henry VIII from 1539–40 is generally regarded as being the beginning of a 'national defence policy' by the Crown as far as gunpowder fortification is concerned. However, it was at a time when England's fortunes were at a low ebb during the Hundred Years War, marked by the reign of Richard II (1377–99), that we first see castles and town defences built or altered to take ordnance, whether small handguns or heavier artillery.[1] Several of the sites involved were royal castles, or new buildings built by local lords which had been the subjects of licences to crenellate. There were also improvements to defences of important towns such as Canterbury and Southampton, where there was also Crown involvement to some extent.

As we shall see, the main period for the provision of fixed gun positions in walls, towers and gates was the last two decades of the fourteenth century. However, it has been argued that the two small circular openings in the north precinct wall of the original Quarr Abbey in the Isle of Wight are the first datable examples.[2] Their construction has been linked to the issuing of a licence to crenellate in October 1365. The two loops were ideally located to protect the approaches to the abbey's north-west gate.

In the fourteenth century not only were there several raids on the English coast by both the French and the Bretons, but there were also alarums over invasion signals. Southampton had suffered a devastating attack in 1338; the town was particularly vulnerable as its defences only covered the landward approaches, on the north and east. In spite of this raid, the conflict between improving urban fortifications and allowing freedom of movement around the mercantile areas of the town seems to have resulted in little or no immediate improvements to

---

[1] It must be emphasized that this paper is basically a summary of the writer's 'Early artillery fortifications in England and Wales', *Archaeological Journal*, 138 (1981), pp. 205–40. There is also more recent coverage of the subject in A.D. Saunders, *Fortress Britain* (Liphook, 1989), pp. 18–21. I have also taken into account more recent studies on individual monuments such as the West Gate at Canterbury and Portchester Castle.

[2] D.F. Renn, 'The earliest gunports in Britain?', *Archaeological Journal*, 125 (1968), pp. 301–3.

Southampton's defences. However, in 1360 it was proposed that the merchants' houses overlooking the west quay should form the core of a defensive wall by blocking the doors and windows, a proposal that did not meet with universal approval.[3] That the works were undertaken is clear from the surviving architectural evidence, although the improvements may not have been carried out until about 1380. This stretch of the town walls is known as the Arcade, for over and projecting in front of the Norman merchant houses a crenellated wall-walk was constructed (plate XV); between the various arches and inserted through the wall were a series of gunloops of the inverted keyhole type, consisting of a vertical slit with a circular opening at the base for the gun muzzle. Although later alterations to the Arcade may have removed the evidence for some of the loops, it seems likely that there was originally a line of embrasures capable of covering the western esplanade.[4] However, as early guns were not known for quick rate of fire, more traditional means of defence are likely to have played as important a role, if not more so, with archers on the battlements of the Arcade, as well as the use of machicolations of the wall itself, through which missiles could be dropped.

The addition of these gunloops to Southampton's walls in the 1380s was the first in a series of artillery defences undertaken in the period under review. By the end of the 1380s Southampton was a walled town, as opposed to just having defences on two sides. Gunloops can be seen in the north-east sector of the fortifications where arrowslit embrasures were converted to take small cannon, and just to the north of the royal castle on the west side, a castle which received a new tower on its motte in the late 1370s, the Catchcold Tower was constructed in the early 1400s. This tower has three embrasures with keyhole gunloops, as well as a vaulted roof, possibly to take the weight of heavier cannon mounted behind the parapets.

Arguably the most important defensive work to be built in Southampton in the terms of the development of early artillery fortification in England was the God's House Tower, situated in the south-east corner of the walled town. This work, under construction before 1417, served several functions. The tower, and the gallery which connects it to God's House Gate, projects from the line of the town wall so that it could flank the east walls, but its main purpose was to protect the sluices under the tower which controlled the water levels of the town moats. It is also clear from the contemporary documents that the tower was also the residence of the town gunner and the town's arsenal.

The earlier gunloops around Southampton's walls were generally slight in form; the eight at God's House were clearly designed for larger guns, cannon mounted on wooden beds set in wide and deep embrasures. It is known that the tower had several guns and other munitions in 1434, and a few years later, in 1457, we have one of the few records of English medieval artillery fortification going into action.

3 CIM Edward III 3, pp. 154–55, no. 425.
4 D.F. Renn, 'The Southampton Arcade', *Medieval Archaeology*, 8 (1964), pp. 226–8. A detailed survey of Southampton's defences can be found in A.D. Saunders, 'The defences of Southampton in the later Middle Ages', *The Southampton Terrier of 1454*, ed. L.A. Burgess (London, 1976), pp. 20–34.

The town records note the expenses related to the burning of candles which provided light for the gunners who fired their guns at French shipping during a night raid.

Other keyhole gunloops in the Solent area can be seen in the front of the West Gate of Winchester (plate XVI), whilst a series of good examples were incorporated into the rebuilding of the main gate of Carisbrooke Castle on the Isle of Wight. In 1380, at the same time as improvements to Southampton's defences were underway, Henry Yevele, the king's mason, was instructed to proceed to Carisbrooke with masons and carpenters, and in each of the upper storeys of the two round gate towers three gunloops were built, designed for handgunners or for small cannon mounted on trestles set behind the openings (plate XVII). The possibility of a French landing in 1384 led to the hiring of five gunners for the castle who brought their own guns, so it seems that Carisbrooke lacked gunners and ordnance at this time.

Further east along the Solent lay the royal castle of Portchester, the inner ward of which was transformed from 1396 into a series of grand lodgings by the king. Before this, in another part of the inner ward, the Assheton Tower was built, named after Sir Robert Assheton, the constable of the castle from 1376 to 1381. Completed in 1385, the upper part of the tower, overlooking the interior and parts of the exterior of the castle, was equipped with several keyhole gunloops, and it has been argued that with this tower we have the 'earliest attempt in English military architecture at all-round command for gunfire.'[5] Nearby, at Portsmouth, nothing seems to have been done until 1420–22 when the Round Tower, a masonry blockhouse, was built at the harbour mouth, and this still stands, although later alterations have obscured its original layout.

The other main area where there was provision for guns in defences in the late fourteenth and early fifteenth centuries is the south-east, in Kent. The medieval walls of Canterbury were under construction from the 1370s until later in the following century, but much had been completed in the closing decades of the fourteenth century, and one section with four towers can be dated to 1390–96. Many of the towers, both rounded and rectangular, were provided with keyhole gunloops, although some are modern replacements. However, the most significant structure of Canterbury's defensive circuit is the West Gate. Work on the gate began in 1380, and it has been described as the earliest building built specifically for gunpowder artillery defence. The twin-towered gate contains eighteen original inverted keyhole loops, positioned about the towers on all the storeys so that external approaches to the gate were covered.[6]

The arrangement of the loops in the West Gate at Canterbury has been compared to that in the inner gate at Cooling Castle in Kent. The builder of Cooling was John, Lord Cobham, a man who was involved with the supervision of the construction of Canterbury's defences. Cobham received a licence to crenellate his mansion

[5] B. Cunliffe and J. Munby, *Excavations at Portchester Castle. 4. Medieval, the Inner Bailey* (London, 1985), p. 95.
[6] S.S. Frere, S. Stow and P. Bennett, *Excavations on the Roman and Medieval Defences of Canterbury* (Maidstone, 1982), pp. 107–19.

of Cooling early in 1381, and around the inner ward a series of keyhole gunloops can be seen (plate XVIII), whilst in the outer gate four circular gunloops were built (plate XIX); lacking a sighting slit these could not be as effective as the inverted keyhole loops, although this style of gun opening tended to dominate fifteenth-century English military architecture. The interest in Cooling is twofold. First, here we have a private castle or fortified house being equipped with gunloops, whereas the examples above have been communal defences or royal castles. Secondly, the contract for the provision of the Cooling gunloops survives, thus giving us the earliest description of English gunloops. The contract is dated October 1381, and is between Lord Cobham and the mason Thomas Crump, and mentions 'x arketholes de iij peez longour en tout et saunz croys oue le paraile deinz et de hors',[7] that is to say, ten gunloops three feet long, without cross-slits, and with internal and external fittings.

At Dover, a couple of small gunloops still survive in the outer curtain, but post-medieval alterations have no doubt removed several other examples. Another south-east castle, Bodiam in Sussex (licence to crenellate in 1385), also has a few keyhole loops in the main gatehouse. Views vary as to just how serious a piece of fortification Bodiam was meant to be.[8] Although a pair of very small loops were angled to cover the original approach to the castle from the north-west side, Dalyngrigge's castle should be seen more in the light of a grand mansion rather than a serious piece of fortification, even if the licence to crenellate did stipulate that Bodiam was to act as a 'defence of the adjacent country against the king's enemies'.

One final example of early artillery fortification deserves mention, albeit not along the south coast. This is the Cow Tower at Norwich, built as a blockhouse in a bend of the river Wensum, detached from the main circuit of the city's walls. In the city's accounts for the late fourteenth century guns for the defences are mentioned frequently, for example in 1385–86 when there were fears of a French raid. The tower is a three-storeyed brick structure, with a series of small gunloops on the upper two floors, distributed to give maximum field of fire. The loops are not of the keyhole variety favoured elsewhere, but small cross-slits. That they were designed for guns is apparent from the building accounts, for one Robert Snape was paid nine shillings 'for 12 shotholes'. Like the later God's House Tower at Southampton, the Cow Tower was built with living quarters, for there are fireplaces and garderobes at various levels. The Cow Tower is one of the most interesting examples of late medieval military architecture, and recent accounts of it have rescued it from relative obscurity.[9]

---

[7] D. Knoop, G.P. Jones and N.B. Lewis, 'Some building activities of John, Lord Cobham', *Transactions of the Quatuor Coronati Lodge*, 45.1 (1932), p. 52.

[8] D.J. Turner, 'Bodiam, Sussex: true castle or old soldier's dream house?', *England in the Fourteenth Century*, ed. W.M. Ormrod (Woodbridge, 1986), pp. 267–77; C. Taylor, P. Everson and R. Wilson-North, 'Bodiam Castle, Sussex', *Medieval Archaeology*, 34 (1990), pp. 155–7; C. Coulson, 'Some analysis of the Castle of Bodiam, East Sussex', in *Medieval Knighthood*, ed. C. Harper-Bill and R. Harvey (Woodbridge, 1992), pp. 51–107.

[9] A.D. Saunders, 'The Cow Tower, Norwich: an East Anglian bastille?', *Medieval Archaeology*, 29

This summary has concentrated on the main extant examples of late fourteenth- and early fifteenth-century artillery defences. Other works of note tend to date to the later fifteenth century, the majority the result of local enterprise in the West Country in the face of raids on coastal towns such as Dartmouth and Fowey. Other defences were more ephemeral and have long since disappeared, such as the bulwark built at Sandwich in 1451, two storeys high, moated about, and armed with cannon. In the same decade two bulwarks or gun platforms are mentioned in Southampton's archives. Also, one must not forget the building which Andrew Saunders has referred to as 'the missing link'[10] between those structures which mounted tension and torsion artillery such as mangonels and those equipped with fire artillery. This was Edward III's castle of Queenborough in Kent, razed to the ground in the seventeenth century. It was built in the 1360s for coastal defence, was circular in plan, and was armed with both types of artillery.

The artillery works described above are associated with structures still very medieval in design, the gunloops simply replacing arrowslits. The architecture is even such that one would on the whole associate with thirteenth-century castles and town walls. Nevertheless, the works undertaken in the reign of Richard II were the first in a long history of coastal defence with gunpowder artillery that continued into the present century.

(1985), pp. 109–19; B.S. Ayers, R. Smith and M. Tillyard, 'The Cow Tower, Norwich: a detailed survey and partial reinterpretation', *Medieval Archaeology*, 32 (1988), pp. 184–207.
[10] Saunders, *Fortress Britain*, p. 20.

9

Artillery and the Hundred Years War: Myth and Interpretation

ROBERT D. SMITH

THE START of the Hundred Years War corresponds closely with the first records of gunpowder artillery in Europe; the former is usually dated to 1337, the latter occurs in 1326. Although there are still gaps in our knowledge, the progress of the war and its various stages are reasonably well known and to a greater or lesser extent understood. The same however cannot be said for the first 100, or for that matter the first 200, years of the history of artillery. The reasons for this include not only the lack of detailed contemporary information about artillery but, equally important, the inadequacy of modern research. The former is due to several causes, not least the use of words and phrases which are open to considerable interpretation. This lack of clarity is however compounded by the latter problem, that of the paucity of much modern research. This was not always the case. In the nineteenth and early twentieth centuries, authors such as Napoléon and Favé, Brackenbury and Tout laid the foundations for future work by bringing to light and publishing many of the documentary references and sources.[1]

Since these early pioneers, however, there has been much less emphasis on new work from primary sources or from surviving examples and later researchers have too often relied on secondary sources, frequently including inaccurate embellishments in their work and too often there has been no critical assessment of previous work. This has led to a situation where unfounded assumptions and statements

Acknowledgments. I must thank several colleagues with whom I have discussed many of the issues raised in this article and who have helped me to develop and refine my ideas, notably Sarah Barter Bailey and Ruth R. Brown. Geoffrey Parnell, Howard Blackmore and Nicholas Hall commented on drafts of this paper. Michelle Brown of the British Library assisted in the dating of the lettering on the Swedish gun. Lastly, and by no means least, I must thank Guy Wilson, Master of the Armouries, and the Trustees of the Royal Armouries who have continued their support of this work.

[1] Napoléon-Louis Bonaparte, *Études sur le passé et l'avenir de l'artillerie*, 1 (Paris, 1846); Louis-Napoléon Bonaparte, *Études sur le passé et l'avenir de l'artillerie*, 2 (Paris, 1851); Favé, *Études sur le passé et l'avenir de l'artillerie*, 3 (Paris, 1862); Favé, *Études sur le passé et l'avenir de l'artillerie*, 4 (Paris, 1853); Favé, *Études sur le passé et l'avenir de l'artillerie*, 5 (Paris, 1871); Favé, *Études sur le passé et l'avenir de l'artillerie*, 6 (Paris, 1871); H. Brackenbury, 'Ancient Cannon in Europe. Part 1', *Minutes of the Proceedings of the Royal Artillery Institution*, 5 (1865), pp. 287–308; and 'Ancient Cannon in Europe. Part 2', 6 (1866), pp. 1–37; T.F. Tout, 'Firearms in England in the Fourteenth Century', EHR, 26 (1911), pp. 666–702.

about early artillery, put forward by one writer, have become the material from which later authors have worked. There has also often been a tendency for authors to write on early artillery from a knowledge of later periods, using data from one to justify arguments about another. In addition insufficient work has been done on artillery as a whole and the published material is often piecemeal and fragmentary. There is, of course, good published material but there is much that is less reliable and it is difficult to separate the wheat from the chaff. It is true to say that there has been no integrated study of the various aspects of the subject and there is no reliable modern synthesis.[2]

Thus while the study of warfare and military history has undergone a sea change over the last two decades, the material that these military historians have to use for their study of the impact of artillery is woefully out of date. For example recent work has suggested that some types of wrought-iron swivel gun, which have in the past been ascribed to the fifteenth century, should be dated to the late sixteenth and seventeenth centuries.[3] And this is not an isolated example. Until the recovery of wrought-iron guns from the gun decks of the *Mary Rose* it was commonly stated that wrought-iron ordnance was obsolete by the beginning of the sixteenth century.[4] More recent work indicates that some types of wrought-iron guns were being used throughout the sixteenth century and that some were still in use until well into the seventeenth century.[5] This leads to the realisation that wrought-iron guns were in use for over 300 years, bringing into question one of the most commonly stated beliefs about early artillery, that it was poor and ineffective. In a similar vein there is a frequently stated opinion that breech loading, using a separate powder chamber, was not efficient and led to problems of both obturation and safety. Again new evidence is making clear that breech loading was in use for about two hundred years, until well into the seventeenth century, so that it is clear that in some circumstances it was highly effective and that neither obturation nor safety were compromised by this method of loading.[6]

This essay is not then, as might be expected, about the use of artillery in the Hundred Years War. Instead it will attempt, by outlining the current state of our knowledge of artillery, from its beginnings in the fourteenth century to the middle

---

[2] Among the more modern works which are reliable are P. Contamine, *War in the Middle Ages*, translated by M.C.E. Jones (Oxford, 1984); and, for the early fifteenth century, M.G.A. Vale, 'New Techniques and Old Ideals: The Impact of Artillery on War and Chivalry at the End of the Hundred Years War', in *War, Literature, and Politics in the Late Middle Ages*, ed. C.T. Allmand (Liverpool, 1976), pp. 57–72.

[3] R.D. Smith, 'Wrought-iron Swivel Guns', in *Archaeology of Ships of War*, ed. M. Bound, forthcoming. This article argues that many of the types of wrought-iron swivel gun, previously assumed to be fifteenth century on little or no evidence, are probably products of the sixteenth and seventeenth centuries.

[4] M. Rule, *The Mary Rose*, revised second edition (Leicester, 1983), pp. 149–83. It is also interesting to note that even after the discoveries of the *Mary Rose* there has been a reluctance to accept the idea that wrought-iron guns had any importance in the mid-sixteenth century.

[5] R.D. Smith, 'Port Pieces: The Use of Wrought-iron Guns in the Sixteenth Century', *Journal of the Ordnance Society*, 5 (1993), pp. 1–10; Smith, 'Wrought-iron Swivel Guns'.

[6] Smith, 'Port Pieces'; Smith, 'Wrought-iron Swivel Guns'.

of the fifteenth, to show that our current understanding and much of the published work on early artillery is founded on poor or piecemeal evidence or on inaccurate assumptions. In summary it will try to show that the amount of reliable information is in no way equal to the task of ascertaining the actual nature, role and effectiveness of artillery in this period.

The fourteenth century

Artillery and gunpowder were introduced into the West some time in the thirteenth or early fourteenth century. It is likely that knowledge about gunpowder came from the East, probably from China.[7] The earliest documentary evidence in Europe is a reference to guns in a decree issued by the Council of Florence in 1326, though the very beginnings of gunpowder artillery must surely be earlier. The earliest pictorial evidence is from a manuscript written for Edward III by Walter de Milemete in 1327. As far as I am aware this is the only known picture before the end of the fourteenth century.[8]

Up until the mid-fourteenth century references are rare, probably a consequence not only of the scarcity of guns at this period, but also of the survival of manuscript sources of this date. After about 1350 however the mention of guns in documents becomes more common. What these early guns looked like is still unclear. Brackenbury deduces from the accounts and inventories available that they were on the whole small. His reasons are based on the price of guns and the supply of powder and projectiles. For example in 1356 the town of Laon bought 42 cannon and 1350 'garros', a form of arrow fired from cannon at this period, for 115 *écus*. Later in the account 'garros' cost 2.25 *écus* per hundred which means that the 42 cannon cost approximately 85 *écus* or about 2 *écus* each. When these guns were taken out of the town and proofed, the amount of powder used was in the region of 10–11 pounds or about 4 ozs each.[9] Brackenbury cites more examples to support this view, that guns at this period were small, and his arguments are persuasive. In fact he is one of the few authors who uses the documentary evidence in a systematic and thorough manner and one which later writers have singularly failed to follow.

Professor T.F. Tout, working on the Wardrobe accounts, provides further information for the same period and his work to a large extent complements and expands on that done by Brackenbury. Again his work is of an extremely high standard and his analysis of the state of artillery in England is thorough and systematic. He too comes to the conclusion that on the whole artillery of this period was small. He prints an account of 1382–8 in which the sizes of guns are stated:

[7] J. Needham, *Science and Civilisation in China*, Volume 5, part 7, *Military technology: The gunpowder epic* (Cambridge, 1986); A.Y. al-Hassan and D.R. Hill, *Islamic technology. An illustrated history* (Cambridge, 1986).

[8] For a very good brief summary of the very beginnings of artillery as well as some of the myths and legends which have grown up around it see the excellent introduction to *Pollard's History of Firearms*, ed. C. Blair (Feltham, 1983), pp. 25–32.

[9] Brackenbury, 'Ancient Cannon in Europe. Part 2', pp. 2–3.

5 cannon weighing 318 lb each
47 cannon weighing 380 lb each
1 large cannon weighing 665 lb.[10]

In this period both iron and 'copper' are referred to, the latter probably being a copper alloy of some kind, either bronze or brass. The normal projectile in this early period of the development of artillery was either a form of arrow, a 'garro', or a stone shot. The use of stone shot has also been the subject of much conjecture. Commonly it is reported that they were difficult to make, expensive and quickly superseded by cast-iron shot when that became readily available. However stone shot is listed in ships inventories till the end of the sixteenth century, long after iron shot became cheap and common place, and periers, guns firing stone shot, are still listed in the seventeenth century. What is clear is that stone shot was seen to have a role to play in the use of artillery.[11]

Apart from what can be deduced from these sources the actual form of guns is impossible to ascertain. The complete lack of surviving early ordnance has led to the Milemete illustration, of 1327, being frequently used as the conjectured model for artillery in this early period. However it must be stressed that this is the only pictorial evidence we have for almost the entire fourteenth century. This dearth of evidence is reflected in the absence of any surviving artillery which can be firmly dated to the fourteenth century. There are one, or possibly two, possible exceptions. The first is a gun in the collection of the National Museum in Stockholm (plate XX). In form it is close to the Milemete illustration and from that is usually dated to the early to mid-fourteenth century. It must be stressed however that it does not come from any dated or dateable context. Unless further evidence is forthcoming its dating must, therefore, be tentative and to draw any firm conclusions about the nature of artillery in the fourteenth century from this slender evidence can only invite problems. The gun itself is made of bronze, 30.5 cm (12 inches) long with a pronounced vase-like form. A second small bronze piece, also found in Sweden, is usually dated to the fourteenth century (plate XXI). This piece is unusual in that it is engraved with an inscription and recent analysis of the script suggests that it dates to the last quarter of the fourteenth or the beginning of the fifteenth century.[12]

At this period it is not only the evidence of the guns themselves which is extremely scarce, we do not know whether the guns referred to were effective or not, how they were mounted or even how they were used – in fact we know very little. It was possibly a period of experimentation – it was important that artillery was owned and used, often possibly for reasons of prestige – but that it was not effective. It is also possible to surmise that it had little impact because warfare and battle tactics were still rooted in the past and there was no place for this new

[10] Tout, 'Firearms in England', pp. 697–8. It is salutary to state that since the work of Brackenbury and Tout, and for that matter of Napoléon and Favé, there has been so little work of a similar standard, combining both original sources with a thorough analysis.
[11] The use and effectiveness of stone shot has not been investigated to any depth and the subject needs to be addressed in more detail.
[12] The inscription is difficult to read in full but includes an invocation to the Virgin. Pers. comm., Michelle Brown, Curator of Manuscripts, the British Library.

weapon, except for frightening horses or possibly for sieges. Even here, of course, gunpowder artillery did not supplant the traditional artillery of mangonel and trebuchet, and both were used, often side by side, well into the fifteenth century. However both of these suggestions must remain as just that until there is more reliable information from this period.

From the last quarter of the fourteenth century the number of references to guns become both more numerous and more informative. It is clear that guns were increasing in size; for example almost a ton of iron was used in the making of a cannon in 1375 which was then used at the siege of St Sauveur le Vicomte.[13] However it is not clear whether this was a sudden increase or whether this was merely the result of a more gradual process of development. The account of the making of this gun lists in some detail its manufacture and its wooden mounting. The barrel itself was made from both iron and steel though what the steel was used for is not specified. It is also clear that it was made from staves and hoops though whether it was muzzle loading or had a separate chamber is not mentioned.[14] Included in this account are the purchases of wood for the bed and mounting of the gun though exactly how these fitted together and how the gun was mounted is not stated and is unclear. What is certain is that it was mounted on a wooden bed and that this was probably supported on a wooden frame of some kind, probably for elevation.

As stated above cannon were made from either wrought iron or from a copper alloy. The latter was poured in the molten state into a prepared mould, much as bell casting had been practised for some considerable time. The method of construction of wrought-iron guns has, however, been an area where there has been a great deal of conjecture and much mis-information. Basically the cannon barrel was made from long strips of iron, the staves, bound together with iron hoops. The common assumption has been that the staves from which the barrel was made were welded together to form a tube over which the hoops were assembled in a variety of ways and/or layers. Recent work has shown conclusively that this was not so. The staves were never welded together but were made to fit closely and then merely butted together edge to edge and were not welded. Over this was assembled a single layer of hoops.[15]

Finally an important, and as yet largely untouched, sources of information about artillery in this period are the accounts of the dukes of Burgundy. Partly transcribed

---

[13] Brackenbury, 'Ancient Cannon in Europe. Part 2', pp. 8–9. The full account of the making of this piece is printed in Napoléon, *Études sur le passé et l'avenir de l'artillerie*, 4, Appendix 5, pp. xviii–xxxvi.

[14] A common assumption has always been that muzzle loading superseded breech loading but interestingly most of the early references to artillery do not mention separate powder chambers and it might be supposed that most of the earlier guns were not breech loaders but were formed in one piece and loaded from the muzzle. Later accounts, from the fifteenth century, however, frequently refer to chambers implying that the pieces were breech loading. Whether this was a real change or not must remain, until further work is done, conjecture.

[15] For more information see: R.D. Smith and R.R. Brown, *Mons Meg and her Sisters* (London, 1989); R.D. Smith, 'Construction of Wrought-iron Guns' in *Manufacture and Technology of Ordnance*, ed. R.D. Smith, forthcoming.

and published by Joseph Garnier in the late nineteenth century they offer a much fuller picture of artillery in the late fourteenth and fifteenth centuries.[16] These accounts, which have rarely been used by modern researchers, reinforce the picture that larger guns were being made in the last quarter of the thirteenth century. In 1376–7, for example, five guns are listed which fired shot ranging from 50 to 130 lb. Again these accounts make it clear that the finished guns were mounted on wooden beds and it is also interesting to note that for many of the larger guns a transport carriage and an 'engine' are also specified, the former to move the gun from place to place, the latter to lift and move it into position.[17]

Apart from the one possible surviving example, mentioned above, guns of this period do not exist or, if they do, cannot be recognised due to our almost complete lack of information. Manuscript illustrations of this period are also rare. The only firmly dated picture shows a small gun mounted on a wooden bed.[18]

The fifteenth century

From about 1400 there is an increasing amount of documentary evidence both about artillery in general and on its use. Guns become far more common and purchases of gunpowder, a good indication of the use of cannon, rise dramatically.[19] However it is still difficult to be sure exactly what type of artillery was being referred to.

A common modern assumption about artillery for this period is that it developed along two lines: smaller pieces, hand guns, and huge siege artillery. The Burgundian accounts do however include a whole range of sizes of artillery from hand guns through to pieces of quite enormous size and weight. For example:

> 30 September 1413, 2 iron cannon, one throwing stones of 17 and the other 11 pounds.
> 31 December 1412, a great bombard throwing stone of 84 pounds.[20]

In addition between about 1410 and 1440, there are numerous references to cannons which fired stone shot of between 5 and 20 lbs. Similarly an important source for this period, Christine de Pisan, writing in 1410, details the guns needed to attack a fortress:

> Item 4 great guns one called Garyte, another Rose, another Senecque, and another Maye. The first casting about 500 pounds weight, the second casting

---

[16] J. Garnier, *L'artillerie des Ducs de Bourgogne d'après les documents conservés aux archives de la Cote-d'Or* (Paris, 1895). These accounts contain a wealth of detail on artillery from the 1370s up to the late fifteenth century.

[17] Garnier, *L'artillerie*, p. 9.

[18] For illustrations from the turn of the fifteenth century see, A.V.B. Norman, 'Notes on some Early Representations of Guns and on Ribaudekins', *Journal of the Arms and Armour Society*, 8, 3 (1975), pp. 234–7.

[19] For example see Contamine, *War in the Middle Ages*, p. 148.

[20] Garnier, *L'artillerie*, p. 41.

about 400, and the other 2 about 200 or more. Item another gun called Montfort casting 300 pounds weight. . . . Item a brass gun called Artycke casting 100 pound weight. Item 20 other small guns casting stone pellets.[21]

Evidently a range of artillery was being produced and used though exactly what form this took and how it developed is still not known in any detail. There are no contemporary descriptions of artillery and few illustrations. Throughout the first half of the fifteenth century stone cannon balls were the norm though cast-iron shot was introduced at some time in the early part of the century. There are also references to lead shot, 'plombee'. Guns were still being made from both copper alloy and from wrought iron. However there are occasional references to cast iron. For example the accounts of the dukes of Burgundy in 1417 include 'a cast-iron cannon, throwing stone weighing about 20 lbs'.[22] The technology for producing cast iron was in its infancy at this period and the use of cast iron for artillery is an important milestone in the history of iron making.[23]

It is clear that artillery was becoming, or had in fact become, by this period, effective, at least for sieges, as there are contemporary accounts which state that artillery played a decisive role. This is not to say, of course, that the possession and use of artillery automatically resulted in victory. It is also worth noting that even up to the middle of the century the traditional siege engines, trebuchets and mangonels, were still being used. The effectiveness of artillery can also be measured by the increased amount of activity on fortifications. At first this was only to modify or supplement existing fortifications but by the middle of the century the impact of artillery had been fully realised and fortifications were being planned to take its considerable power into account.[24]

[21] C. de Pisan, *The Book of Faytes of Armes and of Chyvalrye*, trans. by W. Caxton (London, 1932), p. 154.

[22] Garnier, *L'artillerie*, p. 40.

[23] Early iron production was based on the technique of producing wrought iron from the ore in the solid state, the bloomery process. At some stage, probably at the beginning of the fifteenth century the process was discovered whereby the iron was produced in the molten state, as cast iron, which could be used directly or further refined to make wrought iron. An important consequence of this change was a dramatic rise in the quantities of iron that could be produced. There are considerable problems with the use of this material to make cannon and, although it is clear from documentary sources that cast-iron cannon were being made, they were rare. It was not until the mid-sixteenth century that the process was finally perfected and cast-iron guns made in any quantity.

[24] J.R. Hale, 'The Early Development of the Bastion: An Italian Chronology c.1450–c.1534', in J.R. Hale, *Renaissance War Studies* (London, 1983). It is perhaps worth pointing out that the developments in the design of fortifications which led to the angled bastion and the like appear to date from the mid-fifteenth century onwards. If gunpowder siege artillery was so effective against the traditional castle wall in the period 1400–1450 why did it take so long to influence their design? This problem may be linked to the use of castles and walls as offensive positions. Many of the castles and town walls of the fifteenth century are only pierced with relatively small gun loops suitable only for hand guns and seem to have no provision for larger artillery. However it is also clear that many towns had large stores of artillery. This lag in response to the threat of artillery could, of course, have been due to many factors – possibly the introduction of cast-iron shot, or some other change which is not apparent from our current state of knowledge – which made artillery even more effective.

Taken as a whole the first half of the fifteenth century would appear to be a period of little change in the form of artillery from the end of the fourteenth century, but one of its increasing use and, possibly, effectiveness (though the latter could be merely the result of greater use). Large siege guns were being widely used and smaller pieces were certainly being made. However it is interesting to note that it was not until the middle of the century that its impact was sufficient that new fortifications were being planned to take artillery into account. The major new developments in artillery all appear to date from the period after the end of the Hundred Years War – the use of trunnions, more mobile carriages and longer, lighter guns firing iron shot.

Surviving guns

There are no surviving pieces of artillery bearing dates for the first half of the fifteenth century, and only one piece which can be securely dated. However there are a number of pieces which can be approximately dated and these offer more scope in our understanding of the development of artillery.

The first is a large bronze gun now in the artillery collection in Turin (plate XXII). This can be compared to a gun which has not survived but which was preserved in Brunswick in Germany and which was drawn in the eighteenth century (plate XXXIII). This piece was dated 1411 and appears also to have been cast from bronze. The similarities between the two are startling, both in overall form and in details, such as the raised bands along its length and the lugs on its sides. It seems reasonable then to date this piece to the beginning of the fifteenth century. It is 420 cm (13 feet 9 inches) long with a bore of 69 cm (27 inches) and would have fired a ball of approximately 350 kg (770 lb), a figure which, though extremely large, is not completely out of the question as guns of this size are mentioned in contemporary sources.

The earliest firmly dated gun, Mons Meg, is made of iron and dates from 1449, over a hundred years after the first mention of guns. The piece itself is not dated but the accounts for its manufacture and transport to Scotland have been found.[25] Mons Meg is, like the bronze gun above, a muzzle loader, 404 cm long (13 feet 3 inches) with a bore of 50 cm (19.5 inches) which would fire a stone ball of about 150 kg (330 lb). By their close resemblance to Mons Meg two other large pieces of ordnance have also been dated to the mid-fifteenth century, *Dulle Griet* in Ghent and a piece in the Historical Museum in Basle.[26]

It is worth saying that the earliest dated bronze gun is Turkish, made in two pieces and dated 1464 and now in the collection of the Royal Armouries. The earliest dated western European gun, now in the Historical Museum in Basle, is

---

[25] C. Gaier, 'The Origins of Mons Meg', *Journal of the Arms and Armour Society*, 5, 12 (1967), pp. 425–31.
[26] Smith and Brown, *Mons Meg and her Sisters*, pp. 46–50.

dated 1474. This piece is the earliest known cannon to have trunnions. Thereafter the number of dated or dateable bronze guns increases quite considerably.[27]

This brief summary is intended to show that the amount of direct dating evidence for guns and information about the forms and types of guns up to the middle of the fifteenth century is very slim and that even the available information must be used with care. Extreme caution must be used when trying to identify or date a wrought-iron gun as so little is known. Many attempts in the past have, it seems to me, relied on very scanty evidence, often of a circumstantial nature. For example it is common to find that the a gun is dated to a battle which took place near to where it was found. Several guns in the Musée de l'Armée were said to have been used in the siege of Meaux, outside Paris. On further investigation the association dates from the nineteenth century when the guns were found in the town. Similarly two large guns at Mont St Michel are traditionally associated with the siege of the island by the English in the 1420s. Though it is possible that this statement is true there is no evidence to back it up.

Conclusions

This short essay has attempted to indicate the shortcomings in our understanding of the early history of artillery, shortcomings which are due both to the dearth of contemporary information as well as to the interpretation of what little information there is. An attempt has also been made to show that much of the published information about this early period is based on assumptions which are now either being shown to be wrong or are being called into question. It is worth perhaps repeating an earlier comment that it is now becoming clear that wrought-iron artillery was in use for a much longer period than hitherto supposed, leading to the conclusion that it must have been both effective and relatively safe in use.

What this essay has also tried to show is that our current knowledge of this early period of artillery is not up to the task of answering the detailed questions posed by military historians, for example its form, size, range, and effectiveness. Thus while the study of warfare and military history has taken great strides over the last two decades our knowledge of artillery has not kept pace and is now, in many areas, woefully inadequate.

Let us conclude by outlining how it may be possible to build up a more accurate picture of the early development of artillery. First there is a real need for more work on the available documentary sources. A great deal of these have been transcribed and published but there has been little attempt to bring them together and form an integrated synthesis. There is then a need to relate this source material to actual surviving examples. By so doing it might enable us to try to work out what these early guns were like. As already stated there are very few guns which can be dated to this early period with any certainty. It is likely, however, that some

[27] This dearth of early bronze guns can probably be attributed to two factors. The first is that earlier guns may survive but have not been recognised. The second is that bronze has always been a valuable material and old cannon can be easily melted down and recycled into new.

do survive and by relating the documentary evidence to actual examples it may be possible to identify them. Next we need to look at the material coming from wreck sites. Over the last 10 years more and more information is appearing in excavation reports of wrecks and this is adding to our knowledge. This source is possibly one of the most promising. It has already given us much information; we now know, for example, that wrought-iron guns survived for very much longer than previously thought and that they were being carried as part of the complement of ships well into the seventeenth century, and it from the nautical archaeologist that answers to some of the more intractable problems might come. Finally there is a real need for an integration of material from such areas as fortifications, warfare and tactics. It is only by combining these together that we will ever be able to make sense out of what is probably one of the most misunderstood and yet significant developments of the early modern period.

10

The Longbow

ROBERT HARDY

MY SUBJECT IS the longbow, the weapon itself. Without some understanding of its nature, its development, its deployment in battle, its capabilities and limitations, there must be a sizeable gap in our understanding of the conflicts of the long struggle between France and England during the fourteenth and fifteenth centuries. Study of the weapon must involve some study of the archer, and, so far as possible, the tactics of battle.

Briefly a word as to my qualifications for taking some part in this debate. I am a longbow archer of many years' experience, and in 1976 published a book, *Longbow*, which was the result of ten years' practical and historical research at a time when not a great deal was undertaken in that field. I am currently working with Dr Matthew Strickland of Cambridge and Glasgow Universities on a new and more closely focused book on the great war bow between Hastings and the end of Henry VIII's reign. I am a Trustee of the Royal Armouries at H.M. Tower of London, a Trustee and Consultant to the Mary Rose Trust in charge of conservation and research connected with the large finds of military archery equipment brought up from Henry VIII's ship, sunk during battle with the French fleet in the Solent in 1545, and I am at present also serving on the Battlefields Panel set up by English Heritage in 1993.

First let us look at the man himself – the archer of the Hundred Years War. After Crécy, the great shocks the French had to face were that their chivalry could be shot down, and that crossbows were outranged by longbows. The crossbow of the time, with wooden or composite limbs, was probably not capable of much more than 200 yards. The Genoese could have had the 6,000 that some chroniclers attribute to them,[1] and still the battle would have been no different.

When two such armies met again ten years later at Poitiers the crossbows on the French side appear to have done considerable damage,[2] but were certainly not decisive. They would remain in military use, and the invention of the steel bow would greatly improve their range and penetration, and turn them into a siege weapon or a marksman's bow of high value. In 1901 a 400-year-old crossbow was

---

[1] For example, Giovanni Villani (d.1348). See A.H. Burne, *The Crécy War* (London, 1955), p. 175.
[2] *Chronicon Galfridi Le Baker de Swynebroke*, ed. E.M. Thompson (Oxford, 1889), p. 151, cited in Burne, *Crécy War*, p. 315.

shot by Sir Ralph Payne-Gallwey across the Menai Straits, reaching nearly 450 yards.[3] By the time of Agincourt there is no doubt that crossbows could reach something like 400 yards, and outrange longbows, but with their increase in power came complications in loading, and the hopeless inequality of shooting speed was increased. Tests today, as well as the evidence of history, suggest that a crossbow could only be spanned and shot twice in a minute, while a skilled longbowman can and no doubt could loose up to 20 aimed arrows in the same time.

There is a footnote worth adding to the question of military archery for the armies of the late middle ages. By the time the rifle had reached a speed of fire that equalled the speed of shooting of longbowmen nearly 600 years earlier, most British riflemen carried 150 rounds each in their belts and pouches. There would be a further 100 rounds per man in the ammunition trains for each regiment, another 50 rounds each in Brigade ammunition columns, 50 more in Division columns, and a further 200 each in the base ammunition park and in reserve columns. The total for an infantry rifleman was thus 550 rounds. The long history of the handgun, which replaced the bow, shows that as the weapon became more efficient and capable of faster fire so the number of rounds provided for each soldier increased. In 1338 the King's 'artiller' was Nicholas Corand, who was ordered at one time to buy 1,000 bows and 4,000 sheaves of arrows, to make what he could not buy, and despatch them with all haste to John de Flete, keeper of the King's armour.[4] The proportion of arrows to bows in this instance is either 96 to 1 or 120 to 1 depending upon whether the sheaf in 1338 contained 24 or 30 arrows each. Here anyway is an indication that an archer on campaign could count on 100 shafts, more or less, presumably replenished as often as necessary and possible. I find it impossible to believe that commanders of the calibre of Edward III and Henry V, and the rest, wasted the enormous potential of their infantry weapon by failing to supply their archers with enough arrows. What those archers achieved proves that they had, apart from exceptional instances, enough arrows.

In the wake of the victories at Crécy and Nevilles Cross, Edward III had no great difficulty in raising men and money for his new army to besiege Calais and at the same time hold off any French attempts to attack him or relieve the town. A roll of his forces at Calais exists, based upon transcripts from the now lost Wardrobe accounts of William Wetwang. This roll suggests that in 1347 Edward had cavalry numbering 5,340 and foot totalling 26,963. 20,076 were archers, 4,025 of them mounted.[5] That vast host of 32,303 men must have been the largest English army ever to take the field until that time, if the figures are trustworthy.

Within the year the Black Death had begun to ravage Europe and the British Isles, killing perhaps a third of the population before it died out, and it was a long

---

3 R.W.F. Payne-Gallwey, *The Crossbow* (London, 1903, 1907), chapter 5.

4 *CPR, 1338 40*, pp. 124–5.

5 G. Wrottesley, *Crécy and Calais* (London, 1898), pp. 191–204. For a recent discussion of the reliability of the Calais roll, see A. Ayton, 'The English Army and the Normandy Campaign of 1346', in *England and Normandy in the Middle Ages*, ed. D.R. Bates and A.E. Curry (London, 1994), pp. 263–8.

time before such armies could be equalled again. But whatever the size of the armies, from now the proportion of longbowmen in them was always as high as could be achieved. Proportions of 3,4,5 to 1 were common and sometimes reached as high as 20 to 1. To quite a substantial degree the archer could be seen as replacing the man-at-arms.

The so-called 'Agincourt roll', and another later transcript which is incomplete, number but do not often name archers. Taken together, the Harleian manuscript and the College of Arms roll name about 1,000 men-at-arms and list nearly 3,000 archers. That does not account for the whole army, which totalled between 5,700 and 6,000, 1,000 being men-at-arms and the rest archers.[6] One example gives the general style of the roll:

'Sir Henry Huse with his retinue': then follow 22 named men-at-arms followed by 'lances xvij . . . archers lv'.

Further search brings to light names that are shown nowhere in such published lists. For instance, there exists a complete roll of the archers enlisted for the Agincourt campaign from the lordship of Brecknock.[7] There are 159 named, and resounding some of their names are: Mereduth ap Trahan ap Jouan Vachan (nowadays probably Meredith Trahern, or John Vaughan) and Llewellyn ap Llewellyn ap Rosser. There is Jeuan Ferour 'cum equo cum Watkin Lloyd'; did Jeuan come with his horse *and* with Watkin? Did Watkin come as groom with the horse? However he came, he is not lightly dismissed as 'i archer'. There are simpler names, less proud, or less certain of their ancestry, or perhaps belonging to those less able to explain to the roll-writers: Yanthlos, Res Weynh and David Coch.

From records of wage and other payments, letters of protection, and grants of pardon and reward, over 1,000 names can be listed of those who fought with the Black Prince at Poitiers in 1356. The list is mainly of those who served in the Prince's own company, and so represents only a proportion of a far larger total. A lifetime's search could possibly put together something approaching the full lists of those who fought with Edward III and his son, and for Henry V and his brothers, in their long attempt to win the crown of France.

In December 1355, there was an archer named William Jauderel serving in the Black Prince's army who was given a special pass to return home, signed by the Prince himself: 'Know all that we, the Prince of Wales, have given leave on the day of the date of this instrument, to William Jauderel, one of our archers, to go to England. In witness of this we have caused our seal to be placed on this bill. Given at Bordeaux 16th of December, in the year of grace 1355'. This William Jauderel, a descendant of Peter Jauderel who saw service with Edward I, was almost certainly a member of the Black Prince's elite guard of archers. He bore his own coat of arms; so do his descendants to this day, and they still possess the 'pass', which is

---

6   BL, Harleian Ms 782; College of Arms Ms M1. Several unpublished muster rolls and other material concerning the Agincourt campaign in PRO, E101 (Accounts Various) are catalogued in *PRO Lists and Indexes No. XXXV* (London, 1912).

7   PRO, E101/46/20, 26 June 1415.

written not on parchment but paper, a rare luxury at the time. The Jauderels came originally from Yeardsley in Derbyshire. Jodrell Bank in Cheshire came into the family, taking its name from them, at a later date. William the archer went back to France a few months after the pass was issued, and having possibly fought at Poitiers, on his return to England in 1356 was rewarded with 'two oak trees' from the royal forest at Macclesfield to repair his house at Whaley Bridge in Derbyshire,[8] where the name Jodrell is still to be found and the family blazon can be seen at the 'Jodrell Arms'.

Plainly for a long time some archers had enjoyed a position of privilege above their fellow bowmen, which helps to explain the curious fact that, while the greater part of the archer force was simply and economically equipped, there survive many contemporary illustrations of archers in half-armour of even full armour, unlike their rustic colleagues in leather jacks and querbole helmets (plates XXIV–V).

John Jauderel, William's brother, fought at Poitiers and, with other archers, was rewarded by the Prince after the battle for capturing a fine salt container in the shape of a silver ship which belonged to the French king.[9] The Prince also gave rights of pasture and turf-cutting as well as timber to his archers.[10] A company of bowmen was raised at Llantrisant, in south Wales, from among the hereditary burgesses and inhabitants there, to go to France with Edward, Prince of Wales as part of the archer corps of the royal army.[11] Those who went became known as the Black Army of Llantrisant, and today their lineal descendants, wherever they may be, can apply to be enrolled as freemen. If their claim is justified they will be admitted to a company which embodies a true and living memorial to the longbowmen of the fourteenth and fifteenth centuries.

In March 1338 French ships burned Portsmouth; in October Southampton was attacked; in March 1339 Harwich was burned; and throughout that summer the whole south coast came in for attacks of varying force and severity. Folkestone, Dover, Sandwich, Rye, Hastings, Portsmouth again, and Plymouth suffered. The following year the Isle of Wight was attacked, in spite of Edward's victory at Sluys. The first need was for the muster and array of men for the defence of the realm. In February 1339 the order of array for Hampshire demanded that the county provide 30 men-at-arms (fully armoured, equipped and mounted men), 120 armed men and 200 archers.[12] Other counties had to offer similar forces. In general archers were not to be taken for service abroad from the maritime counties, which were being methodically put in a posture of defence, while the royal army was preparing to attack the enemy across the Channel.

The fourteenth century, in this situation of hostility between France and England, was witnessing the emergence of a kind of national consciousness in

---

8 *Register of the Black Prince*, 3 vols (London, 1930–33), 3, pp. 264–5.
9 Ibid., p. 264.
10 For example, ibid., pp. 238, 239.
11 Records of the Company of Bowmen, Llantrisant.
12 T. Rymer, *Foedera, conventiones, literae et cujuscunque generis acta publica* (Record Commission edition, London, 1816–69), II, ii, p. 1071.

England, certainly an anti-French feeling in general, in which many Welshmen joined. It has been said that those who fought with the two Edwards at Crécy comprised an army that was part Norman, part Saxon, Angevin and Celtic, but which in some way thought of itself as the army of England.[13] Care and effort were taken to explain to people in general, often from the pulpit, often in the market place, what was happening, how the war was going, why the French were liable to invade, and why England must go to war in France.[14]

The war allowed the king to take advantage of the desires of men outlawed for many sorts of crime to regain freedom within the law. In 1339 and 1340, 850 charters of pardon were granted to men who had served as soldiers or sailors. In the year of Crécy several hundred more were granted, both for service in Scotland and in France.[15] It would be foolish to over-emphasize the outlaw element in the armies of the period but from two to twelve per cent of those who fought for England were conditionally pardoned outlaws, some three quarters of whom were likely to have been guilty of manslaughter or murder.[16]

Given the great victory of Crécy, the capture of Calais, the successes in arms of the English in Gascony and the defeat of the Scots at Nevilles Cross (plate XXVI), any English commander could count on a fervent rush of recruits ready to seek fortune and the comradeship of arms on a full tide of national feeling. The capture of a Frenchman of importance could carry a ransom that amounted to a fortune for the soldier responsible. There was every kind of rich finery, weapons, furs, gold and silver, and wine in abundance to be had after a battle or the taking of a town.

The gradual changes in methods of recruitment to the English armies during the early part of the fourteenth century and the whole period under review will be familiar, but it is worth noticing some of the experiences and duties of commissioners of array: in 1341, for instance, they issued a writ to recruit for service 160 archers from Northampton and Rutland. In this case Rutland was charged with raising 40 archers, but the county protested that Northamptonshire contained 26 hundreds, 'whereof the smallest is larger than the whole of Rutland' and an adjustment was made.[17] The number raised often fell short of the number projected, but the arrayers did their best to choose, test for skills the archers should have acquired or maintained at the local butts, and array 'les meillors et plus suffisantz, les plus forcibles et plus vigerous archers',[18] to clothe, equip, and where necessary mount them, to pay them, and send them with a leader to a collecting place, or hold them ready for departure. The feeble were to be avoided and the 'ailing and weakly' were sent home from the ports of embarkation, even from abroad. Men could buy out their services for 'reasonable fines', but, when the

---

[13] H.J. Hewitt, *The Organization of War under Edward III, 1338-62* (Manchester, 1966), chapter 7.
[14] See, for instance, *CCR, 1339-41*, p. 636.
[15] *CPR, 1338-40; 1345-48*, passim; *1354-57*, p. 478, *1358-61*, pp. 5-16.
[16] Hewitt, *Organization of War*, p. 30.
[17] *CCR, 1341-43*, p. 190.
[18] PRO, C76/22 m.21, cited in Hewitt, *Organization of War*, p. 37.

feeling for success was high, the proportion that did so was small. Exemption could be granted where there was need.

It was usual for writs to contain some mention of clothing, 'gowns', 'hoods', 'one suit' apiece and so on, which we can assume was uniform of a kind, though details of such dress are limited. Archers raised in Cheshire and Flint were to be provided with woollen 'short coats' and hats, half green and half white, green on the right, white of the left,[19] and it seems every group raised from those areas during Edward III's reign was so dressed. The uniforms were sometimes delivered at the points of array, sometimes in London.

Cheshire archers, marching to Sandwich for embarkation in 1346, were paid for the period of their journey.[20] Though not all counties treated their men so well, the Cheshire practice became gradually more widespread. In the following year recruits were given 16 days' wages in advance for the journey from Chester to Calais, and in 1355 they had 21 days' wages to reach Plymouth. Obviously advance payment was essential if travelling troops were to eat properly on the journey without ruthlessly living off the land. Sometimes counties paid these travelling allowances to an agreed point, after which they were 'at the king's charges'. The usual arrangement was for arrayed men to march to their county boundaries without pay, from there to the point of embarkation at the county's expense, and from then on to be paid by the king, even if there were delays before sailing.

In 1345, the year before Crécy, while the king was collecting his army of invasion, 125 Staffordshire archers assembled at Lichfield on May 25, and with six days' pay in their pockets (probably 18d) set off for Southampton and duly arrived in a week; 100 Shropshire men met at Bridgnorth on 12 May, and set off for Sandwich with 1s 9d each; but 22 Buckinghamshire bowmen who gathered at Aylesbury on 10 May had to be content with 6d each to reach Sandwich. The organisation of archers and other troops on the march was by 'hundreds' and 'vintaines' of 20, each county contingent going in charge of a leader appointed by the king, who carried the wages and the nominal roll and was responsible for getting his charges safely to their port.

When possible the arrays assembled after the hay harvest, in the kindest time of the year for travel, and if the Cheshire contingent of 1355 is fair example, with their 21 days' pay in pocket to get to Plymouth, men were not expected to march more than 13 miles a day. It could not always be a happy, comfortable spring march these recruits made, in their new uniforms with their bows slung and their first issue of one sheaf of arrows at their back. Archers moved about England in all weathers during Crécy year; August, October, December; and on 2 January 1347, 30 of them left Salisbury for Sandwich (130 miles), another 20 the next day from Cambridge (118 miles), 20 each from Cheshunt and Chelmsford the same day, and one group set out from Somerton, 30 of them, three days before Christmas with a march of 182 miles ahead.

Whenever it was possible to beat the profiteers, contingent leaders and the king's

---

[19] Hewitt, *Organization of War*, p. 39.
[20] For what follows, see Hewitt, *Organization of War*, pp. 40–5.

or magnates' agents would resist the overcharging of recruits, and where bad quality was found stocks would be destroyed, so that the new soldiery should drink good stuff at a fair price. Inns were encouraged to be reasonable in their prices, and at any time when many contingents were going through Kent into Sandwich all markets and fairs were shut down except for Sandwich itself, Canterbury and Dover. Everything possible seems to have been done to make at least the first part of the march to war as pleasant as possible. Arrivals were spread over a period, and usually ordered as days by which men had to be there 'by three weeks from Midsummer', or 'by the first day of September'.

Attorneys were appointed for those with considerable possessions so that their interests could be watched while they were abroad, and letters of protection were issued; where law cases were pending, suspension was ordered until the men returned home. Once arrived, those for service overseas were billeted by agents of the Marshal of England. In 1346 Robert Houel had to lodge all the contingents, arriving in numbers far too large to be absorbed into the town of Portsmouth.[21] There must have been encampments 'outside the verge of the household' (the royal household and retinue) to accommodate the main part of the army. Inevitably there were delays; ships did not arrive on time or the weather was adverse, so payment had to be made to the waiting men. One contingent at Plymouth in 1343, mostly Welsh and consisting of a chaplain, an interpreter, a standard-bearer, a crier, a physician, four vintainers and 100 archers, under the leadership of Kenwrick Dein, were given 21 days' service pay for waiting between 5 and 25 November.[22]

The men had boredom to overcome and new accents to comprehend; there was much more of a language barrier between Welsh and English, much more dissimilarity between the speech and usage of the northern and southern counties of England than today, and the language of the nobility was predominantly Anglo-Norman. It seems likely that waiting period became training periods; archers practising both weapon and manoeuvre, groups and divisions learning their organisation, the men getting used to their new leaders. The best argument for the fact that the armies of the fourteenth and fifteenth centuries were on the whole well treated by the leaders lies in the knowledge that a great proportion of them returned after the campaigns, and a considerable number re-enlisted for further duty.[23]

To feed them huge supplies had to be collected: beef, pork and mutton, salted and fresh (more often salted because of the difficulties of storage), flitches of bacon, masses of cheese, oat and wheat cakes and loaves, peas and beans, and fish (usually dried 'stockfish' or herrings) which were caught in home waters, or imported, often from Gascony. Orders went out to the sheriffs of counties for the collection and transport of food and drink. The county of Lincoln, in Crécy year, sent to William de Kelleseye, the king's receiver of victuals at Boston and Hull, 552.5 quarters of flour at 3s or 4s a quarter, packed in 87 tuns, 300 quarters of oats, 135 carcasses of salt pork, 213 carcasses of sheep, 32 sides of beef, 12 weys of

---

[21] *CPR, 1345–48*, p. 79.
[22] PRO, E101/23/22 m.5, cited in Hewitt, *Organization of War*, pp. 46–7.
[23] Hewitt, *Organization of War*, p. 47.

cheese and 100 quarters of peas and beans.[24] From Hereford went supplies to Bristol port, from Kent to Sandwich, and from Oxford and Berkshire over the Thames bridges and the ford at Bolney. But from Rutland went only half the demanded amounts; once again the tiny county complained she could not raise the total, and relief was granted. Where fresh meat could be had it was eaten in the camps, and the waiting ships were filled with the victuals meant to last. Though armies of the middle ages were expected to live off the lands through which they passed, as much supply as possible was carried, but transport was a grave problem. When an army sat down to a siege, supplies from home by sea and land became vital.

At Yarmouth in 1340, 30 ships were provided by the town for 40 days' service as troopers, and they were victualled at the town's expense. The bailiffs' accounts show that, apart from the foodstuffs, 60,400 gallons of ale, supplied by Johanna Hikkeson, Peter Grymbolp and John Gayter, were taken on board, at a cost to the bailiffs, hence the townsfolk, of £251 13s 4d.[25] The allowance seems to have been one gallon a day to the men in the ships.

From all over Wales and England came the weapons of war – swords, knives, spears and lances from the iron-producing areas, bought and provided by the counties; arrowheads of all the different designs and weights; there were 4,000 from Chester Castle in 1359, 52s 5d the lot;[26] arrowheads had to be 'well brazed, and hardened at the points with steel';[27] shafts and feathers, mostly goose-wing feathers, bowstaves and made bows were constantly demanded. Later orders give an indication of earlier demands: in February 1417 six feathers from every goose in 20 southern counties were to be at the Tower by 14 March.[28] On 1 December 1418, sheriffs were ordered to supply 1,190,000 goose feathers by Michaelmas.[29] Year by year the orders went out to replace the stocks that were sent out to the archers.

Bows were divided into two kinds, 'white', which cost about 1s 6d each or 12 deniers, and 'painted' which were 2s or 18 deniers, a more expensive article.[30] No one knows exactly what these designations meant. Yew bows come into both categories, so if 'white' were fairly raw, not long-seasoned bows – 'green' staves, which in the case of yew would show a gleaming ivory colour on the sapwood back that fades with age –, that would suggest that 'painted' bows were of thoroughly seasoned staves, treated with some sort of paint or varnish, as we treat them now, to inhibit the drying out of the last vestiges of liquid in the wood, that final ten per cent or so that stops a bow becoming too brittle.

As they were collected from local manufacturers, the bows were packed in

[24] PRO, E101/25/16, cited in Hewitt, p. 54–8.

[25] PRO, E101/22/25, cited in Hewitt, p. 52.

[26] *Accounts of the Chamberlain and Other Officers of the County of Chester, 1301–60*, ed. R. Stewart-Brown (Record Society of Lancashire and Cheshire, 59, 1910), p. 273.

[27] *CPR, 1358–61*, p. 323.

[28] Rymer, *Foedera* (Hague edition, 1739–45), IV, ii, p. 193.

[29] *CPR, 1416–22*, p. 178.

[30] PRO, E101/392/14 (account of William de Rothwell, Keeper of the Wardrobe).

canvas and the arrowsheaves corded together for stowage in wooden tuns.[31] These were in turn stacked in carts and waggons which were hired for the purpose, covered with tarpaulins of horse-hide, pulled by teams of two to eight horses, and accompanied by clerks who kept the tallies, saw to the delivery and got receipts in exchange.[32] The orders sent out to counties were not always filled in one consignment. Some would come in early and the rest would be promised to follow as soon as possible; and some orders were never completely honoured. A thousand sheaves of arrows ordered from Hereford on one occasion dwindled to 363 sheaves actually delivered.[33] The orders were not regular yearly demands. In times of truce fewer orders were sent out, but when the war fires blazed the orders flew like sparks and massive quantities of arrows would be received at the Tower of London alone.[34] In 1356 the Chamberlain of Chester learned that 'no arrows can be obtained from England because the King has . . . taken for his use all the arrows that can be found anywhere there'.[35] He then had to get for the Prince of Wales, 1,000 bows, 2,000 sheaves of arrows and 400 gross of bowstrings, requisition all available immediately and make certain that production continued until the order was fulfilled.

Available figures show that in 1359, the year of a new royal expedition, the counties supplied over 850,000 arrows to the Tower, and about 20,000 bows and 50,000 bowstrings.[36] That does not include already existing stocks, nor the fact that the orders continued to pour in to the suppliers for more and more of everything, nor the fact that large quantities of arms went direct to the appropriate ports. If one accepts the idea of 6,000 archers shooting off half a million arrows in one of the rare major engagements, then the production of a million arrows in a year would seem too low a figure, but it should be remembered that, from a million arrows shot off, some proportion would be recovered. Every arrow that quit the string in battle was not a lost arrow.

The cartage problem is a tricky one. A million arrows might weigh about 40 tons, and that, in the waggonage of the day, and in relation to the poor roads and rough country to be crossed, would represent a large and cumbrous part of the baggage train; but the argument of the difficulty of carriage suggesting that carriage was not achieved is a poor one. Armour had to be carried as well, tents and pavilions, food, spare bows, guns, sulphur and saltpetre, the whole equipment of the field kitchens and so forth. Forty tons of arrows, those vital components of English success in arms, may have been hard to transport, but it is quite certain that arrows were carried in great quantity.

By the time Henry VIII was campaigning against the French, taking a leaf out of Henry V's book, we can see many more details of transport. For example in 1513 his massive army of invasion marched in three 'wards' or 'battles' just as in

---

[31] PRO, E372/191, m.11.

[32] PRO, E372/201.

[33] Ibid., cited in Hewitt, *Organization of War*, p. 66.

[34] Hewitt, *Organization of War*, pp. 69–70.

[35] *Register of the Black Prince*, 3, p. 23.

[36] Hewitt, *Organization of War*, p. 69.

Edward III's time, though the proportion of archers to other arms had dropped by then to one in three, or less. In one of these wards, of approximately 15,000 men, there were 90 vehicles allowed for spare weapons and equipment. Five thousand two hundred bows in parcels of 400 were carried in 13 waggons; 86,000 bow-strings in 20 barrels were in two waggons; and 140,000 arrows needed 26 wagons, a little under 10,000 arrows a waggon.[37] Possibly in this case the artillery and its ammunition needed the big waggons, so that small carts were used for arrow-transport, and possibly in the past the bigger waggons with larger teams of oxen or horses were used for bows and arrows, which would have much increased each load and lessened the number of vehicles (plate XXVII).

The great march from Harfleur to Agincourt is supposed to have been made without wheeled transport, for speed of movement.[38] If that is true, then every-thing, including a good part of the crown jewels, which were rifled during the battle by the French raiding party in the rear of the English, and the appurtenances of the royal chapel, had to be carried on sumpter animals. The English must have marched with a minimum of gear, though certainly with enough armour for 1,000 men-at-arms and 5,000 archers. But arrows? Could Henry V have risked cutting his bowmen short of ammunition? It is known that after the armies shocked together the archers threw down their bows and went in with sword and dagger, maul and anything else they could lay hand to. Was that because there were no more arrows? It could be. But I doubt it. Those commanders of experience who had armies in the proportion of five or six to one in favour of the archer arm would have been mad to risk that arm's paralysis.

In this context, 500 whips for 'great horses', 200 leather halters, 400 trammels and pasterns, 200 leather collars, 200 pairs of traces went across the Channel in 1339 from Yorkshire alone, and from Nottingham, 10,000 horseshoes and 60,000 nails.[39] For the same campaign, 80,000 horseshoes with the appropriate nails went from the southern counties via Yarmouth and Orwell. Again, for the retinues of 12 magnates in the campaign of 1359, which represent only a proportion of the whole, more that 6,300 horses went on inland from Calais,[40] the number of those em-barked in England being much increased by animals available in France.

Certainly this rough sketch can be filled with much more detail, but to the quick of the ulcer, the bow itself.

The wreck-site in the Solent of Henry VIII's great ship the *Mary Rose*, sunk during battle with the invading French fleet in 1545, had been re-discovered by Alexander McKee and his team in 1967 and for some years the patient and skilful work of investigating the ship had been going on, under the inspired command of Dr Margaret Rule. The site had been protected from amateur and professional robbers, and from time to time the Press offered stories of artefacts being brought

[37] G.G. Cruickshank, *Army Royal. Henry VIII's Invasion of France, 1513* (Oxford, 1969) p. 78.
[38] J.H. Wylie and W.T. Waugh, *The Reign of Henry the Fifth* (3 vols, Cambridge 1914–29), 2, p. 89 and note 4.
[39] Hewitt, *Organization of War*, pp. 84–5.
[40] PRO, E101/393/11.

to the surface – guns among them, just as there had been when the Deane brothers first investigated the wreck in the 1830s. The Deanes had also brought up longbows. The Anthony Anthony Roll of the King's Ships, at Magdalene College, Cambridge, lists 250 longbows of yew, and arrows and bowstrings in the *Mary Rose* inventory. Dr Margaret Rule was hoping to find some example of everything mentioned in that roll, on board the Mary Rose.

One day in 1979, a diver surfaced alongside 'Sleipnir', the control vessel anchored over the wreck site, with a long, slightly bent pole tapering at each end, waterlogged, black and covered with small marine accretions. Was it a longbow? If it was not a bow it was a very odd pikestaff indeed. At Dr Rule's request, I went down to Portsmouth, with my friend and colleague in research, Professor P.L. Pratt, then Professor of Crystal Physics at the Imperial College of Science and Technology. There was not the slightest doubt: before us lay a longbow of 1545, all the more authentic to my unaccustomed eyes because it immediately called to mind an early photograph of the Hathersage weapon known as 'Little John's Bow'. It was knobbly, where the bowyer for safety had allowed extra timber about the knots and pins; even in its uncleaned state there was faint differentiation between the sapwood of the back and the heartwood of the belly; and it was massive; it looked as if it must in its prime have had a draw-weight well over 100 lb.

As more bows and arrows were discovered in the murk of the silt that covered the *Mary Rose*, and were brought to the Trust workrooms, Peter Pratt and I were joined in our examinations by John Levy, Professor of Wood Science at the Imperial College of Science and Technology. He was already advising the Trust on the timbers of the ship's hull, and brought his vast knowledge and experience of timber to our team, which was now officially appointed as the consultant body on longbows and arrows to the Mary Rose Trust. Our job was to conserve, examine, research and make detailed measurements of all the bows, and when thought advisable, to make experiments on them to determine their strengths now, their degrees of degradation, and so their likely strengths when new. From the beginning, through Professor Pratt we were able to count on the assistance of Dr B.W. Kooi of Groningen University, author of a highly technical work *The Mechanics of the Bow and Arrow*,[41] who has made himself responsible for what we called the computer profiling of the bows.

When the first of two complete bow boxes from the orlop deck was discovered, and then its companion was brought to the surface, it became obvious that we were dealing not only with a reasonable proportion of the 250 bows enumerated in the Anthony Anthony Roll, but with bows of the finest quality imaginable. It was evident that all the bows were made of fine-grained yew timber, cut radially from logs across the sapwood and heartwood boundary, allowing the highly tensile sapwood to remain on the backs of the bows (that is the convex side of the drawn weapon), lying against its own heartwood in the centre and belly of the bows (the

---

[41] B.W. Kooi, *On the Mechanics of the Bow and Arrow* (Drukkerij van Denderen B.V. Groningen 1983).

concave side) which is probably the most resistant timber to compression known to man.

When the bows from the chests were still wet, they had almost the appearance of new wood, though it was only after drying that the pale sapwood took on the true colour that one sees today in a yew bow made fifty or a hundred years ago. The deep reddish brown of the belly lightened as the timber dried through the months, and later gentle oiling and waxing restored to them something of their youthful look. It was possible from the detailed examination of broken fragments to establish that there was a degree of cell degradation in the timber surface, but whether there was vital degradation in the many complete bows could only be revealed by testing their elasticity and strength. It was also clear from the narrowness of the growth rings, in some cases reaching over 100 to the inch, that the timber was extremely slowly grown. This suggested two things: strength, and a foreign provenance; and the average radius of the growth rings suggested that the bowmakers had chosen grown timber of more than eight inches diameter.

During the long months of cleaning and drying, each bow was examined, and preliminary measurements were taken. A complicated system of description and identification was begun to record the idiosyncrasies of each weapon. In many instance, among the best preserved, the extraordinary skill and confidence of the bowyers were apparent. Where the surfaces seemed almost like new wood, as they now did in many cases, the marks of the bowyers' draw knives, or 'floats', were plain to see, even to feel, like delicate fluting on a glass stem. So sure were the bowmakers of their skills and of their timber that they clearly felt no need to work out those last straight marks of manufacture, as we do now.

The bows were found variously about the ship, on the weather deck, in which number must be included those that fell into the ship from the bow and stern castles, either on impact with the sea bottom or during later disintegration of the castles, in the gun deck, and in the orlop. In one chest were 48 bows, in the other 36, almost all in miraculously fine condition after 437 years' immersion. The rapid flow of silt accounts for the good state of preservation, which is probably far better than would have been the case if the bows had been preserved in air, since much of the natural make-up of the timber was sealed in anaerobic conditions.

It was noticed at once that every bow, no matter what condition it was in otherwise, as long as one or both tips remained, showed at the tips a plain differentiation of colour for some five cms. This was clear evidence that the tips had originally been covered by an applied nock of some kind. Since horn is and was the most usual material for such applied nocks, and since horn has been proved to perish fairly rapidly in the conditions of the Solent silt, it can safely be assumed that the nocks were of horn. This is borne out by the fact that of the thousands of arrows recovered, having a slot at the nock end which runs down towards the fletching and which would originally have taken a horn sliver for the purpose of strengthening the force-absorbing end of the arrow, only one or two still have the horn in place. Those few only remain as a result of being protected, for instance by a coil of tarred rope, from the effects of micro-biological and seawater decay. It is also notable that among all the *Mary Rose* finds, no horn buttons have survived, no horn panels for lanthorns, no horn handles, though it is obvious that there had been many such articles in 1545.

In the opinion of the Consultants these *Mary Rose* longbows, whether found at action stations or in boxes in the orlop, were finished weapons ready for use. It might seem unnecessary to make such an obvious claim, but it is necessary because within the archery world a good deal has been said and written expressing the view that the *Mary Rose* longbows are not bows, but bowstaves, unfinished and not ready for use. Apart from the very oddity of the idea that a ship of war, in time of war and actually in action against the enemy, should put to sea for action with no longbows but a large number of unfinished staves, there is the massive evidence of the bows themselves. What started the hare of this nonsense was our first published suggestion of the draw-weights of these bows. It was hard to believe it ourselves. Few believed us when we came up with the first massive weights, arguing that the *Mary Rose* bows ran from about 100 lb draw-weight at 30 inches to 180 lb. Many said these weights were impossible, and that therefore the bows must be unfinished, carrying more timber and hence more weight than they would when completed. That they are completed is now self-evident. By this time we had completed three or four copies of *Mary Rose* bows, or rather 'approximations' (since in following the dictates of individual staves, a true copy can never be achieved) of which we knew all the relevant details. When the vital statistics of these weapons were fed into the Kooi computer their draw-weights came out with absolute accuracy, so we had to believe them.

All the bows were made from yew timber, each from a single unjointed, unpieced stave. The quality of the timber, its density, the extreme fineness of the grain in most cases, suggested that we were dealing with imported staves of a straighter and finer quality than can readily be found in the soft climates of the British Isles. That most of it was imported from the Continent there is small doubt, and several documents from Henry VIII's reign record such imports either through Venice by the Doge's special permission or from elsewhere by special mandate of the Emperor Maximilian.[42] Such timber would be gathered from those parts of Europe – Italy, Austria, Poland – where the yew grew high and fine-grained, and where for centuries timber had been felled and split into staves to supply our military needs.[43] Henry VII was a great encourager of the military use of the longbow, just as he keenly pursued the development of gunpowder artillery. He sent his agents into Europe to choose the finest yew timber, selecting at a time thousands of the best staves which were then stamped with the Rose and Crown for export to England. The orders were almost always large; one part-order was for 40,000 staves to be sent to England through Venice,[44] and the names exist of five

[42] *Calendar of Papers Foreign and Domestic, Henry VIII*, vol. 1, part 1 (London, 1920), nos. 529, 566; *Calendar of State Papers and Manuscripts relating to English Affairs in the Archives and Collections of Venice*, vol. 2, 1508–1519 (London, 1867), no. 78.

[43] Roger Ascham, *Toxophilus. The Schole of Shootinge conteyned in two Bookes* (1545), section on bow woods.

[44] *Calendar of Papers Foreign and Domestic*, no. 757.

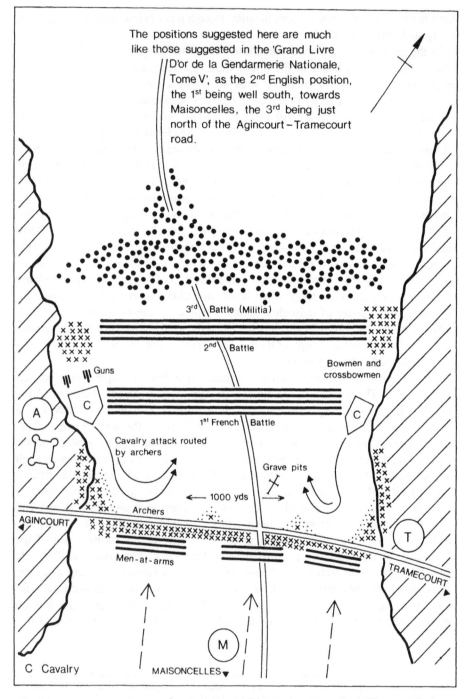

The positions suggested here are much
like those suggested in the 'Grand Livre
D'or de la Gendarmerie Nationale,
Tome V', as the 2ⁿᵈ English position,
the 1ˢᵗ being well south, towards
Maisoncelles, the 3ʳᵈ being just
north of the Agincourt–Tramecourt
road.

3ʳᵈ   Battle (Militia)

2ⁿᵈ   Battle

Guns

Bowmen and
crossbowmen

A

C

1ˢᵗ French   Battle

Cavalry attack routed
by archers

Grave pits

C

← 1000 yds →

Archers

AGINCOURT

T

Men-at-arms

TRAMECOURT

M

C Cavalry   MAISONCELLES

Fig. 10.1 A suggested positioning of the French and English battles at the time of the
French cavalry assault at Agincourt. Whether the English line was finally drawn north
or south of the east-west road is a matter of debate.

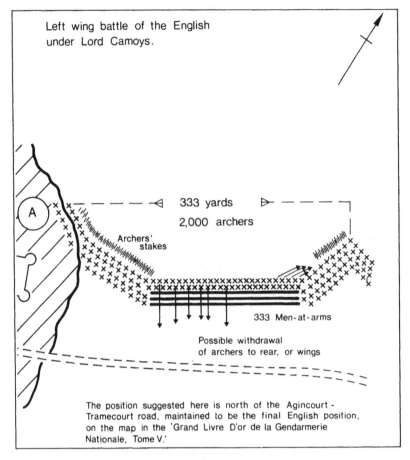

Left wing battle of the English
under Lord Camoys.

A

333 yards
2,000 archers

Archers'
stakes

333 Men-at-arms

Possible withdrawal
of archers to rear, or wings

The position suggested here is north of the Agincourt -
Tramecourt road, maintained to be the final English position,
on the map in the 'Grand Livre D'or de la Gendarmerie
Nationale, Tome V.'

Fig. 10.2 A suggested formation for the men-at-arms and archers on the English left at the opening stage of the battle of Agincourt. This sketch puts the English position north of the east-west road, which from the position of the grave pits is more likely, though it is only a matter of yards.

bowyers who made up 600 of this particular batch of staves into finished bows, for which they were paid altogether £200 13s 4d at a time when a master carpenter was paid 4d a day and beef was about 2d a pound.

After long and frequent examination we came to the conclusion that the bows showed exactly what today's longbows show in the way of age and use. Those in regular use exhibit a slight or a marked 'string-follow', that is they remain curved towards the belly, or 'de-flexed'; one of the deck bows was certainly in use when the ship foundered and the string somehow survived long enough to set the bow in the braced position for good. Others lie almost straight; but a majority of the boxed bows show a 'reflex', a bend towards the back, away from the natural bow shape. The probable reasons for this curvature are either natural, the bowyers selecting timber with a natural bend towards the back, or the fact that when bowstaves are split from recently cut logs they will tend to reflex themselves. The result in either

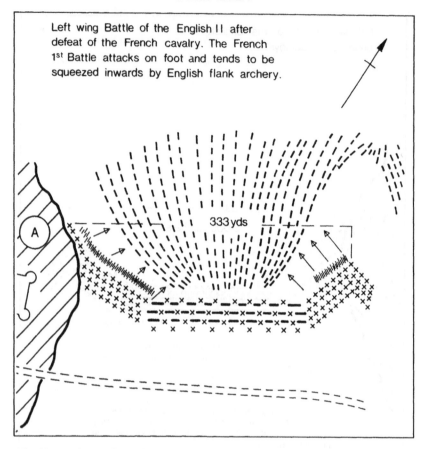

Left wing Battle of the English II after
defeat of the French cavalry. The French
1st Battle attacks on foot and tends to be
squeezed inwards by English flank archery.

333 yds

A

Fig. 10.3 The English left battle or rearguard after the failure of the French
cavalry attack at Agincourt, showing how the French infantry might tend
inwards away from the flank archers, as described by an eyewitness.

case is just what the bowyers were after, timber that would maintain optimum
straightness after much use, which means a longer and faster return of the limbs
from full-draw to the braced position at which the arrow quits the string. The faster
that return the greater the bow's ability to cast an arrow.

The *Mary Rose* bows are handle-less. There are no indications of any binding
being put on them, and it must be assumed they had none. The approximate
position of the 'arrow-pass' is just above the handle position (for even without a
marked handle section, there is of course still a handle position), and it is in very
many cases indicated on the *Mary Rose* bows by incised, pricked, and in some
cases stamped marks. The marks consist mainly of groups of incised dots, as if
made with a chisel corner (perhaps a float blade corner) arranged in pairs, threes,
crosses or little tree-like groups. There is a variety of circular marks: plain circles,
circles with a cross, segmented circles, some apparently made with dividers, one or
two possibly with a tubular stamp. There are variations on the cross: plain, and

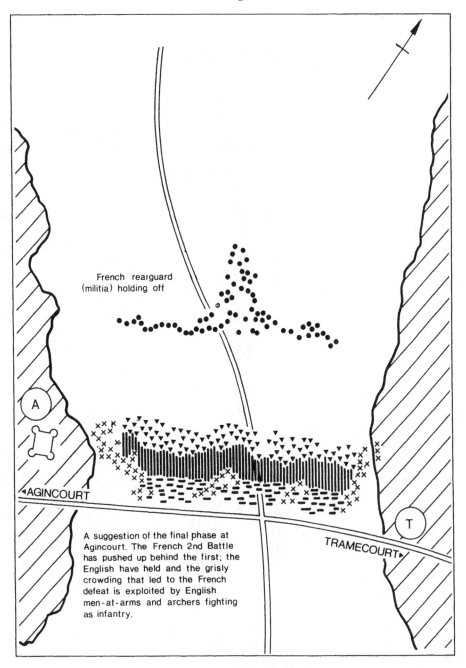

French rearguard
(militia) holding off

A suggestion of the final phase at
Agincourt. The French 2nd Battle
has pushed up behind the first; the
English have held and the grisly
crowding that led to the French
defeat is exploited by English
men-at-arms and archers fighting
as infantry.

◄AGINCOURT

TRAMECOURT►

T

A

Fig. 10.4 A suggestion as to how the French second battle followed up at Agincourt and became inextricably mixed with the first, and of how the English archers and men-at-arms might all have been fighting together, hand to hand with the French, having jettisoned their bows, except for those flank archers who could still usefully shoot into the French flanks. The French rearguard, mostly comprised of *milices*, is holding off.

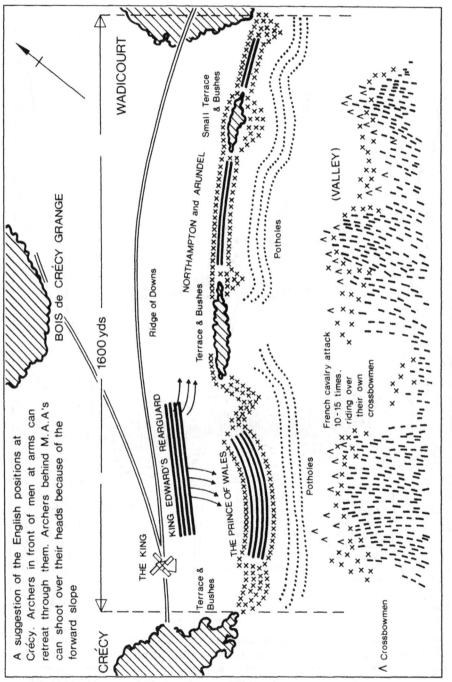

A suggestion of the English positions at Crécy. Archers in front of men at arms can retreat through them. Archers behind M.A.A.'s can shoot over their heads because of the forward slope

CRÉCY

THE KING

Terrace & Bushes

KING EDWARD'S REARGUARD

THE PRINCE OF WALES

Potholes

Terrace & Bushes

NORTHAMPTON and ARUNDEL

Small Terrace & Bushes

Potholes

(VALLEY)

French cavalry attack 10–15 times. riding over their own crossbowmen

∧ Crossbowmen

1600 yds

BOIS de CRÉCY GRANGE

WADICOURT

Ridge of Downs

Fig. 10.5 A suggestion of how the English battles with their archer wings might have been drawn up

with dots in various arrangements. There are other linear marks, often in association with dots, sometimes whole clusters of pinpricks up to 30 or more in number. In general there seems a difference between the heavy marks which suggest a maker's advice or identification, and rather more random markings which could be personal additions. But those bows which are not marked at all, some fifth of the total, do not seem to be generally inferior, or different from the marked ones.

Though it is hard to detect a standard in these marks, it is certain there was hardly a standard bow; yew does not yield to a standard; there are not two dozen bows at exactly 100 lb and two dozen at exactly 110 lb and so forth. There are more standard arrows at predictable lengths; the bow by its nature is personal and unique, first in the timber, then in the bowyer's hands, then in the hands of the archer.

There is a painting in the Christ Church, Oxford, manuscript collection, an illumination of 1326, showing a castle defended by two women, one using a massive crossbow, the other an equally massive longbow. The moral of that is: training can make nearly all things possible! Does anything lead us to suppose that bows of the weights represented by the *Mary Rose* collection would be unusable? The answer must be no. If they were unusable they would not be there. So, if we admit them usable, what is there to suggest that the men who used them were specially selected, specially trained? The answer is: a very great deal. Those skeletons found in the *Mary Rose* which can undoubtedly be linked with archery tackle, and can be presumed archers are large men, six-footers or so, and described by the Senior Consultant Anthropologist to the Trust who examined them as 'huge . . . not necessarily tall, but massively boned'. The shipboard location of skeletons representing the highest percentage of bony changes attributable to the use of heavy bows occurs in the areas most associated with archery equipment. Even with the lighter bows we use for sport today it is in the shoulders, the upper arm and the elbows that things tend to go wrong. The lengths of the bows, from just over 6 feet to just under 7 feet suggest men of some 5 feet 7 inches to over 6 feet, and the arrow measurements, with draw-lengths of 28 inches to 30 inches confirm these likely proportions.

Increasingly today there are to be found those who are teaching themselves to master bows of such great weights. I know of, and benefit from the skills of, young archers who can handle weights well over a hundred pounds, as well as those who have trained themselves to shoot, with reliable accuracy, 20 and more arrows in a minute (plates XXVIII–XXIX). Turn those few into thousands and one begins to get a genuine idea of the formidable power of our archer corps throughout the long years of its military ascendancy. What sort of men could use the *Mary Rose* bows? Young, fit men in constant practice chosen for well-paid military service from a nation to whom the shooting of longbows had been second nature for 150 years at least.

It can be argued that by Henry VIII's reign, military archery was in decline. Can we infer that in these heavy bows rescued from the Solent we have the sort of weapons that were used at Bosworth, at Towton, at Agincourt, Poitiers, and at Crécy 200 years before the *Mary Rose* archers sailed out of Portsmouth? I see no reason why we cannot be confident of that. If decline in the use of the weapon is going to change anything in the weapon itself, it will tend surely to diminish the strength of it, not increase it. We cannot but believe we now have available to see and to study nearly 140 bows that represent the great period of military archery. The *Mary Rose* bows were part of the equipment of the army of Henry VIII, himself a fine longbowman, who went to great lengths to procure the finest timber for his archers; he was also an innovator in the use and development of artillery. Within those terms of reference it seems to me unlikely either that he was demanding from his bowyers the making, and from his archers the use, of either heavier or lighter bows than were previously in general use. Because of the growth of artillery we might expect a downturn in the strength of bows, just as there is a lowering of the proportion of archers to other arms in his army recruitment. It cannot be that there is a drop in bow strengths, because if there is, from what weights, drawable by man, can bows of 180 lb draw-weight have diminished? Can we suppose that he demanded greater weights, greater feats than he inherited from the past of military archery? When it was becoming increasingly difficult to recruit and train archers, it is scarcely credible that the use of the weapon itself should be put beyond average trained practitioners. I see no reason to suppose these bows we have from 1545 differ in general from the military weapons of the Hundred Years War. Therefore I believe we can argue usage and tactics during these wars from the evidence of the weapons that have been recovered from the Solent.

We now begin to know from practical experiments (which are by no means complete) that effective bow range can exceed 300 yards, though not, I think, by much. It depends on the purpose of long range shooting, and the weights and designs of arrows shot. So let us take 300 yards as the length at which the first fall of arrows can begin to be effective. Given the proportion of archers to men-at-arms at Agincourt, or Crécy, what would the commanders have done? Deployed them to best advantage, I take to be the answer. At Agincourt the English and French engaged on a front of approximately 1,000 yards; at Crécy where larger numbers were involved, and again from the lie of the land, which because of terracing would have allowed for a very light defence of the centre, the whole front seems likely to have been almost a mile. If, as is sometimes argued, the archers were placed only on the wings of the entire battle array, then there was at Agincourt at least 300 yards of front which the French could attack, unswept by the fall of arrows; at Crécy something like 1,100 yards. Does that make any sort of sense? We are left with the only sensible proposition: that each 'battle' in the whole army line up, whether it was double or triple, had its own archer wings, so deployed as comfortably to cover the front from the left of the rearguard to the right of the vanguard (see figs 10.1 – 10.5). The fact that I believe archers were often placed in front of the whole line during the early stages of attack, and that drills existed for them to move sideways among their fellows on the wings, or back behind the men-at-arms to re-deploy as needed, will probably not greatly influence those who force contemporary accounts to support their beliefs that the vastly effective English archer forces were only deployed on the extreme wings of the entire battle line, and thus were unable to cover the centre of the field of action. Alas, there are no surviving drill-books. We still do not know quite how they stood, or moved in their formations, how orders were given for general marshalling, or for companies in the roar and din of battle, but we are pushed towards various commonsense conclusions, and guided by – dare I repeat Alfred Burne's extremely sensible phrase? – 'inherent military probability'.

11

Winds of Change?
Ships and the Hundred Years War

IAN FRIEL

THE ANGLO-FRENCH conflicts between 1337 and 1453 would never have been as ferocious as they were if the English and the French had not been able to call on considerable shipping resources. Royal and mercantile fleets made the great English expeditions possible, and facilitated the sometimes devastating coastal raids carried out by both sides.

Although the title of the chapter is 'ships and the Hundred Years War', this is not going to be a nail-by-nail, rope-by-rope anatomization of the late medieval warship. Rather, it will deal with a variety of topics, including ship construction, rig, equipment and armament, but will also look at what ships were used, and what effects their use may have had on the course of events.

The question posed in the title of the chapter also refers to an 'old chestnut' in the history of warfare – the effect of war on technology. The experience of the world since the Industrial Revolution has shown a definite link between the demands of development and production for war and technological improvement: aviation and electronics are just two of the many fields affected in this way. Did the Hundred Years War affect the development of ships?

In the 1330s, two main forms of ship construction and rig predominated in Northern Europe. Very broadly speaking, all major sea-going vessels constructed by native shipwrights in a zone stretching from Scandinavia in the north to at least as far south as northern Spain, were clinker-built. That is to say, their hulls were formed from shells of overlapping plan, built up from the keel, stem- and sternpossts, and fastened at the edges. The nails securing the planks were driven in from the outside, and on the inner face of each plank, they were hammered flat ('clenched' – hence 'clinker') or riveted, usually over a metal washer called a rove. Most of the frames were added at a fairly late stage of construction, and the frames themselves were fairly light – the main load-bearing element in the structure was the shell of planking. There were differences of form and detail with regard to different types of vessel (cogs, for example, had flat bottoms, and clinker sides), but clinker construction was the main construction form in Northern Europe.[1]

---

[1] J. Leather, *Clinker Boatbuilding* (London, 1990), pp. 22–9; B. Greenhill, *Archaeology of the Boat* (London, 1976), pp. 60–88 and 259–61.

Likewise, there was one main form of ship rig. A Northern ship had a single mast, carrying one sail. This sail is known as a square sail, although it was often rectangular in shape, wider than it was deep. The sail was attached to a yard, or 'sailyard' (as it was called in Middle English) which could be raised or lowered as required. The square sail performed best with the wind from astern, or the side, although it did give a ship some limited capacity to sail to windward, or to sail 'on a tack' as it is known. Viking ships were able to do this, and there is little doubt that late medieval ships could also do so. When performing this manoeuvre, it was crucial to keep the leading edge of the sail taut. Viking ships had achieved this using a wooden pole, like a spinnaker pole on a modern dinghy, but by the thirteenth century the bowsprit had been developed. Ropes called bowlines were attached to the bowsprit at one end and to the opposite edges of the sail, at the other end. When pulled taut on one side, the bowlines ensured that the leading edge of the sail did not collapse when sailing on a tack. The importance of sailing to windward, aside from course changes and the avoidance of danger, was that in combat it put one ship in a favourable position to attack another. A vessel to windward of an opponent had the 'weather gage', the ability to choose the time and position of an attack.[2]

The main warlike features of medieval ships – defensive superstructures and the topcastle – were already well-established by the 1330s. The forecastle, at the bow, and the aftercastle, at the stern, originated, probably in the twelfth century, as simple wooden castles erected in ships either to given them a height advantage over smaller opponents, or to nullify the advantage of ships with higher sides. Documentary and pictorial evidence suggests that castles could be installed or removed with some ease: certainly in merchant ships they would have imposed weight and stability penalties that a mariner would not want to suffer for too long, but it is difficult to be sure how much they were or were not a permanent feature of the majority of ships. Most medieval illustrations of large ships tend to show vessels with castles (fig. 11.1), but the reason for this is not hard to seek – they looked better than ships without castles. There is some evidence of English merchant ships being equipped with castles for naval service in the early 1330s, and of English warships in the 1410s having extra castles built on to them, but these may have been temporary expedients.[3]

The topcastle was a small railed platform at the masthead, used for keeping a look-out – a 'crow's nest' – but it also had an important function in battle as a point from which projectiles and rocks could be rained down on to the crew and decks of an enemy ship, when fighting a boarding action. The topcastle was reached by

[2] T.C. Gillmer, 'The capability of single square rig: a technical assessment', in *Medieval Ships and Harbours of Northern Europe*, ed. S. McGrail, B.A.R. International Series 66 (Oxford, 1979), p. 179.
[3] For some of the earliest illustrations of castles on ships, see e.g. H. Ewe, *Schiffe auf Siegeln* (Rostock, 1972), pp. 120, 133, 139, 179 and 180; *The English Government at Work, 1327–1336*, ed. J.F. Willard and W.A. Morris, 1 (Cambridge, Mass., 1940), p. 391; *The Navy of the Lancastrian Kings. Accounts and Inventories of William Soper, Keeper of the King's ships, 1422–1427*, ed. S.P. Rose, Navy Records Society 123 (London, 1982), pp. 214–16, 219–21 and 259.

means of climbing up the standing rigging, or shrouds, and weapons and rocks were taken up by rope. Some ships even had small winches on the topcastle and special bags to carry items aloft.[4]

Although clinker construction was the main technique used by native North European shipwrights, it was not the only one practised in Northern Europe. There was at least one area in which Mediterranean construction and rig techniques were used. Mediterranean shipbuilders employed a technique now called skeleton construction. This involved erecting a skeleton of heavy frames, on to which the planks were subsequently fastened, using iron nails or wooden trenails. The planks were flush-laid, giving the hull exterior a smooth appearance. This method was easier to repair than clinker construction and probably demanded less in the way of skilled manpower, and perhaps even materials, than clinker construction.[5]

In the 1290s the French Crown established a base for galleys at Rouen, called the Clos des Galées. However, these galleys were not the Northern type – large, double-ended warships descended from Viking longships. Rather, they were skeleton-built Mediterranean vessels. These were large oared fighting ships, with relatively advanced rowing systems, and sometimes as many as two masts, carrying lateen sails (fig. 11.3). The lateen was a triangular sail, better adapted for sailing into the wind than the square sail, but much less effective when sailing with the wind from astern. The galleys were built and maintained by Mediterranean shipwrights, summoned from the South of France or Northern Italy. Local Norman shipwrights constructed the clinker-built oared barges that were also based in the Clos des Galées, but there is little evidence that they ever learned skeleton construction from their Mediterranean colleagues. Craftsmen were not inclined to be free with their knowledge.[6]

English and French ship technology was broadly on a par at the outset of the Hundred Years War, and for much of the succeeding period. The French may have had an 'edge' in terms of oared warships, at least in the first instance, but there are few signs of major technological gaps.

Each side used similar sorts of shipboard weaponry, although the English relied on massed archers, using the longbow, as their main projectile weapon, and the French tended to favour crossbowmen. The evidence regarding the use of long-range torsion artillery – rope-powered bows like *springalds*, or stone-throwing machines – is not very clear. The Spanish ships involved in the battle off Winchelsea in Sussex in 1350 may have had some, but they are not commonly found in sources relating to English ships. However, what is certain is that medieval naval battles were seldom decided by anything but the outcome of a host of bloody individual boarding actions, with ships grappled to each other. In these situations,

---

4   F. Howard, *Sailing Ships of War 1400–1860* (London, 1987), p. 30.
5   R.W. Unger, *The Ship in the Medieval Economy 600–1600* (London and Toronto, 1980), pp. 104–5.
6   *Documents Relatifs au Clos des Galées de Rouen et aux Armées de Mer du Roi de France de 1293 à 1418*, ed. A. Merlin-Chazelas, 2 vols (Paris, 1977); C. de la Roncière, *Histoire de la Marine Française*, I (Paris, 1899), pp. 406–7 and n.1; R.C. Anderson, *Oared Fighting Ships* (Kings Langley, 1976), pp. 52–60.

Fig. 11.1   A drawing from an early fourteenth-century English miniature showing two vessels in combat. The ships are one-masted cogs, with their distinctive angular stern and sternposts, and flat bottoms. The cog was chiefly important as a merchantman, but it could also be converted to serve as a warship. Both vessels here have fore- and after-castles, defensive superstructures that could be removed or added, as required. The handweapons – bows, swords and even clubs – are typical of some of the shipboard weaponry used during the Hundred Years War. Rigging detail is minimal, and although the square sail has been omitted from the left-hand vessel, it can be seen clearly on the right-hand one.

the key factor would tend to be who had the largest ship and the largest crew. These men, whether sailors or embarked soldiers, were armed with the swords, spears, axes and other weapons used on land (fig. 11.1).[7]

Cannon were a rather separate matter. Once their initial shock value had gone, it is doubtful if they had the firepower to make a great deal of difference to sea battles, and ships seldom had them in large numbers. The earliest-known use of a gun on a ship – in English service, at least – dates from the very beginning of the Hundred Years War. In 1337–8, Edward III's warship *All Hallow's Cog*, operating in the Channel and the North Sea, was supplied with 'a certain iron instrument for firing quarells and lead pellets with powder, for the defence of the ship'. The gun is unlikely to have been very large, for it cost a mere 3s, the equivalent of 20 darts bought for the vessel. Even the trumpet of the *All Hallow's Cog* cost more, at 5s.[8]

Guns were to remain relatively unimportant at sea until well into the fifteenth century. For example, in the reign of Henry V, the king's naval forces fought two major naval battles in 1416 and 1417, undertook several great expeditions and sea patrols, but only fifteen of his more than 30 ships ever seem to have had guns. The most heavily-armed vessel was the 760-ton great ship *Holigost*, which had seven guns: few of the others had more than three apiece, and these fifteen ships could muster no more than about 42 cannon (mostly breach-loaders) between them. One

---

[7]   Willard and Morris, *Government at Work*, p. 380; Merlin-Chazelas, *Documents*, 1, pp. 95–6; H.J. Hewitt, *The Organization of War under Edward III* (Manchester, 1966), p. 78; *Froissart Chronicles*, ed. G. Brereton, (London, 1978), pp. 113–19.

[8]   PRO, E101/20/27, m.1v; L.G. Carr Laughton, 'The Cog', *Mariner's Mirror* 46 (1960), pp. 69–70.

hundred years later, the biggest of Henry VIII's ships would have been able to out-gun Henry V's entire fleet, *by itself*, but this revolution in naval armament post-dated the end of the Hundred Years War by some decades.[9]

The most common manifestations of naval warfare in the Middle Ages were skirmishes between small groups of ships, and coastal raids. The skirmishes were commonplace, and like the raids, took place during periods of truce as well as during time of war: in some cases they were little more than piracy, or a form of private warfare. Indeed, recent research has suggested that in the early fifteenth century, Henry IV of England was using state-legalised piracy, or privateering, as a controlled form of warfare in the Channel. The French retaliated, and there were losses on the English side. For example, in the early years of the fifteenth century, the small – now lost – port of Gosford at the mouth of the River Deben in Suffolk appears to have lost its entire fleet of tiny merchantmen to pirates.[10]

Coastal raiding was one of the worst manifestations of the war at sea. The suffering of people in coastal settlements could be considerable, repeated in each generation. The port of New Winchelsea in Sussex was attacked in 1337, 1359–60 and 1380, dealing successive blows to the population and economy of a port that was already starting to decline due to silting. The fear of French attack prompted the Kentish rebels in 1381 to order people living within twelve leagues of the coast to stay at home, in order to defend it against the French. English attacks on France and Brittany were carried out with as much ferocity as those by the French against England.[11]

The raids attracted the attention of chroniclers, but it is the great sea battles that are better known, and bulk large in Victorian naval histories and the less critical modern works. As pointed out by Colin Richmond over twenty years ago, it is difficult to call any of these battles 'decisive': they had local importance in time and space, but the main problem was the impossibility, given the limitations of medieval technology and naval organization, of gaining anything like 'command of the sea'. For example, in 1340 an English fleet under the direct command of Edward III destroyed a French invasion force of some 200 ships at Sluys in Flanders: this severely dented French sea power for a time, but did not end it. Sluys was celebrated by Froissart and other chroniclers, as was Edward's other great sea victory, when he sank or captured some fourteen vessels out of a fleet of 40 large Spanish ships (in French service) off Winchelsea in 1350. However, this battle, known as 'les Espagnols sur Mer', achieved little: the Spanish vessels were actually sailing home, and Edward's enthusiasm for ramming tactics – like a demented ten-year-old on the dodgems – so weakened his own ship that he and his

---

[9] PRO, E364/54 and E364/59, passim; M. Rule, *The Mary Rose* (London, 1983), pp. 149–52.

[10] C.F. Richmond, 'The War at Sea', *The Hundred Years War*, ed. K. Fowler (London, 1971), pp. 96–121 (this paper remains one of the best studies of the naval aspects of the war); C.J. Ford, 'Piracy or Policy: the Crisis in the Channel 1400–1403', *TRHS*, 5th series, 29 (1978) pp. 63–77; Gosford: *CPR, 1405–1408*, p. 5 (reference of 6 October 1405).

[11] M. Beresford, *New Towns of the Middle Ages. Town Plantation in England, Wales and Gascony* (2nd edition, Gloucester, 1988), p. 27; *The Peasants' Revolt of 1381*, ed. R.B. Dobson (London, 1970), pp. 126–7.

Fig. 11.2 Ship illustrated on the third seal of John Holland, earl of Huntingdon, as Admiral of England, 1435–42. Huntingdon commanded the English fleet in its second major sea battle against French forces in the reign of Henry V, in 1417. The ship depicted does not have a realistic shape, although the overlapping clinker planking of the hull and the single square sail are fairly typical of English vessels of the time. The object in the aftercastle is an admiral's lantern, which enabled the admiral's flagship to be used as a rallying-point for a fleet at night.

crew had to transfer to the Spanish ship they had just taken in order to escape drowning.[12]

The English did not have it all their own way: an English fleet was defeated off La Rochelle in 1372 by Castilian galleys, in French service, but this humiliation did not cripple English sea power. Likewise, although the English victories over French and Genoese naval forces at Harfleur in 1416 and off the Chef de Caux in 1417 (see fig. 11.2) helped to save the English garrison at Harfleur and ensured a safe crossing for Henry V's invasion fleet in 1417, they did not remove the threat of attack from the English coast. In 1418 and 1419, measures had to be taken to defend the English royal ships in the River Hamble, off Southampton Water, against possible attack by enemy galleys. It was only the conquest of Normandy by English forces that ensured – albeit temporarily – that the French Crown had little seaboard left from which it could mount attacks.[13]

One of the other main uses of shipping in the Hundred Years War – mostly by the English – was to transport expeditions and invasion armies. The numbers of ships in such forces given in chronicles are sometimes colossal – up to 1,600 English ships in the Calais expedition of 1346, 1,500 ships in Henry V's 1415 expedition. The numbers found in government records, where available, are smaller, but still sometimes impressive. In 1340 the French mustered a fleet of 170 sailing ships at Sluys, drawn from the ports of Normandy and Picardy, with 28 large French oared

---

[12] Richmond, 'War at Sea', pp. 98–9; *Froissart*, loc. cit.
[13] J.W. Sherborne, 'The battle of La Rochelle and the war at sea, 1372–5', *BIHR*, 42 (1969), pp. 17–29; PRO, E364/61, G m.1v.

barges and galleys, as well as Genoese galleys. In 1345 the English massed three great forces on the south coast of England, totalling 443 ships: one group was to go from Portsmouth to Brittany, another from Sandwich to Flanders, and the third, some 147 ships, crewed by 2,871 men, took Henry of Lancaster to Bordeaux. One hundred and forty two of these ships were English, drawn from ports as far apart as Cornwall and Yorkshire. One tiny vessel, with a crew of ten, came from as far inland as Doncaster, suggesting that the bottom of the seapower 'barrel' was being scraped. The River Don also supplied at least one vessel to Henry V's invasion fleet in 1417. We do not know the overall size of this fleet, but of 217 ships given leave to depart from royal service in Normandy that year, about half were from Flanders and Holland, and most, by their type names, were small craft. The impression is once again one of resources stretched to breaking-point. The last English expeditions of the Hundred Years War used smaller, but still not insignificant, numbers of vessels. Some 62 ships were gathered at Portsmouth in 1449 for the attempted reinforcement of Normandy, and 81 at Plymouth in 1450.[14]

Did the sizes and types of ships change over the course of Hundred Years War? The most common measure of a sailing ship's size in the fourteenth and fifteenth centuries was in terms of an estimate of how many tons of wine it could carry. Tonnage figures for individual ships are quite common, and whilst these units do have their problems, the overall indication is that there were more large ships in England and France in the first half of the fifteenth century than there had been a century earlier. This is not to say that ships got larger, as if they were organisms. Small ships, vessels of 50 tons or less, had always existed in comparatively large numbers, but it is apparent that shipowners began to require larger vessels as well.

The few overall tonnage figures for large fleets at the beginning of the Hundred Years War period suggest that French shipping had something of an advantage. In 1326, 205 ships were stayed in English ports, on royal orders, and had their tonnages listed for a prospective expedition. Just over half (106) of them, exceeded 100 tons burden (theoretical carrying capacity), and only five were of 200 tons or more, the largest being a ship of 250 tons.

The largest sailing ship in the 1340 French fleet at Sluys was of 240 tons, but here 149 of the 170 sailing vessels were of 100 tons or more, 87% of the whole fleet. The oared barges and galleys used by the French at this time were likewise very large – 22 of them had crews exceeding 100 men (eight exceeded 200 men), suggesting that the numbers of oars they used were probably close on 100. The biggest English royal galley of this period was the *Philippe*, built at King's Lynn in 1337, with 80 oars.[15]

---

[14] M. Oppenheim, *The Maritime History of Devon* (Exeter, 1968), p. 14; F. Taylor and J.S. Roskell (eds), *Gesta Henrici Quinti: The Deeds of Henry V* (Oxford, 1975), p. 20 and n.1; Merlin-Chazelas, *Documents*, ii, pp. 33–54; Hewitt, *Organization of War*, pp. 182–6; T.D. Hardy (ed.), *Rotuli Normanniae 1200–1205 and 1417–1418* (London, 1835), pp. 320–9; PRO, E364/92, A m.1v–B m.2r, N m.1r–O m.1r.

[15] *Calendar of Memoranda Rolls 1326–1327*, pp. 128–33; Merlin-Chazelas, *Documents*, loc. cit.; PRO, E101/19/31.

The importance of large ships in medieval sea warfare was that they were easier to defend, having larger crews and high superstructures, and for the same reason were more effective in attack, as battles were decided by boarding actions. Given the apparent size and manpower advantages possessed by the French at Sluys (the English fleet may have numbered no more than about 150 ships), the magnitude of Edward III's victory, and the errors of the French commanders, seem all the greater.[16]

Larger ships make occasional appearances in the records later in the century: the largest ship in Richard II's tiny royal fleet was the 300-ton *Trinity*. Increasing numbers of ships of more than 250 tons are to be found in the sources of the first half of the fifteenth century; the English fleet at Plymouth in 1450 even included six vessels in the 300–400 ton range.[17]

It may be that this gradual increase in the numbers of large ships over the period of the Hundred Years War was mere coincidence, but one must bear in mind that shipowners would not have commissioned the construction of large ships unless they had good reason to do so. Big ships were very expensive to build, and represented a considerable risk in terms of capital and cargo. There was a precipitate decline in the numbers of large ships in the last few decades of the fifteenth century, and it is tempting to see this as some sort of 'peace dividend' from the end of the Hundred Years War, but it was a European-wide phenomenon, with a complex mixture of causes. However, war at sea and a concomitant decline in the general safety of seafaring, remain a possible cause for the brief rise of the big ship in the first half of the fifteenth century.[18]

The four biggest ships in early fifteenth-century England, and perhaps all Northern Europe, were constructed for Henry V between 1413 and 1420. The first was the *Trinity Royal*, of 540 tons, rebuilt from the old *Trinity*, followed by the *Holigost*, rebuilt from a Spanish ship at Southampton, of 740 tons, the 1000-ton *Jesus* constructed at Smallhythe in Kent, and the gigantic 1400-ton *Grace Dieu*, built at Southampton. All were clinker-built vessels, and the first three saw action in the Channel in 1416 and 1417. They were probably modelled on the great trading carracks of the Mediterranean, and served as a counter to the 400–600 ton Genoese carracks hired by the French: it is surely no coincidence that seven of the eight carracks captured by the English in these years were taken in the battles in which Henry's first three 'great ships' participated.[19]

The *Grace Dieu*, one of the biggest ships in English history before the seventeenth century, was not ready for sea until 1420, and as research by Dr Susan Rose has shown, the only known voyage of the *Grace Dieu* ended in mutiny and fiasco on the Isle of Wight. The *Grace Dieu* was subsequently moored in the River

---

[16] *Froissart*, pp. 62–5.
[17] PRO, E101/42/11; E364/92, loc. cit.
[18] G.V. Scammell, 'English merchant shipping at the end of the Middle Ages: some East Coast evidence', *EcHR*, Second Series, 13 (1961), p. 334.
[19] Rose, *Navy of the Lancastrian Kings*, p. 247.

Hamble: all four great ships escaped the mass sale of royal ships following the death of Henry V in 1422, and were kept afloat for some years. The first three great ships rotted away, but the *Grace Dieu* was struck by lightning in January 1439, and was burnt out. However, that was not the end of the story. The remains of a large, clinker-built ship in the Hamble have been identified as those of the *Grace Dieu*: buried in the mud, and only visible at very low tides, the extant remains are about 40 feet in width and the keel is more than 125 feet long. Each run of clinker planking is composed of three thicknesses of boards, and the whole structure is a testament to the skills of fifteenth-century English shipwrights, operating at the limits of technology.[20]

The type-names of ships come and go in the sources: usually we can work out whether or not a vessel type was large or small, but not always, and it is often impossible to be sure if a type-name represented a distinct hull form, a local name, or some other feature not mentioned in the sources. We know what cogs looked like: with their angular stems and sterns, their flat bottoms and high sides, they were one of the most important cargo-carriers of Northern Europe in the thirteenth and fourteenth centuries. We also know what Mediterranean carracks looked like: the type was actually developed from the Northern cog, built skeleton-fashion, and the hull-form, at least, may have been 're-exported' to the North in the second half of the fourteenth century. Problems arise with the host of vessels described in the sources as 'navis', 'nef' or 'ship': we do not know if the term denoted a distinct type of sailing ship, or was just a catch-all.[21]

Oared ship-type names abound: galley, balinger, barge, great boat, floin, escomer and so-on, but beyond quantifiable points such as crew size or numbers of oars, it is difficult to distinguish between them. North-European ship iconography in the later Middle Ages is strangely deficient in pictures of Northern oared ships. We know what Mediterranean galleys looked like, but their Northern equivalents are something of a mystery. What is known is that in English service the balinger and its (apparently) larger equivalent, the barge, supplanted the galley in English service in the course of the fourteenth century. Balingers ranged in size from 20 or 30 tons up to 120 tons, and they may have had a reputation for speed – certainly they were favoured by pirates. Oared ships were a useful adjunct in battle, and had an important role in reconnaissance (or straightforward spying), but they were seldom significant by themselves. The victory of the Castilian galleys over the English ships off La Rochelle in 1372 was something of an exception.[22]

The Hundred Years War may have had some effect on the sizes of ships, but it is very difficult to know if it had much effect on maritime technology. However, there

---

[20] S.P. Rose, 'Henry V's *Grace Dieu* and mutiny at sea: some new evidence', *Mariner's Mirror*, 63 (1977), pp. 1–6; I. Friel, 'Henry V's *Grace Dieu* and the wreck in the R. Hamble near Bursledon, Hampshire', *International Journal of Nautical Archaeology*, 22 (1993), pp. 3–19.

[21] I. Friel, 'The Carrack', in *Cogs, Hulks and Galleons*, ed. R.W. Unger, forthcoming.

[22] J.W. Sherborne, 'English barges and balingers of the late fourteenth century', *Mariner's Mirror*, 63 (1977), pp. 109–14.

Fig. 11.3 Illustration of a ship from a bench-end formerly in the Chapel of St Nicholas, King's Lynn, and now in the Victoria and Albert Museum. Dated to c.1415 on stylistic grounds, the carving shows a vessel with the profile of a Mediterranean carrack, with two masts. Both sails are furled, but the rig comprises a square mainsail and a lateen mizzen (carried on the sloping sailyard on the small mast behind the large mainmast). The ship is ready for war, with second stages added to the fore- and aftercastles, and bundles of long darts (called 'gads') in the topcastle at the top of the mainmast. The carving illustrates very well the type of Genoese carrack captured by the English in 1416 and 1417, although it is impossible to say if there was any connection.

does seem to be at least one documented example of technical transfer taking place as a direct result of the war. As mentioned above, in 1416 and 1417, English naval forces captured eight great Genoese carracks (fig. 11.3). Two of the carracks were one-masted, like English ships, but the other six were two-masters, each with a lateen sail carried on a mizzenmast behind the mainmast. The lateen was used to help manoeuvre the ship, and this two-masted arrangement had been used in the Mediterranean since the mid-fourteenth century. It represented a technical advance. The first recorded English two-master was the balinger *Anne*, built at Southampton in 1416, and in the period 1416 to 1422, the Crown acquired a few more two-masters, and seems to have experimented with giving some of its other ships a second mast. The English adopted Italian terminology for the mizzen sail and mizzenmast, but in a way that suggests they were very much neologisms for them. Carracks had been voyaging to England since the 1340s, but the sudden appearance of these words in the English sources in the years following the capture of the eight carracks indicates that this was the first time that the English had ever made use of a second mast.[23]

Even more interesting is the tantalising evidence of a third mast making its appearance. The great ship *Grace Dieu* had three masts in 1420, a main and mizzenmast, and a third of unknown location. It is possible that the third mast was in fact a foremast, stepped in the bow area and carrying a small square sail. Certainly the English were using the foremast by the mid-1430s: the small royal balinger *Little Jesus* was re-built then with a rig that used three sails, the third sail being described in Middle English as a *ffoke-* or fore-sail (carried on the foremast), the terminology perhaps suggesting that it was an English invention. One can speculate that the foremast might have originated as an extra mast to help propel and manoeuvre the unprecedented bulk of the *Grace Dieu*: if this was the case, then we have a direct link between the demands of the Hundred Years War and the development of technology. Discussion of the third mast is not mere nautical antiquarianism: the three-masted rig developed to become the basic rig of European ships for the next four centuries.[24]

By contrast, it is fairly clear that neither the English nor the French were able to master the technique of Mediterranean skeleton construction. The French continued to rely on southern shipwrights to build and maintain their galleys at Rouen, until the Clos des Galées was destroyed by the English in 1419. The English, likewise, experienced severe problems in maintaining the carracks captured in 1416 and 1417. Within a year or two they were having to look for Venetian and other Mediterranean craftsmen to carry out the work, as English shipwrights did not know what to do. Some of the carracks were already too far gone: two sank at anchor in 1420 and two others had to be beached in 1421 in order to save them from a similar fate. The adoption of skeleton construction in Northern Europe took place in the mid- to late fifteenth century, and seems to have had little, if anything, to do with the Anglo-French conflict.[25]

So, were the 'winds of change' blowing across the seas from the Hundred Years War really just fitful breezes? Only two areas of maritime technology show evidence of any effect: vessels got larger, and the development of ship rig seems to have been stimulated. Did ships have much effect on the wars? The Hundred Years War was won, and lost, on the soil of France, not in the Channel or the Bay of Biscay. However, the fact that the English had sufficient maritime resources to make recurrent invasions of France, and that both sides could mount major coastal raids, meant that the agony was considerably prolonged.

---

[23] I. Friel, 'England and the advent of the three-masted ship', *International Congress of Maritime Museums, Fourth Conference Proceedings, Paris 1981* (Paris, 1983), pp. 131–5.
[24] Ibid., loc. cit.
[25] Ibid., loc. cit.

12

English Church Monuments during the Period of the Hundred Years War*

BRIAN KEMP

BY THE LATE 1330s the practice of placing or setting up individual monuments to the dead inside cathedrals and churches was in full spate all over Europe. In England it had begun in the first half of the twelfth century, and for about a hundred years was almost entirely restricted to royalty and high-ranking ecclesiastics. However, particularly as the privilege of interior burial was progressively extended to other social groups, monuments to nobles, knights and wealthy landholders began to appear in increasing numbers from the second quarter of the thirteenth century onwards, followed shortly by those of high-ranking ladies. By the fourteenth century the practice had spread to almost all classes, clerical and lay, who could afford the costs involved.[1] This trend was encouraged, not only by a burgeoning desire for permanent memorials, but also to some extent by the growth in chantry foundations, the more elaborate of which in the later middle ages often involved the erection of a monument close to the altar of intercession.

It is not surprising, therefore, that many of the commanders and captains who served in the various phases of the Hundred Years War were commemorated in funerary monuments of differing degrees of size and display. These were either stipulated in their wills or provided by the piety of their heirs, or sometimes devised in their own lifetime. What is striking, however, is that, although the war dominated the thinking of the military classes for well over a century, no special types of monument or particular iconographic conventions were produced for those who took part. Their monuments followed the same basic lines as others, and, for example, knights who had fought were commemorated no differently from knights who had not. This lack of specific iconographic allusion to campaigning

---

* In this chapter all county locations are in accordance with the pre-1974 boundaries.

[1] For accounts of medieval English funerary monuments in general, see F.H. Crossley, *English Church Monuments A.D. 1150–1550* (London, 1921, reissued 1933) (henceforward Crossley); B. Kemp, *English Church Monuments* (London, 1980) (henceforward Kemp), chapter 2. The introduction of monuments to the laity into churches in the twelfth century is discussed in a European context by A. Martindale, 'Patrons and Minders: the intrusion of the secular into sacred spaces in the late middle ages', in *The Church and the Arts*, ed. D. Wood, Studies in Church History 28 (1992), esp. pp. 147–55. For English lay effigies in the thirteenth century, see H.A. Tummers, *Early Secular Effigies in England: the Thirteenth Century* (Leiden, 1980).

had been equally true of military monuments in the earlier period, and was to remain so until at least the end of the sixteenth century.

The only significant difference compared with the thirteenth and early fourteenth centuries is that, during the Hundred Years War, monumental inscriptions gradually came to record the most important military commands and achievements of the deceased. So, for instance, the brass of Sir Thomas Swynbourne (d.1412) and his father Sir Robert (d.1391) at Little Horkesley (Essex) mentions that Thomas had been lord of Hammes, mayor of Bordeaux and captain of Fronsac.[2] The rhyming verse inscription on the brass of Sir John Phelip (d.1415) at Kidderminster (Worcs) describes how, *audax et fortis*, he fought well at Harfleur, but died on 2nd October (i.e., before the Battle of Agincourt).[3] The alabaster tomb-chest with effigy of Sir John Cressy (d.1445) at Dodford (Northants) (plate XXX) goes further, for its inscription refers not only to his captaincy of Lisieux, Orbec and Pont-l'Evêque in Normandy, but also to his having been a councillor of Henry VI in France and to his death at *Toue in Lorenia*, possibly Toul in Lorraine. The most extensive inscription of this kind occurs at Tideswell (Derbs) on a brass, renewed in the early eighteenth century, commemorating Sir Sampson Meverell (d.1462). It records *inter alia* his service to John (*rectius* Thomas) Montagu, earl of Salisbury, 'the which ordained the said Sampson to be a captain of divers worshipful places in France', and his subsequent service to John, duke of Bedford, resulting in his participation in 'eleven great battles in France within the space of two years'.[4] Expeditions to France did not, of course, cease after 1453, the date conventionally taken to mark the end of the Hundred Years War, and some later monuments record exploits in subsequent encounters. A very nice example is that of Sir John Clerk (d.1539) at Thame (Oxon), whose inscription trumpets his pride in a military success over twenty-five years earlier: it states that he 'toke Louys of Orleans duk of Longue ville and marquis of Rotuelin prysoner at ye Jorney of Bomy by Terouane ye xvi[th] day of August in the vth yere of ye reigne of ye noble and victorius Kyng Henry ye viii[th] (i.e., at the Battle of the Spurs, 1513). Apart from giving the date of his death and expressing a wish for divine pardon, it says nothing else.

Nevertheless, despite their interest, the significance of references to military matters should not be exaggerated, for monumental inscriptions tended generally to increase in length in the later middle ages, giving scope for all groups to include personal details if they wished. For example, the brass of John Peryent at Digswell (Herts), placed there after his wife's death in April 1415, has a partially lost inscription, the full text of which described him as esquire of the body and pennon-bearer to Richard II, esquire of Henry IV and Henry V, and Master of the

---

[2] *Transactions of the Essex Archaeological Society*, new ser., 7 (1898–1900), pp. 103–5. The brass is illustrated in M. Clayton, *Catalogue of Rubbings of Brasses and Incised Slabs* (Victoria and Albert Museum, 1968), plate 15.

[3] Illustrated in *Monumental Brasses: the portfolio plates of the Monumental Brass Society 1894–1984*, introduced by M.W. Norris (Woodbridge, 1988), no. 119.

[4] K.B. McFarlane, 'Bastard Feudalism', *Bulletin of the Institute of Historical Research*, 20 (1943–5), pp. 170–2.

Horse to Queen Joan of Navarre, to whom his wife was principal lady-in-waiting.[5] Again, the inscription on the magnificent brass of Sir Simon Felbrigg at Felbrigg (Norfolk), made after his first wife's death in June 1416, calls him standard-bearer to Richard II, whose standard he is depicted holding, and his wife lady-in-waiting to Queen Anne of Bohemia.[6] Comparable examples can be found on monuments of ecclesiastics, merchants, lawyers and others. The recording of military achievements in monumental inscriptions was thus not fundamentally different from the general practice of the period. Occasionally, however, information may be included that is not otherwise known to historians, such as, for instance, the location of Sir John Cressy's death.

The fact that the monuments of those who fought in the Hundred Years War were in no material respect distinctive indicates probably that, as with others, the primary concern was the permanent commemoration of their place and standing in society. In their effigies, for example, personal details other than heraldry were almost entirely lacking.[7] Save in a very few cases, occurring first in the later fourteenth century, effigies were not portraits, but depicted the deceased usually in the prime of life, as ideal representatives of their class, fully armed in the case of lords and knights, and surrounded by heraldic evidence of their rank, descent, marriage and affinity.[8] The iconography of their monuments displayed, not the weaponry or engagements of war – we are not yet in the age when military trophies or reliefs of battle scenes would be carved on monuments[9] – but rather elements drawn from the contemporary repertoire of artistic motifs or the conventional imagery of the Christian religion. It is true that their monuments together made up a significant proportion of the English output in funerary work between c.1330 and c.1460, and that many of them were among the most splendid erected in England during that period. Nevertheless, since those responsible for commissioning them were in the main content to follow contemporary fashions in the design and enrichment of monuments, the subject can best be tackled by examining the range of typical features found on English monuments in these years, with particular but by no means exclusive reference to the memorials of those who had fought in the campaigns.

By the time the Hundred Years War broke out all the elements of the fully developed monument in England had appeared. These comprised the effigy of the deceased, the tomb-chest upon which it was laid, and the canopy which covered and gave extra honour to the other elements. By no means all monuments embraced these three features. Frequently effigy and tomb-chest stood alone without a canopy or, especially where the effigy was two-dimensional, the monument often

5 R. Clutterbuck, *The History and Antiquities of the County of Hertford*, 3 vols (London, 1815–27), vol. 2, p. 325.
6 Illustrated in Clayton, *Catalogue of Rubbings*, plate 17.
7 Several military effigies from the later fourteenth century onwards wear an SS collar, indicating adherence to the House of Lancaster, and a few wear the Garter.
8 Among the earliest portrait effigies is that of Edward III (d.1377) in Westminster Abbey. Not infrequently the heraldry displayed on a monument would include that of the deceased's lord.
9 These first appeared on English monuments in the late sixteenth century.

consisted simply of an enriched slab set into the floor of a church. In the most elaborate cases, on the other hand, the monument formed part of a chantry chapel resembling a miniature building set wholly within the main body of the church, where intercession would be offered on a regular basis for the soul of the deceased. Monuments thus varied considerably in type and scale, depending on the resources at hand or on the degree of ostentation that was desired or considered appropriate. In almost every case, however, whatever the scale of the memorial, some form of effigy of the deceased would be included.

The range of materials used in the production of monuments was equally varied, both as between monuments and often within individual monuments. The predominant material for three-dimensional effigies was either stone of one sort or another (limestone, sandstone, etc.) or alabaster, newly introduced for monumental work on the eve of the Hundred Years War, but occasionally wood (usually oak) was used or, in rare instances, the effigy was cast in gilt-bronze. Tomb-chests and canopies were usually constructed of stone, alabaster or Purbeck 'marble'. Two-dimensional effigies might take the form either of figures incised in stone, alabaster or Purbeck slabs, or alternatively, and increasingly commonly, of brass (or latten) figures cut to shape and set into slabs of one or other of those materials.[10] Any of these substances might occur in various combinations in the one monument. For example, the important monument of King Edward III (d.1377) in Westminster Abbey comprises a gilt-bronze effigy set upon a Purbeck tomb-chest, whose sides are enriched with further gilt-bronze figures, the whole being covered by a flat tester of wood.[11] Again, the monument of Sir Giles and Lady Daubeney at South Petherton (Somerset), dating from c.1430, consists of two-dimensional brass effigies inlaid in a Purbeck slab, which rests upon a tomb-chest of Ham Hill stone. Alternatively, one substance might be employed throughout, as in the numerous cases of effigies and tomb-chests made exclusively of alabaster. Finally, one should note that painting and gilding were applied to many, but not all, parts of three-dimensional monuments, often over gesso on stone and wooden effigies, and that coloured inlays were not infrequently added to two-dimensional memorials.

The vast majority of monuments created during this period incorporated in their composition an effigy of the deceased. In the early stages of the Hundred Years War three-dimensional effigies were still often treated in the rather free manner that had been characteristic of funerary work since about the middle of the thirteenth century.[12] This is particularly true of military effigies and is most frequently and clearly evident in the crossing of the legs. The popular belief that crossed legs indicated a crusader has long been shown to be erroneous. It is to be understood rather as a fashion in the depiction of military figures which coincided mainly with the rise and flowering of the Decorated style in art and architecture, and not as conveying any symbolic message about the deceased's activities, either on crusade

---

[10] By contrast, imported 'Flemish' brasses consisted of completely engraved rectangular plates.
[11] *Royal Commission on Historical Monuments (England): London*, vol. 1, *Westminster Abbey* (London, 1924), pp. 30–31.
[12] Crossley, pp. 177–80; Kemp, pp. 20–22.

or in any other military sphere. By the late 1330s cross-legged effigies in armour were mainly depicted in a relaxed or restful state, lying fully recumbent on their backs and with their hands closed in prayer. An excellent example, and the earliest certain case of a military figure in alabaster, is provided by the effigy of John of Eltham, earl of Cornwall (d.1336), in Westminster Abbey.[13] Earlier, however, such effigies had tended more often to convey an impression of suspended animation, with their hands not in prayer but engaged in drawing or sheathing their swords, the most spectacular case being the well-known but anonymous knight of the late thirteenth century in Dorchester Abbey (Oxon).[14] This sense of movement continued to be a feature of some military effigies down to the middle of the fourteenth century, as can be seen, for example, in the alabaster effigy of a knight at Hanbury (Staffs), once thought to date from soon after 1300 and now convincingly redated to c.1340.[15] A different sort of freedom in the treatment of effigies is exhibited by two Norfolk knights, at Ingham and Reepham, who are depicted in remarkably awkward and strained positions on beds of stones or large pebbles. Both were shown cross-legged and with their arms stretched contrariwise right across their bodies. The earlier is the figure at Ingham of Sir Oliver de Ingham, who served as seneschal of Aquitaine in 1333–43 and died in 1344. An extremely rare feature of his monument is that, at the head of the uncomfortably recumbent effigy, there kneel two angels raising his helm aloft, but whether this was meant to symbolise his particular military career, rather than his chivalrous attributes in general, is very doubtful. The better preserved effigy at Reepham, normally said to represent Sir Roger de Kerdeston (d.1337), is now fairly convincingly identified as that of his son, Sir William, who fought at Crécy and died in 1361.[16]

Other examples of individual treatment of military effigies in the early stages of the Hundred Years War include the figure of Sir William Fitzwarin (d.1361) at Wantage (Berks), which is not only cross-legged but also has the arms laid crosswise upon his chest, and a somewhat similar depiction, but with straight legs, in the effigy probably of Sir Otho de Grandison (d.1358) at Ottery St Mary (Devon); both of these knights had fought at Crécy.[17] Different again is the effigy of an anonymous knight of c.1350 at Clehonger (Herefs), which has uncrossed legs and the arms disposed in an unconventionally free manner.[18] All the effigies so far

13 *RCHM: London, Westminster Abbey*, p. 42 and plate 188; A. Gardner, *Alabaster tombs of the Pre-Reformation Period in England* (Cambridge, 1940), plate 119.

14 Kemp, p. 22. The effigy is illustrated in Crossley, p. 210, and A. Gardner, *English Medieval Sculpture*, 2nd edn (Cambridge, 1951), plate 411.

15 C. Blair, 'The date of the early alabaster knight at Hanbury, Staffordshire', *Church Monuments*, 7 (1992), pp. 3–18.

16 On these effigies, and on a related effigy at Burrough Green (Cambs), see A. Martindale, 'The knights and the bed of stones: a learned confusion of the fourteenth century', *Journal of the British Archaeological Association*, 142 (1989), pp. 66–74 and plates XVI–XIX. For Sir William de Kerdeston's career, see *Complete Peerage*, 7, pp. 191–3.

17 Fitzwarin's effigy is illustrated in Gardner, *Alabaster tombs*, plate 129. For his and Grandison's presence at Crécy, see G. Wrottesley, 'Crécy and Calais from the Public Records', in *Collections for a History of Staffordshire, William Salt Archaeological Society*, 18 (1897), pp. 31, 34.

18 Illustrated in Crossley, p. 213.

discussed adopt a basically recumbent position, but in a famously rare example at Aldworth (Berks), dating from c.1350, the effigy assumes a reclining posture, half-turned towards the viewer and supporting itself on an elbow (now unfortunately missing). In a remarkable way the Aldworth effigy anticipates the fashionable use of the reclining posture from the second half of the sixteenth century onwards, but it was very rarely repeated in the middle ages.[19] Nevertheless, it shows a continuing readiness to experiment in the form of monumental effigies in the early stages of the war.

In spite of that, however, there had been for some years a growing tendency to depict the deceased in a strictly recumbent posture, with straight, uncrossed legs and with the hands together in prayer. In the later middle ages this rigid treatment became the norm for all classes of effigy and, despite the occasional survival of a freer version,[20] its triumph was virtually complete by about 1375. Its ascendancy reflects the supersession of the Decorated style by the Perpendicular. The effigy at Wingfield (Suffolk) of Sir John Wingfield, who was with the king at Crécy and died in 1361, adopts this posture, and its effect can be clearly appreciated on numerous later monuments, including, for example, those of John Wyard (c.1405) at Meriden (Warks) (plate XXXI) and Sir John Cressy (d.1445) at Dodford.[21] The only major exceptions to this rather dull later medieval uniformity occurred in the effigies of kings, who were normally shown holding the symbols of majesty, and on some monuments of knights and their ladies in which the two effigies hold each other by the hand, as in the case of Sir Sampson de Strelley and his wife Elizabeth (d.1405) at Strelley (Notts), although most couples do not display conjugal affection in this way.[22]

In general, the developments affecting three-dimensional effigies applied also to those in two dimensions, especially monumental brasses. The latter, however, particularly in the later middle ages, not infrequently showed the deceased as a demi-figure comprising only the upper third or half of the body. While this was rare for military figures, examples do occur at Cobham (Kent) and Chinnor (Oxon).[23] Again, brasses sometimes depicted the deceased kneeling in prayer before a sacred subject, though not normally on knightly monuments before the early sixteenth century. On three-dimensional monuments such a posture is very rare for the principal effigy, although it is true of the figure of Edward Lord

---

[19] Illustrated in Crossley, p. 213. Two comparable but fragmentary examples are known at Kingsbury (Warks) and Walsall (Staffs); see A.V.B. Norman, 'An Unpublished Fourteenth-Century Alabaster Fragment', *Church Monuments*, 2 (1987), pp. 3–8. A few other effigies are turned on one side without being raised upon an elbow, including Sir Robert de Shurland (early fourteenth century) at Minster-in-Sheppey (Kent) and three knights of c.1320 in Exeter cathedral.

[20] For example, Sir Thomas Cawne (c.1375) at Ightham (Kent) and two unidentified knights (later fourteenth century) at Dorchester (Dorset).

[21] For Wingfield's presence at Crécy, see Wrottesley, 'Crécy and Calais', p. 38.

[22] For the Strelley effigies, see Kemp, plate 35; Gardner, *Alabaster Tombs*, plate 150.

[23] Respectively, Ralph de Cobham, esquire (d.1402), and Sir Edmund de Malyns (c.1385); see Mill Stephenson, *A List of Monumental Brasses in the British Isles* (London, 1926), p. 219, Cobham ix; p. 402, Chinnor iv. Half-effigies in the round occur, uniquely before the sixteenth century, on the monument of Sir Godfrey Foljambe (d.1377) and wife at Bakewell (Derbs).

Despenser (d.1375) in Tewkesbury Abbey (Glos),[24] and is occasionally adopted for subsidiary representations of the deceased, as at North Cadbury (Somerset), where the end of the tomb-chest perhaps of William Lord Botreaux and his wife (d.1433) has the couple kneeling on either side of the Virgin and Child (plate XXXII).[25]

In most cases military effigies appear in full armour of the period but, for obvious reasons, without full defences for the face.[26] Although some examples seem to display armour that was out of date at the time when the deceased died, the evidence on the whole suggests that normally the armour depicted was, as it were, correct at the time the effigy was made. The Swynbourne brass at Little Horkesley, for instance, carefully distinguishes the armour of the father, who died in 1391, from that of the son, who died in 1412, and the differences reflect the developments which are known to have taken place within this period.[27] Where apparent anomalies occur, there may be any of a number of reasons to explain them. It must be emphasised that we know the dates of manufacture of none but a very small proportion of existing military effigies. Exceedingly few contracts for monuments or records of payment to craftsmen in this period have survived, so that one is mostly in the dark as to whether a monument was set up soon after death, up to a generation or more after death, or in the lifetime of the deceased. Detailed contractual arrangements for the elaborate monument of Richard Beauchamp, earl of Warwick (d.1439), in St Mary's, Warwick, have fortunately survived. They serve as a warning against the assumption that monuments were made close to the dates of death, for, although the Warwick monument is admittedly more complex and costly than most, it is nonetheless instructive that contracts for the gilt-bronze effigy were not laid until ten years after the earl's death and those for the tomb-chest not until the 1450s.[28] Wills occasionally make more or less specific provision for a monument, one of the earliest and most detailed being that in the Black Prince's will of 1376, but we do not usually know how speedily such requirements were honoured, and in any case they are far outnumbered by wills which make no

---

[24] See below, p. 208.

[25] They are also depicted in the normal way as recumbent effigies on top of the tomb-chest.

[26] The vast majority wear helmets until late in the war period, but a few earlier examples are bare-headed or wear only an orle, including effigies in the round at Little Munden (Herts) and Erwarton (Suffolk), both late fourteenth-century, and that of Robert Waterton (d.1425) at Methley (Yorks), and the two-dimensional brass effigies of Ralph de Knevynton (d.1370) at Aveley (Essex) and Sir William Tendring (d.1408) at Stoke-by-Nayland (Suffolk). Towards the end of the war, bare-headed military figures become more frequent, including the alabaster effigies of Sir John Cressy (d.1445) at Dodford (Northants) and Sir Reginald Cobham (d.1446) at Lingfield (Surrey) and the gilt-bronze figure of Richard Beauchamp, earl of Warwick, in St Mary's, Warwick, made in the early 1450s, as well as a number of brass effigies.

[27] See above, note 2.

[28] The original contracts are lost, but their contents are printed (inaccurately) from a copy in J.G. Nichols, *Description of the Church of St Mary, Warwick, and of the Beauchamp Chapel, and the Monuments of the Beauchamps and Dudleys* (London, 1838), pp. 29–33, on which see P. Lindley, ' "Una Grande Opera al mio Re": Gilt-Bronze Effigies in England from the Middle Ages to the Renaissance', *Journal of the British Archaeological Association*, 143 (1990), p. 120. It is clear that preliminary work on the design of the effigy had been carried out by 1447–8 (ibid., pp. 120–1).

such stipulation.[29] Where monuments depicting married couples are concerned, and their inscriptions either survive or have been recorded by antiquaries, it is frequently clear that they were ordered after the death of one partner and before that of the other. For example, the brass of Sir Simon Felbrigg and his wife at Felbrigg, mentioned earlier, was made after the wife's death in 1416 and before her husband's, since the inscription has blank spaces for the date of his death. To judge from the lady's dress, the monument was probably made soon after she died and definitely well before Simon's death in 1442. Simon's armour on the brass certainly sits very well with that worn by Ralph Greene's alabaster effigy at Lowick (Northants), which is known to have been made in 1419–20.[30] Occasionally the appearance of 'old-fashioned' armour may be due to the re-use of a formerly discarded effigy that had been left lying in a sculptor's workshop and then brought back into service for a later commission. Such is thought to have happened, for example, in the case of a puzzling effigy at Barmston (Yorks), which may represent William Monceux (d.1446), but which has armour of about a generation earlier and contains evidence that a previously carved SS collar had been removed.[31]

From the little concrete evidence that we have it seems likely that the armour depicted on effigies in no sense represented that actually owned by the deceased. The contract for the Greene monument at Lowick, dated 1419, specified only 'a counterfeit of an esquire armed at all points . . . with a helm under his head', and that for the Beauchamp effigy at Warwick, dated 1450, only 'an image of a man armed . . . garnished with certain ornaments, viz. with sword and dagger, with a garter, with a helm and crest under his head'.[32] Neither contract contains any requirement that the dead man's own armour should be used as a model. It is even likely that the effigies of some individuals of the rank of esquire, knight or above were shown in armour when they may not themselves have possessed anything like a full suit of armour. Just as the facial and other physical features of effigies were not normally portraits but ideal forms, so the armour depicted was not personal to the deceased but that appropriate to their rank in society. It is interesting, however, in this context that, although the Greene contract speaks of 'an esquire armed at all points', and indeed Ralph had not risen above that rank, the resulting effigy wears armour no different from that on contemporary knightly effigies.[33]

[29] For the Black Prince's will, see A.P. Stanley, *Historical Memorials of Canterbury*, 13th edn (London, 1895), pp. 168–74. For comments on some other wills, see M.G.A. Vale, *Piety, Charity and Literacy among the Yorkshire Gentry, 1370–1480*, Borthwick Paper no. 50 (York, 1976), pp. 8–10.

[30] The Felbrigg brass is illustrated in Clayton, *Catalogue of Rubbings*, plate 17, and Ralph Greene's effigy in Crossley, p. 34. An abbreviated translation of the contract for the Greene monument is ibid., p. 30, taken from W.H. St John Hope, 'On the early working of alabaster in England', *Archaeological Journal*, 61 (1904), pp. 230–1.

[31] P.E. Routh, *Medieval Effigial Alabaster Tombs in Yorkshire* (Ipswich, 1976), pp. 17–19.

[32] Crossley, p. 30; Nichols, *Description of the Church of St Mary, Warwick*, pp. 30–31.

[33] This is consistent with the rise of the esquires by the end of the fourteenth century to a social rank immediately below that of the knights and imbued with many of the attributes of knighthood. For a recent discussion, see P. Coss, *The Knight in Medieval England 1000–1400* (Stroud, 1993), pp. 127–31.

This paper is not concerned with providing a detailed description of the developments in armour which took place over the period of the Hundred Years War. Suffice it to say that the numerous surviving and often well preserved effigies in alabaster, in particular, contain much finely carved evidence of what constituted a full suit of armour at different dates within the period. It is, however, worth drawing attention to a curious feature which is found on the bascinets of some three-dimensional military effigies in alabaster dating mostly from the first quarter of the fifteenth century. Although it might be thought especially appropriate for those who had fought in the war, the feature does not seem to occur only on the effigies of such men, and is in any case too infrequent to have had any standard connotation of that kind. It takes the form of a carving immediately above the forehead of the Latin abbreviation for the words 'Jesus of Nazareth' (usually *Ihc̄ Nazaren⁰* or *Ihc̄ Nazar'*). Some of the effigies which have it are not certainly identifiable, and only one can be precisely dated. Nevertheless, among the earliest may be that of Robert Lord Willoughby (d.1396) at Spilsby (Lincs), followed shortly by those of (probably) Sir Thomas Wendesley (d.1403) at Bakewell (Derbs) and (probably) Sir John Arderne (d.1408) at Elford (Staffs), and a little later perhaps by those of Sir John Mainwaring (d.1410) at Over Peover (Cheshire), William Wilcotes (d.1411) at North Leigh (Oxon) (plate XXXIII) and Sir William Marney (d.1414) at Layer Marney (Essex). Other examples include the effigies of the 11th earl of Oxford (d.1417), formerly in Earls Colne Priory (Essex), now in Bures chapel (Suffolk), Ralph Greene (dated 1419–20) at Lowick (Northants) (plate XXXIV), four insecurely identified effigies at Barmston, Darfield, Hornby and Swine (all Yorks), John Beaufort, duke of Somerset (d.1444), at Wimborne Minster (Dorset) and, exceptionally late, Sir Ralph Mainwaring (d.1456) at Over Peover, where however the feature may have been added in imitation of Sir John's effigy in the same church.[34] Alternatively, and especially in the second quarter of the century, the simple *Ihc̄* alone occurs, although I know of only four examples: on three uncertainly identified effigies at Longford (Derbs), Weobley (Herefs) and Swine (Yorks) and on the effigy of William Lord Bardolf (d.1441) at Dennington (Suffolk). In either form the practice seems completely to have died out soon after c.1450.

It was apparently related to a belief that the inscribing of the sacred name on the forehead assured protection from the danger of sudden death. The belief is found, for instance, in thirteenth-century Lives of St Edmund of Abingdon, archbishop of Canterbury (canonized in 1246), which described his youthful vision of the Child Jesus, who told him to write the sacred words nightly upon his forehead as a protection against sudden death, a practice which he regularly followed in later life.[35] His vision may in some way have been connected, however, with a passage in

---

[34] The two words were also formerly present on the effigy of Ralph Neville, earl of Westmorland (d.1425), at Staindrop (Durham), but owing to damage to the head only *Ihc̄* remains.

[35] See, for example, F. de Paravicini, *Life of St Edmund of Abingdon* (London, 1898), pp. 40–45; C.H. Lawrence, *St Edmund of Abingdon: a study in Hagiography and History* (Oxford, 1960), pp. 225–6.

the late twelfth-century 'Vision of the Monk of Eynsham', which recorded in detail the monk's vision of the next world and the conversations which, Dante-like, he had with people he encountered there.[36] One of these, a goldsmith who had died suddenly from drink, told him that the daily writing or marking on the forehead and breast of the words 'Jesus of Nazareth', which he said 'contained the mystery of human salvation', would preserve a person from peril; and he added that after death the corpse should be similarly marked.[37] It is clear from the context that by 'peril' he meant that of dying suddenly without receiving the last rites and being shriven by a priest, an awful prospect to the medieval mind and a clear risk for those engaged in military combat. Judging from the number of surviving manuscripts, including translations from the original Latin into French and later English, the Vision and therefore the goldsmith's advice were quite widely known in the later middle ages. It seems likely, therefore, that both the well-known hagiographical accounts of St Edmund and the Eynsham monk's vision were the sources for the sacred name carved on effigies, where it appears to have signified a safeguard for the afterlife against any shortcomings at the time of death.[38] If this is so, however, it is odd that the feature is restricted to comparatively few effigies and confined to a period of little over fifty years. Since its appearance on Ralph Greene's effigy at Lowick was not specified in the contract, its inclusion may normally have been due to the practice of particular workshops rather than to the express wishes of their patrons.

After the effigy the second main element in the composition of monuments was the tomb-chest. By Edward III's time it had become standard practice to place three-dimensional effigies and their supporting slabs upon rectangular tomb-chests, either free-standing or set against a wall, and this was to remain almost universally the case for the rest of the middle ages and beyond. Two-dimensional effigies, in brass or incised slab, continued normally to be set into the floor until the end of the fourteenth century, but in the fifteenth an increasing number, especially military ones, were similarly raised upon tomb-chests. Ranging in height from about 2 ft to over 3 ft, these tomb-chests provided vehicles for the carving and painting of appropriate iconographic schemes. In their present state most surviving examples preserve only their carved enrichment, although often even this has been gravely mutilated or destroyed. Occasionally the carving retains some of its original polychromy, but what has almost entirely disappeared is the

---

[36] The Vision is printed, with an introduction, in *Eynsham Cartulary*, ed. H.E. Salter, 2 vols, Oxford Historical Society 49, 51 (1907–8), ii, pp. 257–371.

[37] Ibid., pp. 319–20.

[38] Another possible source is the passage in Revelation, xx, 4, declaring that in the heavenly Jerusalem the servants of the Lamb (i.e., Christ) 'shall see his face, and his name shall be in their foreheads' (or, in the Vulgate, 'videbunt faciem ejus, et nomen ejus in frontibus eorum'), in which case the carving would suggest that the deceased had been, or hoped to be, saved. However, while this is clearly related to the idea discussed above, the verse in Revelation is less likely to have been the immediate inspiration for the carving since, to my knowledge, the sacred name never occurs other than on military effigies; if it bore this meaning, one would surely expect to find it more widely employed.

painting that was applied to uncarved surfaces. Tomb-chests which now appear very plain were once no doubt adorned with painted schemes mirroring the iconography of more fully carved specimens. At Goldsborough (Yorks), for example, an early fourteenth-century tomb-chest of a knight appears merely to be carved with a row of trefoiled arches, but close inspection reveals under some of them faded paintings of saints, enabling the viewer to imagine the whole line of small figures which formerly surrounded the tomb-chest.

For the armigerous classes heraldry was a standard ingredient in the iconography of tomb-chests. Armorial shields might be displayed under arcading or set into cusped quatrefoils and the like or, as we shall see, carried or supported by groups of small figures. Not infrequently the armorial bearings upon the shields were both carved and painted, but often they were merely painted and have therefore in most cases long since vanished. Apart from heraldry, the sides and ends of tomb-chests were normally enriched with a variety of other carving selected from a range of motifs which included stylised foliage, miniature blind window tracery or panelling and, most importantly, small human or angelic figures.

These small figures are among the most interesting features of tomb-chest design and called forth some of the finest carving found on medieval English monuments. It was arguably in this area, for example, that the virtues of alabaster and the skills of the alabastermen were most impressively demonstrated. At the time when the Hundred Years War broke out these figures consisted exclusively of 'weepers', males and females representing the deceased's family or associates, and usually accompanied by heraldic shields to identify them. Weepers of this kind continued to be carved on tomb-chests throughout the war and beyond, subtly changing in stance and style as the Decorated period gave way to the Perpendicular. In the 1330s they were still full of life, as it were, and often depicted in swaying or animated poses, with hands and legs in varied positions, as on the beautiful monument of John of Eltham (d.1336) in Westminster Abbey,[39] but in the later fourteenth century weepers adopted a more rigid, upright and four-square stance which they essentially retained until the end of the war period.

By that time, however, the range of carved tomb-chest figures had been augmented by the introduction of angels and saints. Standing in different ways for the spiritual world, they symbolised the heavenly powers and saintly virtues surrounding and assisting the deceased on the journey to eternal life. Angels were the first to appear, towards the end of the fourteenth century, followed by saints in the first half of the fifteenth century. They are thus features solely of the Perpendicular period and in consequence are normally shown standing frontally, although angels may sometimes adopt other postures and individual saints like St Christopher or St Martin may exhibit some sense of movement. Down to the end of the Hundred Years War angels were invariably vested in albs, and this continued generally to be true thereafter, but some late medieval angels were to be depicted in feathered suits in imitation of costumes worn in contemporary mystery plays. Typically angels

---

[39] *RCHM: Westminster Abbey*, plates 75–6. For a discussion of 'weepers' in general in the fourteenth century, see A. Martindale, 'Patrons and Minders', pp. 155–65.

hold heraldic shields in front of them, as can be seen, for instance, on the monuments of Ralph Greene (d.1417) at Lowick and Sir Edmund Thorpe (d.1418) at Ashwellthorpe (Norfolk), the latter having died during the siege of Louviers in Normandy.[40] Occasionally, on the other hand, angels may be shown kneeling in pairs and supporting a shield between them, as on the end of Sir John Cressy's tomb-chest at Dodford, or seated and holding up a shield beside them, as on the tomb-chests of Robert Waterton (d.1425) at Methley and Sir Richard Redman (d.1426) at Harewood (both Yorks).[41]

Figures of saints, particularly those carved in alabaster, are often among the most accomplished enrichments of fifteenth-century tomb-chests. They have also fared less well than weepers or angels at the hands of religious iconoclasts of the sixteenth and seventeenth centuries. Nevertheless, a surprising number have survived. A very fine example is the tomb-chest of Sir Richard Vernon (d.1451) at Tong (Salop), which has saints alternating with angels.[42] Such combinations of different categories of figure were fairly common, for, while some tomb-chests continued to be surrounded by weepers alone or opted only for angels, others juxtaposed weepers and angels, weepers and saints or, as at Tong, angels and saints. The Tong saints, like all others, are identifiable from their attire and from the distinguishing emblems which they hold.

In the fifteenth century a further feature, closely related to angels and saints, began to appear on tomb-chests, particularly those made of alabaster, namely, sacred imagery relating to the Holy Trinity, to Christ or to the Virgin Mary. An especially fine and beautiful instance is the tomb-chest of Sir Hugh Willoughby (d.1448) at Willoughby-on-the-Wolds (Notts). Its sides have rows of angels set in arched panels, but the ends have, respectively, the Trinity and the Virgin and Child, each flanked by angels (plates XXXV–XXXVI).[43] The Trinity is of the standard late medieval form, comprising the frontally seated figure of the Father, a cross between his knees bearing the Son crucified and, above the cross, a small dove for the Holy Spirit. The Virgin is seated frontally, but her head turns in adoration to the Child on her left knee and she holds in her right hand a flowering branch, upon which a dove has alighted and to which the Child reaches out with an apple in his hand.[44] Both images embody familiar and fundamental teachings about the redemption of the world by God's power and love, and are thus wholly fitting on a monument, but they are here executed with an unusual degree of

---

[40] The Lowick monument is illustrated in Crossley, p. 34. For the Ashwellthorpe monument, see D. Purcell, 'The De Thorp tomb at Ashwellthorpe', Norfolk Archaeology, 36 (1966–9), pp. 253–8. For Sir Edmund's service and death, see J.S. Roskell, L. Clark and C. Rawcliffe, The House of Commons 1386–1421, 4 vols, The History of Parliament (Stroud, 1992), 4, p. 600.

[41] Gardner, Alabaster Tombs, plates 17–18, 27.

[42] Ibid., plate 72.

[43] See plates XXXV and XXXVI.

[44] The flowering branch with the Dove alludes to the Virgin Birth, while the apple held by the Child symbolises his role as the Redeemer of humanity from Original Sin; see T.A. Heslop, 'The Virgin Mary's Regalia and 12th-century English Seals', in The Vanishing Past, ed. A. Borg and A. Martindale (Oxford, 1981), pp. 53–62; J. Hall, Dictionary of Subjects and Symbols in Art, 2nd edn (London, 1979), p. 330.

refinement and sensitivity. Other examples include the less accomplished Trinity on Robert Waterton's tomb-chest at Methley and a much mutilated Crucifixion on that of William de St Quintin at Harpham (Yorks).

The more costly and ostentatious monuments were completed by the addition of a canopy. As with tomb-chests alone, canopied monuments might be either free-standing or, more commonly, set against a wall into which the tomb-chest was to a greater or lesser extent recessed. In either form the design of the canopy reflected the contemporary architectural style, whether Decorated or Perpendicular, and, particularly in the finest examples, the effect was to raise above the tomb-chest and effigy (or effigies) a rich display of cusped arches, crocketed gables and ascending pinnacled shafts. The exuberance of the late Decorated period is well represented in the towering free-standing canopy of the Crécy veteran, Hugh Lord Despenser (d.1349), in Tewkesbury Abbey (Glos).[45] A little later, the transition to early Perpendicular can be seen in the canopied wall monuments of two knights who each fought at Crécy and died in 1361, Sir William de Kerdeston at Reepham and Sir John Wingfield at Wingfield, mentioned earlier (plate XXXVII); in both canopies the upward thrust of the main gables is counteracted by crested or crenallated horizontal mouldings. Later Perpendicular canopies firmly asserted the basic rectangularity of their designs, though often with a wealth of subsidiary carving, as on the wall monument of John Lord Bourchier (a veteran of, among others, the Black Prince's expedition in 1355–6, who died in 1400) at Halstead (Essex) and that probably of Sir Maurice Berkeley (d.1464) in St Mark's, Bristol.[46]

In addition to architectural details, the subsidiary carving on canopies of all periods commonly included heraldic shields and crests, and not infrequently angels or other small figures as well. High up on one side of the projecting Kerdeston canopy at Reepham, for instance, an angel holds a shield; and in a similar position at both ends of the Bourchier canopy at Halstead two shields are each supported by a kneeling angel and a wyvern. Again, amongst the dense carving on the so-called 'Percy tomb' of c.1340 in Beverley Minster (Yorks) appear small figures of knights and ladies with shields, and from the gables on each side little men reach out to support brackets bearing angels.[47]

In the case of wall monuments the back-plate – that is, the area of wall behind the tomb-chest and below the over-arching canopy – was normally left uncarved until some way into the fifteenth century. Such back-plates now appear completely plain, but it is virtually certain that most, if not all, were originally painted with

[45] Illustrated in B. Kemp, *Church Monuments*, Shire Album 149 (Princes Risborough, 1985), p. 5. The monument, which had become much dilapidated, was faithfully restored in 1828; see J. Bennett, *The History of Tewkesbury* (Tewkesbury, 1830, reprinted Dursley, 1976), pp. 160, 162. For Lord Despenser's career, see *Complete Peerage*, 4, pp. 271–3.
[46] The Berkeley monument is illustrated in Crossley, p. 12; J. Evans, *English Art 1307–1461* (Oxford, 1949), plate 76. Both attribute it to a Thomas Berkeley (d.1461), but for the probably correct identification, see I.M. Roper, *The Monumental Effigies of Gloucestershire and Bristol* (privately published, 1931), pp. 52–7. For Lord Bourchier's service, see *Complete Peerage*, 2, p. 247.
[47] Illustrated in Crossley, p. 2; Evans, *English Art 1307–1461*, plate 79.

appropriate designs. In some cases the design may have been heraldic or religious in content, or it may have depicted the salvation of the deceased's soul, in a manner to be discussed below. Alternatively, to judge from a hunting scene which was still partially visible in the early nineteenth century on Sir Oliver de Ingham's monument at Ingham (mentioned earlier), the painting may have shown some event or episode, either actual or perhaps fictional or allegorical.[48] It is just conceivable, therefore, that some monuments of Hundred Years War veterans, especially in the fourteenth century, included scenes of their military exploits painted on the backplate, but this can be no more than an intriguing possibility. However, some idea of the sort of effect that has otherwise been almost entirely lost can be gained from the monument of an ecclesiastic, John Wotton (d.1417), at Maidstone (Kent), where the remarkably well preserved painting on the back-plate depicts him kneeling before a representation of the Annunciation flanked by saints.

Related to canopied monuments were chantry chapels of the type comprising separate structures within the body of a church or cathedral. In these cases the effigy-bearing tomb-chest, if present, was normally either wholly contained within the chapel or incorporated into one of its sides. No surviving example is earlier than the Perpendicular period and many of those dating from before the end of the war were made for bishops or archbishops.[49] Of those commemorating heroes of the war, three are worth special mention on account of their unusual features. The first, in Tewkesbury Abbey (Glos), is that of Edward Lord Despenser, who died in 1375 after a distinguished record of service under the Black Prince in 1355–7 and later under Edward III himself.[50] The chapel has no tomb-chest, but on its roof Despenser's effigy appears in a uniquely kneeling posture under a canopy, while in addition he and his wife are depicted in a rare painting on the east wall of the chapel, kneeling on either side of the Trinity with censing angels. Tewkesbury Abbey also has the more sumptuously carved chantry chapel of Richard Beauchamp, earl of Worcester, mortally wounded at the siege of Meaux in 1422.[51] It is both notable for the rich tabernacling of its superstructure and unusual in having in its western half two storeys, the upper of which may once have contained effigies of the earl and his widow, Isabel, since no access to this level is provided, but if so they have not survived.[52] Finally, the chantry chapel of the war's supreme hero Henry V (d.1422) in Westminster Abbey is utterly *sui generis*, being inserted at mezzanine level above the ambulatory to the east of Edward the Confessor's

[48] For the Ingham painting, see C.A. Stothard, *The Monumental Effigies of Great Britain* (London, 1817), plate facing p. 56.
[49] Crossley, pp. 5–6; Kemp, pp. 35–7.
[50] For his service, see *Complete Peerage*, 4, pp. 274–6.
[51] Ibid., 1, pp. 26–7 (under Barony of Abergavenny, II).
[52] It has been suggested that the effigies may have been kneeling, but on the other hand Countess Isabel's will (made in 1439 after the death of her second husband, Richard Beauchamp, earl of Warwick) provided for a naked effigy of herself (probably a cadaver) accompanied by figures of saints; these were apparently made, but precisely where in the chapel they were placed is uncertain (Bennett, *History of Tewkesbury*, pp. 163–4). For Isabel's will, see F.J. Furnivall, *The Fifty Earliest English Wills in the Court of Probate, London*, Early English Text Society, orig. ser. 78 (1882), pp. 116–19.

shrine, with the tomb-chest and effigy on a platform beneath. The monument itself was complete by 1431, but the chapel was not begun until 1438 and, mainly because of its complex structure and what has been called 'the extreme elaboration of its decoration', not finished before about 1450. Every surface is indeed covered with carving, including images of saints and other figures, heraldic beasts, angels holding shields and depictions of the king at his coronation and fully armed on horseback. Even so, in all this wealth of decoration there is no specific allusion to Henry V's achievements in the war with France.[53]

One last aspect of the subject remains to be considered. As we have seen, medieval monuments were erected primarily to perpetuate the memory of the deceased and to celebrate the station in society which they had occupied when alive. The hope of all, however, was for the ultimate passage of the soul to eternal life, aided by propitiatory prayers and masses on earth to reduce the pains of purgatory. From well before the outbreak of the Hundred Years War monumental inscriptions had included a plea for divine mercy upon the deceased's soul, and this tradition continued, but in the later stages of the war an increasing number directly requested the reader to pray for the soul, in the hope thereby of adding to the treasury of intercession offered up on its behalf. But medieval monuments could also express the desire for eternal bliss iconographically, in the form of an angel or angels bearing a naked representation of the soul in a napkin. A number of carved or engraved versions survive, and a few painted depictions are known,[54] but, since the theme was a familiar one in medieval devotional art, these no doubt represent only a small proportion of the numbers once existing in either medium. In its fullest form the convention showed two angels presenting the soul to a seated figure of Christ or, according to some authorities, God the Father. It so appears, for instance, on the canopy of the Percy tomb (c.1340) in Beverley Minster and on the brass of Laurence de St Maur, rector (d.1337), at Higham Ferrers (Northants).[55] A variant form occurs on the later fourteenth-century tomb-chest of Sir Roger and Lady de Bois at Ingham (Norfolk), where single angels individually offer the two souls to a much damaged figure of either Christ or the Holy Trinity (plate XXXVIII).[56] More frequently, however, no divine personage was represented, even though the idea behind the image remained the same. Thus two angels bear up the soul at the foot of the effigy in Lincoln cathedral of Bartholomew Lord Burghersh, a veteran of Crécy and Calais who died in 1355, and on the famous brass at Elsing (Norfolk) of Sir Hugh Hastings, who fought at Crécy and died during the siege of

[53] W.H. St John Hope, 'The Funeral, Monument, and Chantry Chapel of King Henry the Fifth', *Archaeologia*, 65 (1913–14), pp. 129–86; *RCHM: Westminster Abbey*, pp. 71–3 and plates 129–40. It is possible that the castles and fortifications which appear in the vigorous equestrian images of the king refer in a general way to his French exploits (see St John Hope, p. 175 and plate XXI).

[54] Painted versions are recorded on early fourteenth-century monuments at Dodford (Northants) and Winchelsea (Sussex).

[55] The St Maur brass is illustrated in *Monumental Brasses* (see note 3), no. 25.

[56] The figure's mutilated condition makes identification difficult. It is sometimes said to be Christ, but M.R. James, in his *Suffolk and Norfolk* (London, 1930), p. 152, read it as the Trinity.

Calais in 1347.[57] By contrast, a single angel performs the task on the canopy of an unidentified knight of c.1425 at Lutterworth (Leics).

Another manifestation of concern for the afterlife involved the depiction of the deceased as a decaying corpse in its shroud, which is found on a limited number of English monuments from the second quarter of the fifteenth century onwards. In the earliest examples a 'cadaver' effigy of this kind formed part of a two-fold representation, which displayed the deceased in earthly rank and honour on an upper tier and, below, as a corpse deprived of all worldly accoutrements and naked save for its shroud. In its grim portrayal of the body's corruption after death, the cadaver performed the function of a 'memento mori', with the spiritual purpose of shocking the living into a realisation of their own mortality and urgent need for reform in their lives. It served not only to elicit prayers for the soul of the departed, but also to focus the minds of others on the fate of their own souls.[58] Despite that, or rather perhaps because of its very gruesomeness, the cadaver did not enjoy a wide appeal, being confined to a comparatively small minority of monuments, at first mainly those of bishops. It does occur, however, on that of one of the most renowned soldiers in the later phases of the war, John, earl of Arundel (d.1435), at Arundel (Sussex), where the earl's fully armed military effigy rests upon a slab above the representation of his corpse. The date of the monument is unknown, as is the reason why it took this unusual form, although it may have been connected with the circumstances of his death. Known as 'the English Achilles', he had served valiantly under the duke of Bedford in the early 1430s, but died as a prisoner of the French after being severely wounded at the siege of Gerberoy near Beauvais in May 1435.[59] The only comparable monument of a former soldier in the war is that of John Golafre (d.1442) at Fyfield (Berks), but he is not known to have served after a short spell in Normandy in 1417–18, and in his case the choice of a two-tiered design with cadaver may have resulted from his links with a particular Lancastrian circle which seems to have favoured it.[60]

In any event, the presence of cadavers on these monuments, especially on the earl of Arundel's, is but a further instance of the adoption of existing forms (whether long established or newly introduced) for the commemoration of those who had served in the war with France. It is another illustration of the fact that, as a group, monuments of war veterans were distinctive neither in design nor in

---

[57] Lord Burghersh's monument is illustrated in Crossley, p. 67; for his service and death, see *Complete Peerage*, 2, p. 426. For Sir Hugh Hastings' brass, see Clayton, *Catalogue of Rubbings*, plate 4, and for his service and death, see *Complete Peerage*, 6, pp. 352–3.

[58] For an excellent recent discussion, see P.M. King, 'The cadaver tomb in England: novel manifestations of an old idea', *Church Monuments*, 5 (1990), pp. 26–38. See also E. Duffy, *The Stripping of the Altars: Traditional Religion in England c.1400–c.1580* (Newhaven and London, 1992), pp. 306–8.

[59] *Complete Peerage*, 1, pp. 247–8.

[60] For his career, see Roskell et al., *House of Commons*, 3, pp. 199–202. See also P.M. King, 'The English cadaver tomb in the late fifteenth century: some indications of a Lancastrian connection', in *Dies Illa*, ed. J.H.M. Taylor (Liverpool, 1984), pp. 45–56, esp. p. 54. The much restored monument of the war veteran, Sir Sampson Meverell (d. 1462), at Tideswell (Derbs) – see above, p. 196 – also has a cadaver, but in this case without a separate depiction of the deceased as in life.

decoration. They served the same function as other monuments of the time and made use of the same range of forms, techniques and iconography as was available generally. This does not make them any the less interesting or precious, however, for together they provide us with an enormous amount of artistic and historical detail, not least in their effigies. But more than that, they enable us to catch at least something of the valour and pride, perhaps even chivalry, of those who joined in the campaigns against France.

INDEX OF NAMES AND PLACES

Printed and bound by CPI Group (UK) Ltd, Croydon, CR0 4YY

13/04/2025